CLOSING THE EQUITY GAP

FREADA KAPOR KLEIN
AND MITCHELL KAPOR

CLOSING
THE
EQUITY
GAP

Creating Wealth and Fostering Justice in Startup Investing

HARPER
BUSINESS

An Imprint of HarperCollins*Publishers*

FIRST EDITION

Title page art courtesy of Shutterstock / Flas100

Library of Congress Cataloging-in-Publication Data has been applied for.

ISBN 978-0-06-326851-7

23 24 25 26 27 LBC 5 4 3 2 1

To the rising generation of gap-closing entrepreneurs,
fund managers, and scholars, who are creating inspiring solutions
for the millions who face unfair obstacles, injustice, and bias.

CONTENTS

1   Our Urgent Proposal   1

2   Solving Silicon Valley's Meritocracy Myth:
     Irma and Jake   25

3   World on Fire: Donnel and Davida   47

4   Dignity for All: Phaedra's Promise   73

5   Breaking into Tech: Ruben   95

6   Investing in Mental Wellness:
     Matthew and PK   119

7   The Price of Loyalty: Uber   139

8   Fork in the Road: Mandela and
     the Changemakers   165

9   Partnership: Ulili and Brian   191

10   Lessons Learned   213

     Acknowledgments   247

     How We Invest   251

OUR URGENT PROPOSAL

On any given day in the United States, a mother who has been laid off from a factory job will start learning how to build websites, her first step toward a higher salary, stability, and security. A retired teacher with chronic, untended medical needs will find an affordable health plan and start getting care. A deeply indebted family facing water shutoffs will get a call from their utility offering to help with payments. Boxes of healthy, organic cereal, peanut butter, breads, and soup will replace dollar store junk food in a veteran's kitchen.

Behind these promises of a better America is a new community of mission-driven entrepreneurs, visionaries who themselves survived life's worst challenges only to grow up determined to solve them. They have no time for complacency. They're motivated, passionate, and making a difference.

These CEOs and founders, who collectively run companies worth billions of dollars and are sought out by mainstream Silicon Valley investors, include the children of immigrants, descendants of enslaved people, men and women who grew up disenfranchised, unentitled. One grew up in foster homes; others saw loved ones addicted or incarcerated. In the young white male–dominated landscape of tech startups, they're considered outsiders. Their businesses are considered misfits. They'd all heard hundreds of "No thanks" from investors early on; rather than seeing their potential, those investors looked for a pedigreed college diploma, a well-connected set of industry contacts, and a proven track record.

Their companies are different, too.

No one is building robots that make bankers' lives easier, or hawking Internet of Things–connected kitchen appliances. They have different goals: to avoid utility shutoffs and sky-high interest fees, to bring clean energy to low-income communities, and to connect untapped talent to tech opportunities. Every single one of them has created a business that closes gaps between haves and have-nots. We are proud to say that all the companies were launched with significant initial investments from Kapor Capital.

During a summer week on Martha's Vineyard in 2021, we had gathered with a dozen of these entrepreneurs for intensive workshops, meetings, and networking. Although some were just getting started, as a group these entrepreneurs had raised many hundreds of millions of dollars, employed thousands, and were well on their way to improving the lives of people around the U.S. and beyond. Together they were buoyed by each other's work, and they challenged, questioned, and encouraged each other. They stayed up late whiteboarding a plan to team up and tour around the U.S., collectively pitching their various solution-oriented products and services to cities. They shared their goals of improving generations of lives in underserved communities. They shared their outrage over injustice and inaction, and they marveled at how quickly they were making progress: just one generation ago, there weren't any Black and Latinx tech startup founders and investors. Their numbers were still paltry, but this week these men and women filled a house.

When former president Barack Obama stopped by for a visit, he fit right in. Their visions aligned, he said, to harness technology to confront the biggest challenges that America faces.

CHALLENGING ASSUMPTIONS

When we made a commitment to invest $10 million per year of our own money for a decade in an investment fund, we set out on a singular quest to find a better way to invest dollars in people. This is the backbone of our work in venture capital. Now we're finding answers that can have repercussions reaching far beyond the finance industry. Venture capital–backed companies drive the U.S. economy, stimulating the creation of companies worth trillions of dollars. When that big money benefits the already advantaged and fails to benefit society, especially those on the lower rungs of the ladder, it's exacerbating the growing divides that separate us. We're seeing it happen right now. Investors and corporations are making record profits, as the stock market, even during rocky times, demonstrates a long-term rise. We're gravely concerned that the not-so-hidden costs of that success threaten the promise of America.

Consider this: the Federal Reserve Board in 2021 found that a typical white family owned about $184,000 in family wealth, a typical Black family owned $23,000, and a typical Latinx family owned $38,000. The average wealth gap between Black and white families, $12 per $100 of white wealth, pretty much hasn't changed in decades; the gap for Latinx families, $21 per $100 of white wealth, has only slightly improved. Oh, and women? There has been a lot of talk about how women's salaries are finally closing in on their male counterparts, but there are still gaping gender disparities in basic wealth, bank savings, property, investments. Also, even within any given racial group, women tend to make less than men. And white women still make more than their Black, Latinx, and Native women counterparts.

Generations ago, women were largely confined to a narrow choice of work: secretary, teacher, or nurse. That's changed, somewhat. Today's young women have a broader range of work opportunities than baby boomers had before them. Unfortunately this is not the case when race is taken into account. Opportunities for people of color in the U.S. haven't really improved over the decades, according to a 2020 analysis by the Washington Center for Equitable Growth. The types of jobs Black and Latinx people in the U.S. tend to work in remain low-paying and devalued, which further entrenches inequality.

Nowhere are these imbalances more obvious than in the technology industry, where some of the world's greatest fortunes have gone disproportionately to white male founders. This remains the case even as, collectively, global corporations have been spending $6–8 billion per year on "diversity and inclusion" commitments. We can say, objectively, that money has been largely wasted. Fewer than 5 percent of big tech employees are Black or Latinx. Women are also lagging. It's been that way for decades.

When we launched Kapor Capital more than a decade ago, we committed to doing things differently. We are an impact investment firm seeking to bring about positive, measurable change with our funds, along with financial returns. Impact investment funds aim to do good, often founded with a specific mission to address environmental or social issues. In recent years impact investing firms in all asset classes—venture capital, private equity, real estate, public equities, and more—have soared in popularity. More and more people from different generations and different walks of life want to see their money invested in a manner that aligns with their values. Universities and foundations hear from their communities about the importance of investing their endowments consistently with their missions. Private workers are keenly interested in what their 401(k) retirement accounts are investing in. Nevertheless, all of this interest in impact investing has resulted in a lot of rebranding without substantial changes in how that money is invested, who receives it, and how success is measured. Many of the large private equity (PE) and venture capital (VC) firms that have opened divisions focused on impact investing still rely on the same investment committees to approve their transactions. "Impact" has become a feel-good, catch-all category with little rigor in definition or metrics.

That's why Kapor Capital's funds stand out in the arena. When we started our impact investing effort, we established clear criteria: the core business had to be a tech business that closed gaps of access, opportunity, or outcome for low-income communities and/or communities of color. We had already founded and/or invested in multiple tech companies, seeing firsthand how the venture capital process worked to launch successful businesses—and where it failed. And we had already been highly successful investing in tech startups for years, noticing along the way how many of our competitors missed investment opportunities that served low-income consumers or were founded by people of color.

We had also started questioning whether our industry's definition of "success" was enough. We saw our industry ignoring or even worsening the problems that kept us up at night, like the digital divide, health disparities, education achievement gaps, housing discrimination, biased policing, environmental justice, and global warming. We watched as investors with the power and resources to change the world rejected opportunities to solve big problems, and instead bet on esoteric forms of financial speculation (cryptocurrency) and new kinds of entertainment (the metaverse). Venture capitalists like to say they're improving our world, but for most the real focus is making as much money as possible today with the promise to give it away

5

later. When pressed, they'll donate to an alma mater or favorite cause, but the investments themselves often exacerbate problems, not solve them. We're all for giving; in fact, a significant part of our lives is focused on our own nonprofit and philanthropic work. But, as study after study demonstrates a growing wealth gap that relegates Black, Latinx, and other marginalized communities to poverty, we remain frustrated with the status quo—the traditional investors' method of evaluating companies using standards that implicitly—or explicitly—disadvantage them. Is "success" measurable only in market capitalization? Or is it something bigger and more long-lasting—building businesses that make a difference in people's lives, that might help bend the arc of the business world toward justice? For us, the central questions for evaluating a new venture are: What is the fundamental purpose of a business? If it succeeds, who benefits and who suffers? Does it improve the daily lives of people who struggle to make ends meet or face a myriad of obstacles as they work to improve their lives? Does it widen the gap between the haves and have-nots or provide opportunities to level the playing field?

In 2011 we launched our own venture capital fund devoted to tech startups that would bring positive social change alongside "venture scale returns," that is, at least doubling or tripling our investment and nothing less. Over the years, "gap closing" would become the signature phrase for Kapor Capital. Closing gaps of access, opportunity, and/or outcome have been part of our investment criteria for more than a decade. Our intention was to take everything we knew about building tech businesses, and everything we'd learned about how traditional venture capitalists have failed underrepresented entrepreneurs, and use it all to support businesses that yielded vital social impact while driving significant financial returns. In addition, since 2016, every entrepreneur we've backed has signed on to our Founders' Commitment—the first one in venture capital—requiring them to build a diverse team and an inclusive culture. The impact they create must be first and foremost for the communities being served. Secondarily, we want to diversify the tech and VC ecosystem. Creating a group of wealthy Black and Latinx women and men entrepreneurs and investors is also a by-product of this approach, but not the primary motivator.

When we told other financial leaders about our new fund, most of them smiled politely and reacted as if we'd announced a new charitable project rather than a disruptive new business model. "Oh, that's venture philanthropy," they might say. While few would admit it in public, conventional wisdom in our industry is that prioritizing either impact or diversity is a liability rather than a strategy. In the parlance of the industry, it's "concessionary," sacrificing financial returns in favor of impact.

Although many observers and industry leaders expected that our well-intentioned, bleeding-heart initiative would lead to embarrassment and financial loss, we were confident that our new fund would do well *and* do good.

And now time has proven us right. It's time to share how we did it.

DOUBLE BOTTOM LINE

A dozen years ago we began laying out a series of specific principles that we would adhere to with every investment that Kapor Capital made, a different set of criteria than any other venture capital fund.

Venture capital firms are judged on their financial returns, as measured in a variety of ways, including their "internal rate of return," the percentage increase of cash invested year over year. Keep in mind we're making what we hope are long-term investments in unproven, private companies—often really just an idea—that may not make a profit for years, so measurement looks a little different than a standard 401(k) account. In the last ten years, Kapor Capital's internal rate of return has been a steady 29 percent, putting us in the top quarter of all similarly sized venture funds, impact or not, diverse or not. The financial success is proven.

More importantly, we have made good on our commitment to equity and inclusion. Across the industry, an estimated 4 percent of venture capital investors are Black, and only 20 percent of venture capital firms have even one Black investor on their team. Today, at Kapor Capital, every person involved in making the fund's investment decisions is a person of color. On the flip side, from the perspective of entrepreneurs, we're also doing it right. In corporate America, 1 percent of venture-funded firms have a Black founder/CEO, and 3 percent have a founder/CEO who is a woman or person of a racially underrepresented background. At Kapor, 60 percent of our first-time investments have a founder/CEO who's a woman and/or a person of a racially underrepresented background.

So, making money? Check. Increasing diversity in venture capital and tech? Check.

Our most significant success has been in an even more important mission: social change. Millions of lives are impacted in a positive way through businesses in Kapor Capital's portfolio, from access to health care to dignified ways to build credit scores and obtain loans to alternative educational pathways to tech.

Finally, we didn't just found Kapor Capital to have a direct impact. We risked our own dollars and reputation for this test case, to prove that this could be done—and that in fact our methods and priorities would lead to greater financial return, because they led us to find opportunities that others missed. Our goal was to leverage our success into influencing others to change the way they do business.

Systemic racism in big tech and finance has got to stop. And as we call for others to join the fight to stop it, we're putting into motion the final piece of our plan for Kapor Capital: stepping back from day-to-day management to empower our younger partners and successors to run the fund—two of whom you'll meet in Chapter 9. What we did isn't magic, it was strategy and rigor, and the work will continue without us. We want to use our time now to share the hard lessons we've learned to get here, and to share our plan so others can use it, too.

WALKING THE WALK

To understand our sense of mission, our purpose and dedication to equality in tech, we want you to know how we came to our core values.

Freada: I was born in Kansas City, Missouri, to a physician-in-training father and a homemaker mother, but ours was no standard Midwest family. Five of my aunts and uncles had been slaughtered in Russia's anti-Jewish pogroms. My mother's family fled Eastern Europe before I was born, but I knew those grandparents and their story. It's a fundamental value of mine: none of us are free until all of us are free.

When I was just three, in Biloxi, Mississippi, my brother, seven, came home bloody and beaten after his classmates accused him of killing Christ because we were Jews. A few years later in Tulsa, Oklahoma, we were the only Jewish kids in our elementary school and the hostility there was at times palpable. Our parents had to ask the public school principal to excuse us from singing "Jesus Loves Me" every morning. We settled in California's San Fernando Valley, where Mexican American farmworkers were organizing, fighting for better working and living conditions. Even as a young teen, I could see that these families, who were core to our community, bringing food to our tables, were being treated terribly. One day in middle school I had had enough. I grabbed my stuff and just walked out of class, joining men and women of conscience in a Cesar Chavez–led United Farm Workers picket line. It was an awakening for me, one of many to come. As the nation roiled in the civil rights movement, the Vietnam War, and the rise of feminism, a friend of mine and I, at sixteen, joined our first feminist consciousness-raising group at the University of California, Los Angeles. I quit being head cheerleader and made my choice of colleges based on the strength of their political movements. That's how I chose the University of California, Berkeley, roiling with 1960s activism. Once there, I found a major I thought most focused on social and racial justice: criminology. Still a teen, I trained as a peer counselor at one of the country's first rape crisis call centers, counseling women who had been assaulted, usually by men they knew. Frustrated and shocked, but not necessarily surprised, the more I learned about sexual assault, harassment, and discrimination, the more I wondered about solutions. And by 1977 I was raising my fist alongside Gloria Steinem and consulting with companies about how to deal with sexual harassment, having cofounded the first group to focus on sexual harassment in the U.S. in 1976.

Recognizing the need for hard science to support the work I was doing, I went back to school at Brandeis University, earning my PhD in 1984 in record time. For decades I was a go-to expert for the *Wall Street Journal*, NBC News, *Washington Post*, and others, from the 1980s, when sexual harassment lawsuits and scandals began breaking, to the #MeToo era. The United Nations brought me in to conduct a survey in its six official languages to identify cross-cultural definitions of harassment. The World Bank called me to train peer counselors in its offices around the world to act as ombuds when staff were harassed. When top leaders at Harvard Business School got caught sweeping a sexual harassment case under the rug, you guessed it: they called me. Quantifying the bias through hard research in a variety of workplaces and institutions gave me leverage to push for change. Even as an investor, I rely on research and often conduct my own surveys to take the pulse of a company. In the late 1990s, as the U.S. grappled with a president's sexual relationship with an intern and corporate America's human resources departments realized they needed to define boundaries, the *New York Times Magazine* asked me about sex and power. I told the reporter that the overwhelming majority of corporations haven't established safe cultures, where workers don't fear retribution and can safely report concerns. "Don't Even Think About It. (The Cupid Cops Are Watching.)" read the headline.

Although the media liked to focus on gender equity, focusing on white women, I always asked "Which women?" because workplace bias never happens in a silo. Women were also Black, Latinx, and LGBTQ, and they faced unfair obstacles along multiple dimensions. Along with their male counterparts. The scale and complexity of the biases was measurable but most organizations wanted a simple fix.

In 2001 I pivoted, starting a series of broad and growing programs to bring underrepresented students of color, in small cohorts, into the world of science and technology, and to support them through college and into careers. I celebrated their successes and built a network of relationships to help them achieve their individual ambitions. But when I looked at the tech industry, the students I worked with and people like them weren't present. What the industry needed, I felt, was proof that things could be done differently.

There was such a stark disconnect—and I saw it even with Mitch. Before my eyes, he was becoming unhappy and disillusioned with his work as a top Silicon Valley investor. At the same time, I saw how engaged he was when he met the kids I worked with. He's always had a sixth sense for potential, and he was on his toes with them, asking about their families, their childhoods, their hopes and dreams. His favorite interview question of high school students of color from low-income backgrounds was "If you could invent anything, what would it be?" Mitch was always drawn to stories of inspiration and overcoming adversity, but he was spending his days investing vast sums in companies that make up the clicks and bricks of the Internet, many led by and working in service of already wealthy people.

So, I came to him with a proposition: "What if we invested in something that would give you joy? What if one of the metrics you assessed potential investments by was whether a company does something that helps kids like them and their families?"

Mitch admitted to me later that his knee-jerk response was: If I do that, I could miss out on some of the most exciting deals. While my consulting work had kept me steeped in the research showing that diverse teams posted better returns, Mitch was surrounded by a venture capital mindset that said that "good works" and "good money" were mutually exclusive. But he kept thinking about the question.

THE MOST PROGRESSIVE EMPLOYER

Mitch: I was born in Brooklyn and raised on Long Island. My grandparents and great-grandparents were Eastern European Jewish immigrants seeking to escape persecution and find a better life in America.

I was a smart kid who showed an early talent for math but whose social skills lagged behind. I skipped second grade, leaving me isolated in a classroom of kids two years older than me. It cemented my outsider status all the way through high school.

And then there was my father. He'd grown up very poor in the Great Depression, on the outskirts of New York City, but he got a shot at higher education at City College of New York because it was free and he could commute from home, ninety minutes, each way every day, by subway. That was a life lesson for me: there aren't a lot of opportunities for people living on the margins, and when there are opportunities, that's a Big Deal. An education can impact generations, and it did. My father had an ethically centered life. He didn't make a big show of it; he was very down-to-earth, but you'd never see him cut a corner or take advantage for his own gain and that was an important part of his legacy to me.

In 1966, as the U.S. was trying to catch up with the Russians after the launch of Sputnik, the first artificial satellite, I was extremely lucky to land in a six-week National Science Foundation summer science program in California. Here was my Big Deal opportunity. We were a cohort of kids who wanted to do things in science and technology, kind of like the underserved kids Freada would bring into our fold decades later. When she started summer science and tech programs, I understood from my core how transformative that could be. The opportunities don't have to take years, but everyone deserves a chance to really dive into their passion.

At the start of the personal computing era in 1978, I bought an Apple II and, with my friend Eric Rosenfeld, created Tiny Troll, a one-hundred-dollar software program that let users for the first time manage their own data and produce charts and graphs without relying on someone else to do the computer programming. I got a foothold in the embryonic PC software market with Tiny Troll. Our logo was a cute, bearded gnome stepping out of a hollowed apple. Get it? Apple?

From there it was a wild ride from Cambridge, Massachusetts, to Silicon Valley and back again as I got in on the ground floor of the personal computer software industry.

A short four years later, in 1982, along with Jonathan Sachs, I founded Lotus Development Corporation. Following on the success of VisiCalc, the world's first electronic spreadsheet, we developed

Lotus 1–2–3, a next-generation product aimed squarely at the new IBM Personal Computer. I was the designer and product manager, Jon the technical architect and implementer. We had no idea we were sitting on top of a volcano about to explode.

The estimate I gave to the venture capitalists who invested in us was to make $3 million our first year. In fact, the company saw $53 million in revenue in its first year and had a successful initial public offering. My forecasting error was 1,700 percent, but fortunately the variance was in a favorable direction. In 1984 sales tripled to $156 million, making it the largest independent software company in the world.

With this unexpected success, I saw the opportunity to create a company in which misfits like me felt included. That was my dream and here was my big chance. I set out to hire help on this, with a job description: "Make Lotus the most progressive employer in the U.S."

Well, thought Freada, who was being recruited based on her impressive reputation and her twenty-thousand-subject dissertation. That's interesting.

She took the job and that's how we met.

And Lotus was progressive. Here was Freada's chance to put all of her experience and education into action. There were confidential or anonymous channels through which to ask questions or raise concerns, proactive attention to gender and racial issues within the corporate culture, discussions of values and morale. We did anonymous surveys and managers were rated as to how well they lived the values day to day. Employees thrived, as did the company.

I stepped down as Lotus CEO and chair in 1986, feeling trapped by our rapid growth, huge size, my inexperience as a manager, and most of all my lack of desire to preside over an empire. We had three million spreadsheet customers, but for me, the innovation and creative work was gone. IBM bought the company ten years later for $3.5 billion.

After I left Lotus, like many other successful entrepreneurs, I found investing in new startups and helping their founders to be very gratifying. Putting dollars on the table gave me skin in the game, but the real reward was always to be part of creating something new and different.

You're either going to be really wealthy or homeless, an investor told me.

Freada and I once went to a Stanford Business School class where Google's then CEO, Eric Schmidt, was teaching a case on Lotus 1–2–3. When he introduced me, he said, "Mitch is a guy who sees around corners." If I have a superpower, that is it.

In 1992 I was among the first investors to put money into the Internet, which I saw as a tremendous global opportunity. In 1994 I was the first outside investor in a streaming media company—RealNetworks went on to lead the first generation of businesses delivering audio and video over the Internet before the giants stepped in. Early on, I was also concerned with the risks to society of the Internet. That's why I cofounded the Electronic Frontier Foundation (EFF) in 1990 to protect freedom of expression and other basic rights, and also why I became the founding chair of the Mozilla Foundation, the creator of the open-source web browser Firefox, which offers privacy and security.

Freada and I worked together in the 1980s. In the mid-'90s we got together as a couple after my marriage ended. Then, in 2000, Freada and I moved to the Bay Area so I could join Accel Partners, a well-known venture capital firm and early backer of Facebook.

It was an eye opener. It didn't sit well with me that so many venture funds consistently push their entrepreneurs to grow as fast as possible, even if it causes nine of ten to fail. While one big success can return 10x, 100x, or even more, I came to see that "go big or go home" imposed unacceptable costs time after time. VCs claiming to be founder-friendly in fact made decisions based on expected financial outcomes to the exclusion of other factors in ways that benefited themselves and their limited partners but not the founders they invested in or the visions they believed in. In this fashion, business models were routinely abandoned as not being aggressive enough, and founders were similarly tossed aside. In moments of candor, individual VC partners sometimes expressed regret about a state of affairs that troubled them but not enough for them to do much if anything about it.

As an Accel partner, I was frequently in the company of other Silicon Valley venture capital partners and investment bankers. I was also astonished to hear the type of discussion going on now that I was in the inner sanctum where people were unguarded. For example, one day some partners were sitting around the table discussing companies they were considering investing in. After hearing about a pitch from a company founded by an Indian immigrant, a partner said, "You know Indians, they're good engineers but they have no management talent, no executive talent. Pass."

I could not believe that somebody would actually say that. And it was during that time that I really began to understand the undeveloped state of thinking about big issues of diversity and inclusion in the heart of Silicon Valley. I concluded that the standard VC playbook is just not consistent with either treating founders and their teams well or enabling them to create the great products and services that make a difference in people's lives.

So, when Freada came to me with that proposition, investing "in something that would give you joy," I did keep thinking about the question. She was right, of course, and so after a bit of nudging we went for it. Together we refined ideas for crafting an investment practice that would evaluate investment opportunities on whether they were gap-closing. Conventional wisdom said it couldn't be done. Then again, we'd never found success by heeding conventional wisdom.

Today when we counsel the entrepreneurs we mentor and fund, we tap back into our decades of lessons, looking at what worked and what didn't. Certainly, every year there are new issues out there in the world that we have to consider, along with how they intersect with business. The issues have changed but the basic approach is similar, stemming from the same place. For example, one challenge in ethical, positive workplaces we've seen emerge, consistently over decades, is issues of entitlement within organizations. If someone can provide a workplace with good benefits, a culture where you listen to people's concerns, seriously, there's an inevitable tendency—if you don't do something to check for it—for people to become entitled.

It's a pitfall that we work with our founders on. Employees start to think, This workplace ought to be about me, instead of about the company's mission in the world.

Even at Lotus, there were times when people thought, if they didn't like the decision the manager made, it ought to be discussed more, because that would be more democratic. But that's fundamentally not accepting the premise, under our common mission, that there is a power hierarchy. We try to be respectful. But if leaders don't have the ability to actually make decisions and carry them out, they can't be effective as an organization. These are the types of lessons we like to share with our CEOs.

A GAP-CLOSING ECOSYSTEM

Today, in the heart of downtown Oakland, you can find our head-quarters, also unconventional. In a redesigned century-old building, every day teams of entrepreneurs, investors, students, teachers, and advocates are accomplishing what the public and private sector rarely pull off: they're closing gaps. Gaps of access, gaps of opportunity, gaps of outcome. The building itself is a manifestation of our ideals, from a rooftop garden that brings visitors face-to-face with each other, to a large theater where graduations and achievements are celebrated. There are solar hot water panels, the world's first bioplastic chairs, and reclaimed wood conference tables. On any given day, tech leaders and teenagers may brush shoulders on the sweeping, circular staircase, or a group of Black computer science majors might gather on high stools for a meal in the open, friendly kitchen.

Behind the preserved, 1920s facade are our three different, overlapping entities all working to remove barriers to diversity in tech.

First, Kapor Capital, our investment arm and the focus of this book, is our venture capital firm committed to only investing in businesses that are designed to close gaps and improve society.

We start every funding decision with four investing rules we developed, refined, and solidified.

Any company we invest in must:

1. *Close gaps of access to information or goods and services.*

2. *Expand economic opportunity in the workplace and the marketplace.*

3. *Produce significant financial returns.*

4. *Build a diverse team and inclusive company culture.*

Armed with these, and lots of data, due diligence, and gut checks, our small, sharp team ferrets out one amazing entrepreneur after the next.

Second, Kapor Center is the research, community engagement, and foundation arm, whose staff consult and collaborate to spark equity in communities and run a small but mighty team that studies barriers to diversity and devises practical inclusion solutions. One example: our groundbreaking Leaky Tech Pipeline study, led by the foundation's CEO, Allison Scott, PhD, finally and definitively framed increasing diversity in the technology ecosystem as an "urgent national priority." We drew on social science research and data, and the experiences of tech professionals, to identify the specific "leaks" in the tech pipeline that create barriers to access, from pre-K to venture capital. Then we identified recommendations and have been working to support those multilayered solutions.

Third, we launched the Summer Math and Science Honors (SMASH) Academy, a fundamental piece of our work, as a youth-centric arm focusing on supporting Black, Latinx, and Native American students from ninth grade through college and into the workforce to pursue jobs in STEM—science, technology, engineering, and math. Over the course of three high school summers, our students—mostly from underserved communities—live and learn on a college campus, gaining confidence and skills as they prepare for higher education. Over twenty years of supporting SMASH, we've watched every single one of our participants graduate from high school, and almost all have gone on to college, defying the odds. Almost half of our alumni are working full-time in STEM jobs, eight times the national average.

The layered ecosystem we've created at the Kapor Center collectively works to increase diversity in technology, using research-backed programs and projects to solve specific barriers, to benefit everyone from toddlers in preschool to CEOs in the executive suite. We see potential everywhere, and in everyone. The next Elon Musk or Steve Jobs may well be a kid living in East Oakland, and every day we're battling the unequal systems and misplaced priorities that allow people with potential to fall through the cracks, end up in the criminal justice system, or worse. For years we've said it in private and in public: America must hold up a mirror to its own biases. Now we've done just that, and the payoff in uplifting people—and building wealth—is indisputable.

Part of what makes the Kapor Center work is our own unique journeys, which is why we share them. People are talking today about Internet 3.0, but Mitch helped build Internet 1.0 and 2.0, and everyone working and excited about tech today grew up using these technologies. At the same time, Freada, who has been on the ground protesting, is a genuine advocate and bold role model who is never afraid to call out things that are wrong. Our DNA is embedded in the center. We are deliberately not on Sand Hill Road, the Palo Alto hub of elite venture capital investing. And we live our truth; everyone who walks into our building comments on the palpable vibrancy of the environment and the diversity of the team. We even invited our favorite restaurateur, Octavio Diaz, to open his second Oaxacan eatery on our ground floor, featuring delicious mole made with the recipe his grandmother taught him. Many have said that coming to our building is like glimpsing the future. That's not to say we're easygoing. We expect our staff and founders to do their homework, and to recognize that our shared purpose is gap-closing in the world. This is not a place to coast. We expect them to be as committed to their work as we are. As one member of our team says, "Mitch and Freada outwork everyone." It's not true. We are in awe of the relentless work, passion, and commitment we see in our founders. But collectively, we know this work matters and can make a difference.

ETHICAL SHARK TANK

If you've seen the reality television show *Shark Tank*, you know some basics of how venture capital works. You've seen panels of stern, mostly white faces listen to pitches and consider whether they want to invest, how they would value the company, and how much of the company they want to own, in exchange for how many dollars. You've seen entrepreneurs choose between offers based on both the investors' visions and dollars on the table. Of course, this glosses over the less entertaining parts of venture capital investing: due diligence, reference checks, poring over spreadsheets, hard questions, backgrounding, and more.

Some of the *Shark Tank* investments exemplify the lack of social and moral value placed in making money: heat-free hair rollers, ugly Christmas sweaters, blankets with hoods. There are few discussions of closing gaps, expanding opportunities, diversity, and inclusion. The focus is entirely on financial returns, just as it is in the "real world" of venture capital investing.

The current model pushes tech startups to get as big as possible, as fast as possible, which is such a misalignment of incentives. Entrepreneurs often do better in the long run if they're more thoughtful, building something with more meaning, even if it takes more time. After seeing this pattern play out for years in the venture capital world, we kept thinking about how many of aspiring and passionate entrepreneurs might have succeeded if they'd had a different kind of support. What world-changing ideas never got off the ground? Which great entrepreneurs were told they were "too early" or didn't have the right track record, simply because they looked different? And what opportunities were big investors missing by refusing to work with people unwilling to commit to a business model that prioritized fast growth at any cost?

Welcome to our accelerated course in Venture Capital 101, providing basic facts alongside nuanced context on venture capital investing. It's important to understand traditional tech investment practices, because that shows how we've steadily redefined some of the assumptions surrounding venture capital, keeping what works while flipping three major assumptions that perpetuate discrimination. Our hope is that other investors might consider whether this route is an option for their own projects, on any scale.

So, to begin, what is venture capital? Every year, Americans create close to one million businesses. From software companies to frozen yogurt shops, most are funded with personal savings, but about ten thousand new companies a year are funded by specialized investors: venture capital firms. You can think of a venture firm like a mixture of a mentor and a bank. Like a mentor, venture capital firms advise founders on how to set and accomplish goals. Like a bank, they provide money up front to help get a company started. But instead of paying back a loan with interest, entrepreneurs give VCs an ownership stake, equity, in the company. If all goes well, the VCs can eventually sell their ownership stake through an "exit" that pays them back their original investment and then some.

There are a few key stages in a company's life cycle when venture capital firms invest, and most firms specialize in one of these stages. Kapor Capital's sweet spot is the first cash a founder gets from a professional investor. We invest when we love an idea, it has some initial positive customer feedback, we see evidence of robust capacity for growth, and it meets our Kapor Capital principles. We write a check in exchange for future equity and occasionally a seat on the board of directors. This seed-stage tranche helps entrepreneurs further develop their product, buy equipment, hire colleagues, perhaps get an office, and start to expand. Without a seed investment, it's impossible for an idea to grow.

If a company proves "product-market fit"—evidence that customers find the product or service truly valuable—other venture capitalists get an opportunity to invest in expanding it further. We work with our companies to set a valuation so they can sell shares to investors. Companies can roll through multiple rounds of financing, often named Series A, Series B, even C and beyond before they exit by going public, being acquired, or failing and going out of business.

The money that venture capital firms use to invest comes from limited partners. This can be anyone from a wealthy individual who likes the firm's track record and investment style to a pension fund, university or foundation endowment, or large corporation seeking to build wealth.

The concept for venture investing dates back decades, but the practice took off with the tech boom in the 1990s. When the Internet was first becoming accessible to the public, thousands of new online companies formed to profit off this vast, new community of consumers. These startups were perfect for VC: great ideas, little proof of concept, and an opportunity to potentially strike it very rich as billions of people moved onto the World Wide Web.

CHALLENGING EVERY SINGLE ASSUMPTION

Those are the basics: done well, venture capital helps great ideas get off the ground. So why are we arguing that the system is broken? Because the way it works in practice builds in bias, and some strongly held assumptions make it extremely difficult for the tech world to diversify. Among them:

ASSUMPTION #1: *"Impact" and "diversity" mean there will be financial concessions. By definition, the story goes, if you're investing for impact or trying to be a company that more accurately reflects our racially and ethnically diverse communities, you're going to give up financial returns. So companies seeking these qualities don't historically get the attention they deserve.*

ASSUMPTION #2: *Financial returns alone define success. Most big players in this overwhelmingly white world of investors have plenty of money and don't need to work anymore. But still they measure victory with dollar*

23

signs, and they're in it for the win. There are some who will seek that win at any cost.

ASSUMPTION #3: *To be worth meeting with, an entrepreneur must have networked enough to get a "warm introduction." It's easy to network into a meeting through the cousin of your Stanford University roommate or your father's former colleague. They know someone who knows someone. But what if you grew up in a housing project in Pittsburgh? Or paid your way through college picking lettuce before dawn in Central California? This system bakes in bias from the very beginning.*

Our approach challenges all three of these assumptions. We've shown that impact and diversity do not result in financial concessions, but financial gain. We've shown how real success can create multidimensional value for communities, not just monetary wealth for founders and investors. Finally, we've democratized the path for founders who believe that their startups fit our investment criteria. They don't need to know someone who knows us; they can just submit their pitch deck via KaporCapital.com. We were the first to do this and many others have followed suit. Click a button, fill out the form. We might not fund them, but we'll assess their business plans and respond to everyone, equally.

Now we want to inspire other leaders and people with capital to use that leverage to create change, and to inspire entrepreneurs left out of the traditional system to demand better. From angel investors who can tie a strict set of principles to early stage investments to small business owners looking for ways to live their principles to anyone whose 401(k) or IRA includes corporate shares—this same concept can spread well beyond finance and tech.

2

SOLVING SILICON VALLEY'S MERITOCRACY MYTH

IRMA AND JAKE

When we first met Irma Olguin Jr. and Jake Soberal, we were moved by how deeply the company they'd cofounded, Bitwise Industries, was rooted in their personal stories. Both Irma, an engineer, and Jake, an attorney, had found their way into the technology industry entirely by accident. The daughter of Central California farmworkers, Irma had earned enough scholarships to be the first in her family to leave for college. Jake grew up one generation removed from the immigrant story, and held his parents' struggles close in mind. Both Fresno locals, they left the area and gained education and experience before returning with the shared hope of building equity and restoring justice in their hometown. They devised Bitwise as a multifaceted business that could revitalize America's struggling cities and make the tech industry diverse and inclusive. Their company was training underrepresented communities for tech jobs, breathing new life into blighted neighborhoods, and providing well-paid jobs by the thousands, but they'd been rejected by hundreds of VCs before we met them. Why? Because Silicon Valley's pernicious myth of "meritocracy" denies people like Jake and Irma the opportunity to come up with tech-enabled solutions.

Irma and Jake were convinced that the paths to success in tech they'd stumbled on could be paved and publicized. Anyone should have the right to earn not just a living wage, but one where they could begin to develop generational wealth for their family and community. So how could they analyze serendipity and turn it into a system? That was the question they wanted to answer with Bitwise Industries.

Like so many of the founders we invest in, Jake and Irma have family stories that have inspired their goal of pulling thousands of people out of poverty, and providing them with education and meaningful work. Empathy, born of proximity, explains why so many of our entrepreneurs design successful solutions where others have failed.

ON A DIFFERENT PATH

Grapes and almonds, peaches and pomegranates—Irma Olguin could wander any which way as a child and there would be acres of trees. For passersby, the fertile orchards of the San Joaquin Valley are part of the California dream. But for Irma's parents, and her grandparents before them, migrating to one of the most productive agricultural regions in the world meant day and night crippling physical labor, generational poverty, and a deep-set belief that this was their only option. Irma's parents had a loving home—although there wasn't much money—and there was security. Still, all she could see in her town of two thousand people was a future in the fields.

But Irma was on a different path. She identifies as queer, and found a diverse community in Fresno, the nearby city Irma and her friends would visit when they wanted to have a night on the town. One day in high school she heard an announcement that students could miss half a day of school if they wanted to take the PSAT. She jumped at the chance to miss class and ended up scoring so high on the test that she was offered a full ride to college. She chose the University of Toledo because it looked familiar, like Fresno. She chose her major, computer science, because it was the shiniest building in a school brochure. Only after she went there did she realize she was at the College of Engineering.

Irma had a full scholarship, but that didn't include money to get there. And so she picked up bottles and cans, worked in the fields, and took any job she could to scrape together seventy-eight dollars for the Greyhound bus ticket to college. Once she arrived, Toledo wasn't anything like Fresno. She didn't hear a lot of Spanish, and she couldn't find a taco truck parked on every corner. But what she did find in Toledo, Ohio, very similar to her own Fresno, was a place and a people with heart and grit and pride and so much history. She felt like she had found kindred spirits across the country. The idea of being from a so-called secondary city, she's come to learn, sometimes creates in people a feeling of needing to get out, to go somewhere else to do their highest and best. But what she has learned, along with Jake, is that the people most equipped and motivated to make a difference in those so-called underdog cities are the people who know them best, which is why she eventually returned to Fresno. Today as a dynamic, out and proud co-CEO and founder of Bitwise, she's an emerging celebrity in the world of tech. Her blue and purple hair, jeans and sneakers, and slogan T-shirts ("No one belongs here more than you," or "The future is female") make her a standout. When it was time to take a group photo with former president Barack Obama, he put his hands on Irma's shoulders and asked her to stand in front.

In the photo, Irma is smiling broadly. Her T-shirt? "Woke Up Gay Again."

CALIFORNIA'S NEGLECTED HEARTLAND

Together, Jake and Irma have created a thriving, mission-driven business—one that not only draws on their individual strengths and their family's stories but is also contributing to and helping revive their hometown of Fresno, a community all too often ignored by traditional venture capitalists.

Fresno sits smack-dab in the center of California, hours from the sandy beaches and well below the snowy peaks of the Sierra Nevada mountain range. It is the homeland of the Yokuts and Mono peoples, as Fresno State University publicly acknowledged in 2018. Fresno is, on paper, both a very rich and very poor place. Agricultural production value in Fresno County totals more than $7 billion, the highest of any county in the country. But nearly one out of four people lives in abject poverty. Air quality is terrible; gangs and violent crime are disproportionately high compared to other California counties. The city itself was established in colonies, or tracts, and so while a few lovely neighborhoods are filled with tree-lined streets, historic homes, and shady lawns, many other neighborhoods are blighted, with gutted buildings, boarded-up storefronts, and like many U.S. cities today, sprawling encampments of homeless people.

Jake and Irma see nothing but opportunity.

Although they both left their Central California communities to attend university, they were drawn back. Jake returned to Fresno for a summer gig during law school expecting to find a dried-up old cow town. But when he arrived, overwhelmingly, immediately, he had a sense of a calling. He was home. The pull was so strong he couldn't even make sense of it. But he listened to his heart and threw himself into revitalizing the community, especially the desolate and dreary downtown.

For Irma, returning to Fresno from Ohio was literally starting over.

Suddenly her lucrative computer science and engineering internships were done. She was back in California with no money in her pocket, cleaning out garages and pantries to sell things at the flea market to get enough cash to put gas in her tank so she could get to job interviews. But even while scraping by, coming back made sense. Not just to support her family, but also from what she describes as "the heart agitation standpoint." She had left Fresno and, for a period, stepped into a privileged world where she would even consider stopping for a cup of coffee. She wondered: What can I do about the folks in my own hometown who won't ever see what I just saw?

For almost a decade, after returning to Fresno, Jake and Irma took separate paths toward building justice in their hometown.

Irma tried teaching, and soon settled into a series of tech initiatives that blossomed under her inspired leadership. 59DaysofCode launched companies, taught coding, dispersed cash grants, and brought together the existing tech enthusiasts in a coworking space. There were more computer engineers in town than any one of them had realized, and they reveled in their newfound sense of community. She launched Geekwise Academy, a Central Valley tech boot camp, where participants could learn basic coding in six weeks.

It was the predecessor of a much larger Bitwise initiative, and her early mistakes and pitfalls led to greater success down the road.

Meanwhile, Jake was starting to attract clients as one of the few intellectual property attorneys in town. But he was also pouring his energy into uplifting Fresno. When the city elected Ashley Swearengin as its new mayor, she articulated her ambitious vision that the future of Fresno was dependent upon a robust and thriving downtown. Jake started getting involved with projects, from colorful murals to street cleanups, that helped improve the downtown area in some way. Soon the mayor asked him to launch an "I Believe in Downtown" grassroots campaign advocating for revitalization and redevelopment. He helped start the Boomerang Project, to reverse brain drain from Fresno with a simple first goal of bringing ten of Fresno's best and brightest back to the city in one year. He sat on nonprofit boards and met with local leaders. One day Irma Olguin called him. She needed an attorney and had heard he was good.

Jake was astonished by the work Irma was doing, and she was impressed by his vision for Fresno's future. They told us they began meeting up because they both really wanted to build something together. Their question: How do we build the company that creates the future in our city that we want?

On nights and weekends, they hashed out an ambitious model. Then they broke it down, identifying what it would take to get it off the ground. They were thinking very big. Slowly, bit by bit, they devised Bitwise Industries, which, as Irma puts it, could do what it takes to cause an entire city—and not just a select few people in it—to thrive.

They understood that first-generation immigrants and the children of migrant farmworkers were often blocked from careers in tech because they hadn't learned programming skills, but they also knew, inherently, that those roadblocks had much more to do with practical barriers like child care, food insecurity, and rent. As Irma pointed out, how do you justify learning to write code when there are bills to pay? Wouldn't it be better for your family if you just got a job at McDonald's and put in as many hours as you could? Irma and Jake weren't Silicon Valley kids, yet they were succeeding in tech. They knew it could be done.

"I remember thinking to myself, if it can happen to me, a poor, queer Brown woman from nowhere, why can't it happen to entire cities of people like me?" Irma would later say in a TED Talk that aired on National Public Radio.

They asked themselves what might happen if the potential of the sons and daughters of farmworkers was unleashed? Would people who were traditionally left behind in tech create even more jobs? If so, shouldn't they be lifting them up? Simply put, that's exactly what they have done. They have built a multifaceted business that exposes what it takes to cause an entire city, and not just a few select people in it, to thrive.

BEYOND GOOD INTENTIONS

The cornerstone of Bitwise Industries is job training. The communities they work with are very poor, including unhoused, undocumented, formerly incarcerated, and veterans, people looking for life beyond the body-breaking field work surrounding Fresno. But Jake and Irma have been down that path, and have thought this through. They deploy a fleet of vehicles to pick students up and take them to class. They provide child care, boxes of food, loaner computers, health benefits—various levels of wraparound support that address the system-wide roadblocks that stand in the way for so many immigrant and vulnerable communities.

Irma and Jake have devised a unique three-stage training process that diverges from traditional programs, and each stage—self-evaluation, pre-apprenticeship, and apprenticeship—has a purpose, with clear, attainable exit criteria.

To begin with, Bitwise doesn't wait for students to come. They recruit them, by building relationships with organizations that serve their ideal candidates: formerly incarcerated people, food-insecure families, single mothers. They invite potential students to participate in a self-evaluation, where they're introduced to what it might look like to be a technologist. The idea is to give recruits the agency to make an informed decision about whether they want to pursue a tech career. There are also four basic requirements. Students must be able to read, write, and speak at a junior high school level in English, Spanish, or Hmong, a dialect of Vietnamese prevalent in the area; check email in a web browser; type on a keyboard; and divide by three. (They offer remediation programs for each of these.)

With that, Bitwise participants enter their second stage of training, a pre-apprenticeship program, and they begin six-week, stackable lesson modules that build toward entry-level competency in the tech industry. The training is self-guided and flexible, which reflects the variety of in-demand tech jobs—from front-end development to web design, cybersecurity, or project management. These days Bitwise also trains for jobs adjacent to tech, such as customer support and sales. All these paths will lead to a high-growth, higher-wage job, and all use evidence-based achievement, where the work that students produce is evidence of their achievement. Most students participate in four to six of the courses before continuing on to stage three, an apprenticeship.

An apprenticeship is a paid, one-year, fully benefited program. Students work under the tutelage of a developer fellow who serves as a kind of "player-coach." Through Bitwise's tech consulting arm, apprentices may work on real-world projects. The emphasis is placed on delivering a tangible work product to show what the students have learned and are capable of. Fancy certificates may be nice, but demonstrating that you can do the job at hand is far more convincing to potential employers.

Workforce development based on apprenticeship has been widely adopted in European countries for a long time and has lately become increasingly popular in the U.S. Typically, apprenticeships offer paid, on-the-job training that leads to higher-wage work, while meeting employers' specific needs. Until recently they've largely been limited to tradespeople like electricians, plumbers, and construction workers, but there's been widespread recognition of their effectiveness and scalability in tech, health care, and other fields struggling to fill their workforce. Kapor Capital's portfolio includes several apprenticeship or training programs, and some of the firms in our portfolio are even collaborating with each other. All of this fits with our core beliefs: the distance traveled in life is a better metric of potential than pedigrees and employee referral programs, which are inherently biased. At Bitwise, after a year, apprentices graduate from the third stage to full-time work with either Bitwise or another employer. Bitwise pays their students a living wage, $17 an hour in 2022. It gives them real work and that all-important first line of experience on a resume. We are staunchly opposed to unpaid internships as they are inherently gap-widening because they can only be pursued by people who don't need to feed, clothe, and house themselves—let alone take care of other family members. Yet they build networks and resumes, giving those already privileged yet another unfair advantage. At Bitwise, Jake and Irma understood this, and make sure their paid students are supported by a student success team, specifically focused not on the technical needs, but the other life needs. The six-week tech classes are taught by recent graduates, people who have come from where the new students came from and can relate to their situations.

Almost a decade into its founding, Bitwise Industries has worked with thousands of trainees, with 80 percent of their students employed in tech-related fields. Those students typically earn about $70,000 annually, which enables them to move into a middle-class lifestyle, build savings accounts, go out to lunch, or buy a better car. The remaining 20 percent of Bitwise students who don't fare as well are often blocked by issues of poverty: a death in the family, changes of custody, health issues. Others decide tech is not for them, or just don't reach requisite mastery. Among those who do complete the program, some find jobs in their hometowns or Oakland, but many go to work for Bitwise itself. Jake and Irma also serve companies that are desperate for trained tech employees, and teach specific courses to their systems. And they look to philanthropies that want real results, not policy briefs. But job training itself isn't a job, and Bitwise has a plan for that.

These new techies, whether from Central California or any of the underestimated cities across the U.S. that Bitwise serves, look nothing like your typical Silicon Valley tech team. Bitwise's tech consultants are women, people of color, young and old, whose life experience informs their work.

Bitwise consultants also handle large government contracts, and are uniquely positioned to outperform competitors. For example, during the pandemic, New Mexico launched a $3.2 billion emergency broadband benefit to help bring Wi-Fi to low-income households—largely aimed at the Native American communities. Bitwise won the contract to run a call center that would reach out to potential customers. In Fresno, a team of Black and Latinx talent built and delivered the underlying contact center as a service solution. Then Bitwise trained dialers in New Mexico, tied to their new Las Cruces Bitwise location, to work the phones with Native speakers. In their first ninety days, they added ten thousand additional households to those intended to receive broadband access.

On his first day as California's governor, Gavin Newsom signed a small stack of executive orders. One of them, inspired by and cowritten by Irma, who was cochair of the governor's Transition Technology Council, empowered government agencies to bring their challenges to tech companies, and then allowed the companies themselves to create solutions. This upended a deeply ingrained and flawed practice that has government officials—not necessarily innovators—coming up with outdated, anemic tech solutions, and then contracting with private firms to build them.

It sounded simple, but just a year later, when COVID-19 slammed the world and close to a million Californians found themselves unemployed overnight, it proved to be groundbreaking. Governor Newsom knew there were plenty of jobs and training programs still available, as well as support for rent, utilities, and food. But he needed to immediately connect all of these resources with Californians. Before his executive order, a team of bureaucrats might have needed to design a potential solution, put it out to contractors to build, and then see if it would work.

This time, however, Jake and Irma, in partnership with our nonprofit Kapor Center branch, were able to get to work; they had a team of twenty-five of their own, Bitwise Academy graduates, all women and people of color—from web designers to software engineers—ready to go, and they hired more than 250 additional people to enter data. Less than two weeks after Newsom issued a statewide shelter-in-place order, OnwardCa.org, an intuitive, interactive, resource-packed website, was launched. It wasn't a static list of resources; rather it was a place that could match users with resources according to zip code and desired skills. Their goal was to help 10,000 people in the first month, but in the first twenty-four hours, 100,000 people visited the website and in the first week, nearly 250,000 were matched with open jobs, available training programs, or emergency services such as food or child care.

Jake and Irma were just getting started. After the incredible response in California, they realized this resource was desperately needed in many other communities around the country. Together we went to work on OnwardUS. In the darkest days, we had something to cheer about. Jake teamed up with us to seek large corporate donors, who were looking for ways to contribute; Irma focused on the tech.

It's worth noting that during this time, as we sought philanthropic dollars for the project, we made sure there was a clear wall between our Kapor foundation employees and Bitwise, our portfolio company.

We never cross those lines, because that's what's called self-dealing, using philanthropic dollars to shore up a for-profit company.

As Irma was powering through a firestorm of activity, understanding that Bitwise had something significant to offer during a pandemic, Mitch advised when he could and offered support.

"Someday you're going to tell us how you did this," he said to Irma, impressed.

Irma, who had been working around the clock, paused for a moment. This was the energy she needed to keep going.

Within three weeks, OnwardUS launched, providing a national solution for displaced workers across the country. Here was a website created out of necessity, by software developers from communities most impacted by the crisis, who are often overlooked by the technology industry, and who were now serving our country in its time of need.

MAKING DOWNTOWN THE PLACE TO BE

Ultimately, Bitwise is really about place. A vibrant and supportive workspace for their students and their tech consultants didn't exist in downtown Fresno. So that was part of their plan. Jake and Irma have purchased one large building after the next, vacant cold-storage houses and dilapidated packing plants, and turned them into inviting, creative classrooms for their tech students, contemporary, light-filled offices for their tech consultants, flexible coworking spaces for the next entrepreneurs, and, most importantly, high-ceilinged, wood and glass paneled commercial spaces for other companies to rent. In Fresno, they're in four large buildings within a few blocks of each other, and by hiring local artists, they've created the Bitwise Mural District. Outside, the huge walls are painted with colorful murals, beautifying the community. "MOTHERSHIP of technological education, collaboration and innovation in Fresno," reads one sign. Brew pubs are popping up nearby, to accommodate the workforce. Inside the walls are also bright, with exposed brick, more stunning murals, and artwork from locals. There are podcast chambers and meditation rooms, and a private doggy door for Irma's pooch, Bruce, Pup Executive Officer. Each building has its own café, open to the public, and they've held on to the historic pieces of their properties: a car dealership's indoor ramp is now a stunning indoor theater, with leather seating and reclining chairs. Community groups and nonprofits use the spaces, and local elected officials come and go. There are teams in business suits and teens in sweatshirts. There's a cutting-edge, affordable coworking space, where entrepreneurs can take calls in private spaces or launch a show in a podcasting booth. Businesses, from tech startups to nonprofits, lease offices, and Bitwise has a waiting list for tenants.

They'd moved beyond Fresno by 2022, repeating their model across the U.S., in Bakersfield, Merced, and Oakland in California; El Paso, Texas; Las Cruces, New Mexico; Greeley, Colorado; Cheyenne, Wyoming; Toledo, Ohio; and Buffalo, New York, and work is under way to launch in many more cities. Jake and Irma have very specific selection criteria for how they define an "underestimated city" where they want to serve. They're not looking for a place where things are working well. In many respects, they're looking for the opposite, a city with the sort of economic challenges they've confronted in Fresno. They look for per capita income less than $30,000 a year, a population between 250,000 and 1.5 million, and a place where tech is not flourishing. They choose midsized cities, or parts of cities, that have all the elements that contribute to poor health outcomes: from critter-infested housing and food deserts to air pollution and jobs that don't pay living wages. Tax incentives, while welcome, aren't very helpful for a startup that needs immediate cash flow. And they look for versions of their former selves, people engaged in and respected by their communities, to lead the initiatives.

"We have cities across our nation full of too many hungry, thirsty, overlooked, underestimated and systemically oppressed human beings. Meanwhile, in the tech industry you have hungry, thirsty, blind and spendthrift companies in dire need of talent," they wrote in a 2021 post after receiving $50 million in Series B financing led by Kapor Capital. "It's time to stop expecting tech giants to be better and instead become a giant ourselves. We're going to keep raising money, keep building and shipping world-class software, keep moving into underdog cities and keep training up the scrappy and talented technology wizards that are the future of their hometowns. We're done trying to convince big, medium and little tech to hire folks from these places. They can if they want, and if they do, they won't be disappointed. But we're saving our breath and our energy for more important things. Instead of sending a handful of our apprentices to shiny Silicon Valley companies, we're keeping them." They proceeded to hire one thousand people the world has overlooked in the next eighteen months.

A DIFFICULT PATH TO FUNDING

Fresno is a few hours from the Bay Area, but as we've described, it's a very different place from San Francisco and Silicon Valley. And although we had heard about what Jake and Irma were doing with Bitwise, and were interested in the business, we weren't in a rush to make the trip; it was challenging to fit into our regular routine. But we're so glad we did.

On our first visit, we were struck by the synergy between the two.

Irma is really the heart and soul of the company, and Jake is more what you would think of as a conventional CEO, negotiating deals, signing contracts. What's impressive is their chemistry, their mutual respect, and their ability to argue with each other, constructively. So is their plan. They're creating a workforce of people who can handle information technology jobs at every hospital, every city agency, or every school—the kind of jobs that are needed in every single community. What's more, they are creating a tech ecosystem with the potential to transform Fresno's economy. Every time they create a new job, there's a follow-on effect of creating additional jobs and injecting new money into the community.

When we visited, Irma and Jake were seeking expansion capital to show that they could take their model beyond Fresno. When we looked at what they were doing, we found common purpose. Their business plan was robust as well, with multiple sources of income all reinforcing each other.

But that's not what most investors saw. Many conventional venture firms had already turned them down again and again; they were skeptical about this complex business model and wary of entrepreneurs whose educations and life experiences diverged dramatically from their own. Jake and Irma admit now that they were naïve at first and not great at telling their story in a language that traditional investors understood. They also faced a lot of disbelief when they proposed scaling a venture-backed company out of Fresno, California, an irrigated desert. Finally, they weren't plugged in to the existing VC community, so they didn't have the same cachet and instant recognition that other entrepreneurs did when they showed up to make their pitches.

"I mean, look at me," says Irma. But actually they weren't looking at her. Literally hundreds of times she and Jake, a tall, white-presenting attorney, would be sitting in a room with a team of white, affluent investors and there were no questions for Irma even though Bitwise is a tech company and Irma is the technologist, not Jake. Even if Jake deferred to her for an answer, the follow-up question went back to Jake. It was as if she was invisible. Jake is skillful at redirecting attention to Irma, but they are both humble and pragmatic. They use their resources, personal and organizational, strategically. If Irma's style resonates with people, she'll be the storyteller. If investors are connecting to Jake, he takes the lead—both of them playing their parts in service of the Bitwise mission. As she tells her staff, "Do you want to be right or do you want to get what you want?"

We initially planned to make a small seed investment in Bitwise. After we visited, and had seen all parts of the business, we understood it, and we loved it. Jake and Irma had already secured what seemed like a solid commitment for $5 million from a VC firm in San Francisco that fashioned itself as caring about impact, and was ready to lead the deal. We wanted in, but with a smaller stake, an amount more consistent with first checks we usually write.

Jake and Irma were excited, but also perplexed because days and then weeks passed, but no check arrived from their lead investor. At this point Bitwise's annual revenues were $15 million, but, like so many startups at this stage, they were also perpetually on the brink of running out of money. The early days of an ambitious and expanding startup are exciting and desperate times. People need to be paid. Leases need to be signed. They were scrambling and, as Irma likes to say, "Cash is king."

When we looked into it, we found that the lead VC kept moving the goalposts.

The San Francisco firm had told them that they would make a large, $5 million investment but first they'd need a colead, someone putting in an equal amount of money. Jake and Irma found someone: a Black, successful business owner and venture capitalist looking to invest in existing and aspiring women of color entrepreneurs. He was ready to hand Bitwise Industries $6 million.

Irma and Jake couldn't get back to the Bay Area fast enough to meet with their original firm, excited and ready to roll. But that's when it got really ugly.

Their original investor told them they had found the *wrong* colead. "We really need a credible colead."

Credible? What was that supposed to mean?

Jake called us for advice. We were furious. What in the world was a credible colead if not a successful entrepreneur turned seasoned investor ready to give them $6 million? And how could their lead investor in San Francisco change the criteria after making a commitment? Each pitch had taken Jake and Irma dozens of hours of preparation and meetings, not to mention exorbitant amounts of time and money spent traveling to VC offices to share their story in person. To have two firm commitments was a great achievement at a very critical time. We wondered how to respond.

"Jake," we said, "we need to think about this, but we're thinking of doing something major. Just give us the night."

The next person to call Jake that night was the original investor, outraged that we had even been consulted because, from their perspective, an unspoken code of confidentiality had been broken.

"You don't know what you have done!" the investor yelled at Jake. "You have compromised your entire relationship with Mitch and Freada. They're going to walk away from this deal and it's clear you don't understand what you're doing, because it's not like Mitch is going to lead this deal."

Jake was now terrified. What would he tell Irma? Had he blown it completely? In the morning, he talked to us again and shared the threat from his lead investor.

To hell we won't lead this deal, we thought. And so we committed to $5 million, far more than we had originally planned. We had deliberately never invested that much in a single deal, nor come in that far along in any company's cycle—Bitwise was more than six years old. We prefer early-stage companies whose founders are highly engaged with us, so we can help them bake in the equitable, gap-closing, positive-impact principles we believe in. Also, Mitch would need to take a board seat, a significant commitment.

Traditionally, venture capital takes a shotgun approach to the startups in its portfolio, expecting that most founders will fail but with those losses offset by a handful of very lucrative winners. Our philosophy, on the other hand, is to only invest in companies we believe are going to succeed, and then we work with them to help make that happen. We made the decision because we realized that in order for Bitwise to achieve its potential it needed good investors, and if we stopped at our seed investment it wasn't going to work. We realized we needed to step up.

For Jake, it was a pivotal moment. To hear one investor try to create fear, and then to have us just have his back, meant everything. At the time, investors were telling them they weren't making enough money. We told them they were extraordinary. We still think so.

And we're still fighting for them. Months later, we were invited with Jake to a meeting with a major U.S. financial firm that had expressed interest in working with or investing in Bitwise. Freada went in with Jake, but the executives in the room wouldn't even look at him. The questions were all for Freada. Like Irma before him, Jake was becoming invisible, and we couldn't stand it.

"You guys are treating Jake like he's a kid in the corner," Freada said sharply. "He's building the fastest-growing workforce company in America, and I'm lucky just to be invited to this party."

Jake sat up straight. Everyone did. But Freada wasn't done.

"Jake is in charge! If you don't want Jake to be in charge, get out of here," she said. Right in the middle of the meeting, she waved her arms and pointed to the door.

Well, thought Jake, I have no idea what to say next. But inside, he was punching his fist in the air. And that's who we want to be for our founders, their biggest advocates. But it took Jake a while to get here. A year after we got involved with Bitwise, Jake and Irma confided that they'd actually seen us before.

It started with a confidential email. Jake and Irma were invited to an exclusive conference in San Francisco, "A Day of Inclusivity." They couldn't transfer this invitation, and they had to keep it "super-secret," as Irma says, laughing. Jake and Irma were not well networked in the Bay Area, and so they figured this would be a good opportunity to get to know some people. All too many speakers took the podium with misguided, out-of-touch, aspirational speeches touching on platitudes and clichés. Irma felt that the day had largely been a waste.

But Freada spoke that day, too, and to Irma and Jake, she'd made a lot of sense. Irma wondered, How are we ever going to get close to a person like that? When Freada heard that they didn't feel comfortable approaching her as she left the stage—as so many others in the audience had done—she was heartbroken. We always want to be in conversation with those who are passionate and have a vision, rather than those who are entitled and transactional.

This story illustrates the depth of self-doubt instilled by outsider status. The nagging question of "Do I have a right to be in the room?" deprives all of us of the products and services that are waiting to be invented by those who don't feel they belong.

Many conversations have taken place about "impostor syndrome" in the tech and VC ecosystem in recent years but too often the distinction is lost between a widely held, understandable fear of stumbling and being the recipient of systemic, lifelong messages that one isn't competent to play on the big stage.

MORE THAN THE MONEY

People often ask us what we're looking for in a founder. Our answer is that we're looking for founders whose own life experiences compel them to create companies and build wealth that will solve the difficult problems that they personally had to overcome. Lived experience brings insight, and technology brings scale.

Take Homar Cardenas. Homar had lived a lifetime of typical Fresno poverty and violence and trauma and gangs when police ordered him to pull over for driving erratically in 2017. He didn't. He kept going, the wrong way up a one-way street, all around the city, and finally, after forty-five minutes, through a fence that stopped him short. He backed up, right into a squad car. Three Fresno police officers opened fire, a barrage of thirty-three gunshots.

Homar was hit in his face, his shoulder, and his arm. Amazingly, he survived, only to face a three-year prison sentence, which ended up including two years in solitary confinement. This can't go on, he thought. I've got to change.

"It's hard though," Homar says. "Everybody says 'I'm done' when they're in prison, right? But when you get out, that's when you have to know what to do and what not to do."

His family wasn't able to support him, and when he was released, he was scared. He was directed to attend a meeting for parolees that just happened to be hosted in one of Bitwise Industries' classrooms. After their meeting, a Bitwise recruiter came in and explained what they had to offer.

"For me, as an ex-con, I was like, that sounds too good to be true," said Homar.

And he really had no idea how to follow through. He went home, thought about it, but was too shy to make the call. That didn't matter. Bitwise called him, and soon he was in a free course offered to formerly incarcerated people, taught by people who had been incarcerated themselves. Homar began learning to code, from someone who had traveled the same road, someone he could relate to.

"To be honest, what really got me was the community, because I've never seen so many people be interested in someone that they didn't know," he said. "I just walked in and everybody was interested in me, genuinely interested in me being better and being happy with myself and progressing."

By 2022, Homar was thirty-five, parenting his two teens and working as an online marketing buyer in Bitwise Industries' Fresno office, alongside hundreds of other colleagues. The Bitwise vice president running all of Fresno operations is Thilani Grubel, who juggles a thousand balls to keep her employees happy, her buildings safe, her operations growing, her tenants content, and the business intact. One day she's convincing an impoverished student to use their bathtub to wash their clothes rather than drop out because they're worried about how they smell. The next she's launching a child care center, not just for her staff but also for the community.

Thilani's mother died when she was twelve, and her father was so mentally unstable that she had to move out at sixteen. She didn't go to college and couldn't even begin to understand how to manage the bureaucracy of applying. Plus she was broke, except for her computer. She did have Photoshop, so Thilani taught herself to be a graphic designer, and for fifteen years she freelanced at various Fresno area firms. She applied to Bitwise's marketing team but didn't expect a call back. After all, she didn't have that college degree. But she was offered a job, with great compensation and supportive colleagues.

They told her, "Everyone we hire, we look at the distanced traveled, not at a piece of paper." And when she said she wasn't sure she could do the work, they told her, "We know you don't know how to do this yet, but we will teach you."

Bitwise leaders soon noticed her talents. When they promoted her to vice president of Bitwise Fresno, Thilani was petrified. Her work was to lead her teammates, with a relatively small staff but lots of influence. Here she had a wonderful job, she was thriving, and, most important, after all that turmoil, she had stability. She was ambitious and believed in her leadership potential, but after a lifetime of uncertainty, what if she failed, she asked Irma. Would she be fired?

"If you fail, which I don't think you will, then we will fail together," Irma told her. "But that's not going to happen because we'll be alongside you, at your side, and together we will make this work."

IT'S A RELATIONSHIP

Bitwise's story and our role in its growth are instructive. We tell founders: look for what we call "aligned capital"—money from investors who are aligned with your values and your goals. Your choice of an investor is very important. We can appreciate that founders feel like they have to take what they can get, and that they're the weaker party in the negotiations.

But we want them to think about venture capital partners as seriously as they would weigh a very senior hire. It's the beginning of a big relationship, we tell them, and it's not just a financial relationship. If all goes well they'll be working together for ten years, longer than most marriages survive. The costs of a bad relationship with an investor are extreme, and even more so when you're building a gap-closing business. It's just as important for founders to know what to look for in an investor as it is for investors to know their investment criteria. That's how you buttress yourselves against feelings of powerlessness.

3

WORLD ON FIRE

DONNEL AND DAVIDA

Tech was taking off in 2004 in ways we had both foreseen and never imagined, for the good and the bad. Facebook and Myspace launched that year, Google had an IPO and began offering Gmail, *World of Warcraft* took the gaming world by storm. Mitch was deeply involved with Mozilla as it launched Firefox, a free, open-source browser that couldn't be tracked and sought to give everyone access to the web. Meanwhile, former vice president Al Gore—who had been a huge proponent of what the Internet could bring—was telling anyone who would listen that the planet faced imminent devastation from global warming. We invited him to our original Kapor Center, occupying two floors of a building south of Market Street in San Francisco, to hear his concerns.

"We already know everything we need to know to effectively address this problem," Gore told our gathered friends and colleagues. "Future generations may well have occasion to ask themselves, 'What were our parents thinking? Why didn't they wake up when they had a chance?'"

We sat and listened, absorbing what he was saying. That presentation, which he would make more than one thousand times around the world, had a big influence on us: we understood, deeply, that the threat of climate change was dire and severe. And we weren't the only ones powerfully moved by his message. A few years after his visit, Gore's slide show was made into the film *An Inconvenient Truth*, which became a blockbuster in theaters, won two Academy Awards, and is still one of the most influential documentaries ever released.

In Durham, North Carolina, Duke University student Donnel Baird saw the documentary too and was inspired. "I just knew that we were in the middle of a climate crisis and that I, personally, had to do something," he thought.

In San Diego, California, Davida Herzl, a recent law school graduate, saw it, too: "I'm responsible for fixing this. I'm going to need tools to create a more balanced existence with natural resources," she said.

Donnel and Davida didn't know each other then, and we'd certainly never heard of them when that film debuted. None of us could have foreseen that in the coming years it would be Davida and Donnel launching some of the most ambitious companies tackling climate change in the world. These founders are dedicating their lives to technologies that we support, closing the climate gap and curbing the looming environmental disaster.

Gore's message also rippled through elite gatherings of Silicon Valley's VC investors during those heady days. Between 2005 and 2006, the National Venture Capital Association reported that investments in what was then called CleanTech went from a few hundred million dollars to $1.75 billion. And over the next five years, tens of billions of dollars poured into the sector, backed with more than $100 billion in tax breaks, low-cost loans, and subsidies.

"Avarice, altruism, and policy had aligned to fuel a spectacular boom," said *Wired* magazine.

As happens so cyclically in VC, the boom was followed by a bust. Ten years after Gore visited our office, "the sector suffered a string of expensive tax-funded flops," said *60 Minutes* correspondent Lesley Stahl. Suddenly *CleanTech* was a dirty word.

The poster child of CleanTech's downfall was Solyndra, a solar panel startup in the heart of the Silicon Valley that raised over $1 billion from private investors and won a $500 million federal loan backed by the Obama administration. The company failed in large part because raw materials used by overseas competitors with conventional solar panel technology dropped 80 percent; Solyndra simply couldn't compete. But there were other issues the cast doubt on the entire sector. A review from the Department of Energy's inspector general found the Solyndra loan application was somewhere between reckless and intentionally deceptive. Many other CleanTech companies failed as well, from poorly conceived car companies to battery technologies that simply didn't work. Entrepreneurs and tech investors had been overconfident, even arrogant, that what had worked in hardware, software, and networking would work in CleanTech. In the passing years, as Donnel and Davida conceived and built their own complex, multilayered companies, it became clear that tackling climate change would have to be dealt with on its own terms.

Not every company tanked, and eventually the sector evolved. By the time the pandemic hit the globe, new and improved ideas, better technologies, and a tranche of new federal stimulus funds again uplifted what was now called Climate Tech. In 2021, Climate Tech startups raised $40 billion, twice the investment of 2020, according to analysts at Climate Tech VC.

At the same time, a new and urgent activism was emerging, inspired by Greta Thunberg, who was asking exactly what Gore had warned us about more than fifteen years earlier.

"You all come to us young people for hope," she said. "How dare you? You have stolen my dreams and my childhood with your empty words."

Our foundation had always supported environmental causes, and our investment fund supported many Climate Tech companies; we understood the growing inequity and disparity that our human pollution was already causing. We also supported projects to raise public awareness; for example, we invested in a film about the health hazards of vinyl, just as the toxic product was becoming ubiquitous. The filmmakers showed that factory workers, those living downwind of the factories, and even people whose homes had vinyl siding were being exposed to dangerous chemicals, and were disproportionately low-income people of color. When disasters hit, whether it's wildfires, deep freezes, or hurricanes, disadvantaged groups suffer disproportionate physical and financial harm. Climate injustice won't be solved by any one entity, but gap-closing tech must be part of the solution.

DECARBONIZE THE PLANET, ONE BUILDING AT A TIME

You can't talk with Donnel Baird for long before he laughs at his own audacity. After all, he is tackling climate change, environmental justice, the digital divide, and racial disparity every day. His mission is to decarbonize millions of buildings nationwide—buildings that produce 20 percent of U.S. greenhouse gases and 30 percent of carbon emissions—in need of $1.2 trillion in energy-efficient upgrades with solar panels, heat and cooling pumps, and more.

Donnel grew up in a small apartment in the Bedford-Stuyvesant section of Brooklyn, sharing a bedroom with his little sister and his parents, his father an engineer, his mother a teacher. They had fled Guyana when it was rocked by violence and political assassinations in the 1980s, and were starting from scratch. The family heated their stuffy space in the winter by turning on the gas oven and opening its door. Because the building's shared bathroom was down the hall, his parents kept a potty in the bedroom for the kids to use at night so Donnel and his sister wouldn't walk past the open oven. Here was yet another consequence of not having reliable energy in their home. His community of low-income Black families were cold in the winter, hot in the summer, and plagued with high utility bills. Donnel was a gifted student who saw the worst America has to offer as a child—toxic housing, dilapidated schools, violence, and grinding poverty. He couldn't visit friends because there were drug dealers and gunfights on the streets outside his apartment. When his mother witnessed a woman and her baby shot on the street, she fled a second time, taking Donnel, who was ten, and his sister to Atlanta. There he fought for a series of opportunities to attend private school, immersing himself in white, privileged communities where he saw, firsthand, the stark disparities in this country.

While Donnel was in college at Duke, his best friend, a climate activist, demanded he take an environmental science class and watch *An Inconvenient Truth*, twice. Donnel majored in history, political science, and government, and he studied how Gore sought strategic policy fixes to solve global warming. Gore had held the first hearings on climate change in Congress when Donnel was still a toddler, and as vice president he pushed for a carbon tax. In 1992, Gore helped broker the Kyoto Protocol, a treaty aimed at curbing greenhouse gases. At the time, the Internet was an emerging phenomenon and Gore also made tech a priority. Mitch, who had cofounded the Electronic Frontier Foundation, advised the vice president to make sure the then-immature web didn't create a growing information gap between the haves and have-nots.

When Gore left politics he cofounded a sustainability-focused public and private equity firm, Generation Investment Management, with David Blood. Each of the Generation cofounders had already worked with one of us—Mitch met the vice president in the early days of the Internet, and Freada met David when he asked her to develop customized diversity programs for Goldman Sachs, where he was a senior executive, in the 1990s. Gore asked Mitch to join Generation's advisory board, and Freada served as a consultant to the firm on human capital matters for more than a decade. We have been investors in the firm since its early days; Generation, now with more than $35 billion under management, has led follow-on funding in several Kapor Capital companies.

As Generation Investment Management was founded in 2004, Donnel was graduating from Duke. He returned to New York to work as a community organizer, where he recognized two problems that were the basis for each other's solution—many unemployed people desperate for work and training, and dilapidated buildings in critical need of better heating and air-conditioning systems. He joined President Barack Obama's campaign, and when Obama won, Donnel was able to run a pilot program of his emerging vision, to hire unemployed people in the District of Columbia and train them to retrofit homes to be more energy efficient. With $2.5 million in stimulus funds, they hired and trained twenty people who updated four hundred homes, dramatically reducing their emissions.

Donnel went back to school, this time getting an MBA at Columbia Business School, where he made good use of his classes to refine his remarkable business, BlocPower.

When we met, Donnel explained that BlocPower's real asset is a highly sophisticated software system that can identify the energy efficiency or inefficiency, building by building, in a low-income neighborhood. It does so by examining information like building permits and utility bills, not by sending inspectors to make an expensive and time-consuming site visit. The software can group buildings into a "Bloc," and then analyze what technologies are going to most effectively and inexpensively retrofit the schools, apartments, churches, or nonprofits to increase the efficiency. Many need solar panels, and all-electric heating, cooling, and hot water systems. Closing another gap, the installers are formerly unemployed people, many traumatized by violence in their communities, now earning living wages and benefits while solving their neighborhoods' biggest problems.

Building owners don't pay up front for the retrofits. Instead, BlocPower offers zero-down financing and building owners pay off the loans with the money they save from lowered utility bills. This means building owners can switch to fossil-free energy without any up-front costs and no annual budget increases.

BlocPower is a quintessential example of a gap-closing company that leverages tech to achieve scale and efficiency.

MAKE SURE YOU HELP PEOPLE

In March 2020, New York City was slammed harder than anywhere else in the country by the pandemic. COVID-19 hospitalizations and fatalities overwhelmed the city, and Donnel and his family fled upstate to a small community. His first task was finding a satellite and installing their Wi-Fi system.

With Wi-Fi up, he checked his email, and saw we had been trying to get in touch.

We hopped on a Zoom, relieved that Donnel and his family were safe. Then we talked about his business.

Mitch told him investors might be reluctant to spend in the coming months. And we told him it wasn't clear what BlocPower would be able to do as the crisis grew. We left him with a challenge: "No matter what, make sure you're helping people," we said. Donnel hung up the phone and thought, Well, how can I help people?

He had just finished installing his own Wi-Fi on his rental house.

Now he decided he needed to get Wi-Fi to the millions of people back in his own childhood neighborhood who were locked down and not connected to the Internet. As the world moved online, they couldn't go to school, they couldn't work, they couldn't even see doctors who had pivoted to telehealth.

Donnel came up with a plan for BlocPower to bring Wi-Fi, and good jobs, into underrepresented neighborhoods. Within months, as the pandemic raged on, he partnered with the Mayor's Office of Criminal Justice and began hiring and training thousands of people to install broadband and clean energy in underserved neighborhoods, block by block. The so-called Civilian Climate Corps moved into communities at high risk of gun violence and put thousands of people to work. Then he scaled up, signing contracts in more U.S. cities.

We invested in BlocPower early, in 2014, because we saw Donnel's genius. He combined an impressive array of talents, bringing together deep insight, lived experience, tech know-how, and best practices as a community organizer. When people ask us what we mean by "empathetic tech" and "investing in people who come from the communities they want to serve," Donnel is an obvious example. We invested to save the planet and to help communities dramatically reduce their fossil fuel use and their energy bills. We invested to train disenfranchised people for the jobs of the future.

Over the years, Donnel has scaled up to managing city-wide contracts across the U.S., covering tens of thousands of buildings from Atlanta to Oakland. Hypergrowth like that is risky, and Donnel has had some very scary times. Growing rapidly to meet all these needs creates one execution challenge after another. He's nearly run out of money, had teams walk away, and dealt with investors who lost faith. The *Washington Post* described him as "tenacious." Donnel says a Black man in America has to be.

We believe in Donnel's vision. He exemplifies our investing philosophy. If he hadn't, himself, grown up in those apartments, with the oven door open and the drug dealers outside, we don't think he would have seen this gap-closing business idea. And because of his background, including being constantly underestimated as a Black man, we don't think standard U.S. investors would have seen him, heard him, and believed in him.

I'M NOT MANAGING

A few months into living in upstate New York, Donnel was out on his daily jog when a white truck pulled up next to him. The driver, a white man, rolled down his window and asked, "Hey, are you from around here?" Donnel scowled and told him he was living with his family in the yellow house down the street. His wife's father had owned a home in a nearby town for decades.

The driver looked closely at Donnel and said, "Well, you know, there's been a lot of robberies around here and we're really concerned."

What an idiot, thought Donnel. He put on his headphones and headed home, where he saw that his best friend had been calling and texting: there was a brutal video circulating online, unbelievably terrible. They needed to talk.

Donnel logged on and watched as Ahmaud Arbery, a twenty-five-year-old Black man, was stopped while jogging on a rural Georgia road by men in a white pickup truck. They shot and killed him. It was all there on the video. This looked all too familiar.

Deeply shaken, Donnel immediately tried to jump back into work, but he describes himself as a ferocious person, and we saw some of his business communications that day were pretty angry.

The next day on a call, Freada asked Donnel how he was processing the grueling videos of Black men being murdered in broad daylight by white men. She talked about the long list in a few short years, beginning with Trayvon Martin, George Floyd, and now this video emerging months after the murder of Ahmaud Arbery.

"I think this is really getting to you, as it understandably should," said Freada. "I'm distraught. I can't imagine what this is like for you."

"I'm not processing this," he told us. "I'm not managing."

He actually wasn't aware, until Freada brought it up, that he had been affected. Now he realized that the ferocity he was bringing to his business negotiations with wealthy white men was influenced by a deep and intense need to protect himself.

When we invest in a company, we invest in the founder and their team. Part of our responsibility is to support those people at every level; that's simply the decent way to work with someone, and it's built into our investment strategy. When terrible news like this hit, we invited all of the Black founders in our portfolio into a Zoom meeting to talk through their feelings with both a mental health professional and a facilitator we hired to support them. We obviously didn't join them, but we were told they spent an intense three hours together.

Nothing came of it immediately, but eighteen months later some of those same founders were gathered at Martha's Vineyard with us, and they recalled that time together, how it built trust between them. They talked about how President Obama had just inspired them, and made plans to work together, pitching smart city technologies around the country. Donnel knew he had a company that could decarbonize the planet. Now he talked with another one of our founders, who said she had an extraordinary new tool to measure his impact.

BREATHABLE AIR

"When astronauts view earth from space, they are awestruck by the glowing thin blue line that surrounds the planet," said Davida Herzl, when she started her pitch to us at our Kapor Center. "That incomprehensibly thin line is the layer of air that makes life here possible—a limited and precious resource. We pollute this treasure every day."

We ask our founders to think really, really big, and now this first-time CEO, a mixed-race Jewish woman, was aiming to solve the greatest challenge of our time, climate change. How in the world could she do this? we wondered.

We were spellbound. Her understanding of our planet, and her responsibility as a human to care for it, were so clearly defined, determined, and technically brilliant. We would later learn of the complex and remarkable path she'd taken to become such a visionary. When she gives talks, she likes to begin by describing the vulnerability of the sixteen thousand feet of breathable air on the planet. Just like water on earth, she'll say, that air is all we'll ever have.

"If the earth were an apple, the layer of skin on that apple would be breathable air," she says. Audiences gasp as she shares slides that lay bare the fragility of the planet's atmosphere.

During her pitch to us, Davida explained that she had set out to solve three integrated challenges with her company Aclima.

The first was to create an air quality sensing system that identifies what pollutants people are breathing at a very local level, block by block through an entire city or region, over time. Most cities had just one, or a few, air quality sensors for miles, or even hundreds of miles, of sprawling homes and businesses, industrial parks, and protected forests. Those stationary air monitors offer extremely limited coverage, and don't tell communities very much about what people are breathing on their neighborhood block, especially about air quality in lower-income communities near freeways, factories, or ports, where emissions can be sky high. They also don't measure greenhouse gases, which cause climate change by trapping heat and pose severe environmental and health issues.

Sitting in our Oakland offices, we knew that thousands of kids in our city had asthma, and that it disproportionately impacts low-income children who are Black and Latinx. Years before we met Davida we invested in Propeller Health, which pioneered an asthma inhaler that sent data to the cloud every time it was used. It could help individuals and their health care providers track their usage and prevent traumatic and expensive emergency room visits. About the same time as our investment in Propeller, research was emerging on the causes of asthma in low-income communities, focusing on the allergens in homes. Asthma caused children to miss school and their parents to miss work, compounding their poverty and lack of access to health care.

"You've found the key to the puzzle," we told her. "Actual data that shows what was in the air they were breathing on their playgrounds, in their parks."

"Right," she said. "That's the second challenge we're solving: once Aclima identifies pollutants, it's critical to understand the impact they have on humans."

It turns out that the same emissions that are transforming our climate go straight back into our lungs, she explained.

"We're like fish in the ocean that have forgotten that we live in water, and those health impacts are transforming human well-being around the planet," she said.

The third integrated problem she aimed to solve was the uneven distribution of local pollution; low-income communities of color are disproportionately impacted. Black people in the U.S. are three times more likely to die from diseases that are induced by exposure to pollution. Now Davida was telling us that she thought this could be addressed, by generating the data and the measurement infrastructure to target solutions in a quantified, efficient, and effective way.

She showed us a map of West Oakland; it turns out that pollution varied by up to 800 percent from one block to the next—groundbreaking research by Aclima that the team published in 2017. This meant that someone's address, where they live in proximity to those emissions, can have long-standing health outcomes for them and their families.

Mitch likes to say that genius is evenly distributed across zip codes, but access and opportunity are not. Now Davida was laying this out on her map.

PLANETARY HEALTH IS HUMAN HEALTH

By the time we met, in 2016, Aclima was doing groundbreaking work. Davida talked about looking at the impacts of the expansion of warehouses as the result of e-commerce growth. Tens of thousands of new eighteen-wheelers and delivery vans were racing across the country—what did that mean for the planet? Aclima could identify gases emitted from abandoned wells, spot natural gas leaks in pipelines, and understand impacts of landfill emissions.

"Planetary health is human health," she said.

She explained her technology: air-sensing devices about the size of a carry-on bag that rode in Aclima's hybrid vehicles and some of Google's Street View cars. This was a technical tour de force, to shrink an air quality monitoring system, typically the size of a shipping container, to a small suitcase.

And there was one more critical layer: when Aclima received contracts from a government or a utility or a company to map their air, they hired drivers and technicians from the communities hit hardest by pollution.

"We're not only helping to catalyze emissions reductions, but we're also lifting people up, we're lifting communities up," she told us.

Davida had already interacted with a lot of venture capitalists in Silicon Valley by the time we met. On that day, she grew emotional talking to us; we could see how passionate she was about the planet. She told us later she was also deeply moved that day by the level of diversity in Kapor Capital. It was the first time she had actually stepped into an office where she felt seen and heard.

We told her we were only investing in companies that were solving big social problems, and she pressed us about our willful, intentional strategy around investing in entrepreneurs who came from underrepresented communities and nontraditional backgrounds. Freada talked to her about how the distance a founder has traveled told her more about their potential than their degree or family name. Davida later shared that on the day she came to Kapor Capital, seeing a set of investors proactively trying to chart this completely new path made her feel like she was home. That's certainly what we were aiming for.

For years, Davida had been pitching to white men in hoodies, over and over again, including one who didn't take off his sunglasses until she finished, when he asked, "Are you tired? Are you really going to have the energy to keep this up?"

She told us there was zero resonance with what she was trying to do.

"It was like I was talking into a vacuum," she said.

Davida was one of many of our founders who had a tough time raising funds while facing scrutiny and skepticism from mainstream investors. Latinx women founders received less than half a percent of the $400 billion in VC investment between 2009 and 2017, and only fifty-eight of those women ever raised more than $1 million, according to ProjectDiane, a demographic study that provided a snapshot of Latina and Black women founders. Aclima had raised tens of millions over a decade, a testament to Davida's commitment to her ambitious mission. She'd had to overcome a lot in convincing VCs to write her a check.

Although her first customer was Google, government funding

began to make up a substantial portion of her revenue, which some investors falsely claim is an unreliable and difficult customer base, subject to the whims of politics, and not highly scalable. Behind this myth is a darker belief in Silicon Valley that government itself is a problem, and that elected officials and those who serve them interfere with innovation. We believe the opposite. Given that government at all levels—federal, state, and city—increasingly has mandates to track and reduce emissions, especially as they impact low-income communities, we see Climate Tech backed with government funding as a growing field and potentially a source of significant revenue.

Investors are biased against women, and even more biased against women of color; in our own study of female founders, 77 percent told us they experienced rudeness, condescension, or unfriendly behavior from investors during pitches. Davida told us she faced even further discrimination for her women-led team of scientists building hardware. Many VCs are wary of hardware and components to begin with, but this inequity was compounded by the downfall of Elizabeth Holmes, the former CEO of Theranos, convicted of criminal fraud for raising hundreds of millions of dollars by touting fake blood-testing equipment. At its peak, Theranos was valued at $9 billion, and while yes, Holmes was lying, the blue-chip investors and supporters were a large part of the problem. It's grossly unfair that the high-profile taint of Theranos's lies and rip-offs would ever cast a negative pall over remarkable businesses like Aclima, where Davida has built a team of world-class scientists from top institutions, including NASA.

We had the opposite reaction. A bull's-eye company is one whose central purpose is gap-closing, and when Davida told us about Aclima, we saw a company that was nailing it. It's a central mission that all Kapor Capital portfolio companies share, proving their thesis that they can address multiple dimensions of disparity at the same time. Aclima aimed to close equity gaps in race, the environment, economics, education, and health by quantifying disparity as it relates to the quality of air people breathe.

"You can't manage what you can't measure," she told us. "Our mission is to enable a more environmentally intelligent society—for public health and planetary health."

By the time we invested in 2018, Aclima was growing rapidly, and when wildfires battered the Bay Area, it offered the only definitive information pointing to what was in the thick, orange-brown smoke that smothered the region. There were gaseous pollutants like carbon monoxide, and on those dark days, particle pollution, the greatest threat to public health.

In 2020, as she was closing a new round of fundraising, wildfires in Northern California turned the Bay Area skies dark orange. Davida, who understands that our global economic system has translated into some people breathing healthy air, and some people breathing the most toxic air on the planet, looked around and had a visceral reaction.

She thought about the animated, croaking frogs in *An Inconvenient Truth*, when a hand scoops them out of a pot of water just as it starts to boil. On this day, as the thick, eerie smoke blocked the sun, she wondered if VCs were finally going to understand the connection between air pollution and climate change.

"Look outside!" she said, calling investors. "This is why we need to do this work. This is why you need to send that check."

When it comes to big, urgent problems like climate change, we need big, creative solutions. The business of Aclima was so squarely on the mark, so needed, and such a good application of tech.

WHAT'S ON THE SHELVES

As a child, Davida would later recall in a blog, she became obsessed with extinction and the role humans have in stewarding our natural resources. She collected *National Geographic* articles, and tracked stories about the manatees in Florida being killed by boat rudders, the fate of the golden toad in Costa Rica, and how 60 million American buffalo were reduced to 1,000 in just a few years. Carl Sagan, who called earth a "pale blue dot," was her childhood hero. When bees built hives in her home, her parents eventually had to take the walls apart and, at nine, Davida was astonished by the magnificent honeycomb structures, vertical cities dripping with honey and the thousands of bees inside them, working in unison. Every year Davida looked forward to science projects, where she explored visible and invisible patterns in nature. Life was held together by networks, by invisible rules, in a balance that she deeply wanted to understand.

Davida's parents were binational, and borders were nothing more than a bridge between cultures. Her entrepreneurial family was a dealer of global goods, supplying, delivering, and sourcing components and products for a range of industries and customers. The oldest of four, Davida says "a colorful, global upbringing" shaped her thinking.

When Sony needed components for remote controls, the Herzls could import crates of high-quality, low-cost pieces from Southeast Asia, and then get them delivered to a manufacturing plant south of the border. When a blue jeans company needed denim, boxes of sample swatches from Vietnam, Cambodia, and Thailand would arrive at their door. She would cut the lids open and smell another country, feeling the fabric, for thickness, softness, quality. When an infant formula maker needed dry powdered milk, her dad—during dinner—facilitated a deal with a manufacturer in Australia who was just waking up. Pots and pans, pressure cookers, stuffed animals, bags of flour, plastic pellets: she'd watch where they came from, who made them, and where they went. She'd wander through stores gazing at the shelves, knowing where each component first came from.

Today a massive e-commerce website, Alibaba.com, launched in

1999 by a Chinese schoolteacher Jack Ma and his students, has automated this work and sees more than $100 billion a year in revenues. At the time, however, companies relied on families like the Herzls to broker the shipments and trade.

On vacations, the Herzls headed to the forests, and Davida developed a profound love of nature on their camping trips and hikes. But when they weren't taking a break, Davida's parents traveled to factories across the Pacific Rim. Back home, Davida would run the office on school nights, typing and editing letters and sending purchase orders via fax machine. When she was eleven years old, her parents trusted her to communicate with business partners in other countries, conferring an unusual level of responsibility on a preteen. It gave her a visceral understanding of how the world worked and her part in it.

Davida was deeply moved by a series of trips she took with her father, who was serving on a U.S. Department of Commerce team working to convince American companies to invest in the maquiladora region south of the U.S.–Mexico border. Early on, she'd see the small, impoverished neighborhoods and meet local families who only saw opportunity in the concept of building large American factories in their dusty open spaces where cows and goats grazed. At the time, the North American Free Trade Agreement gave U.S. companies tariff breaks on items made in these Mexican manufacturing areas. Low wages and few environmental regulations enticed U.S. companies, offering the chance to reap even higher profits. As globalism boomed, factories sprang up. From her home in San Diego, Davida watched Tijuana become the television manufacturing capital of the world, where Samsung, Sony, Panasonic, Matsushita, Hitachi, and others built TVs from tube to screen.

Davida recalls a day when she and her father returned to a particular site where a small community was now a factory town. Industrial waste poured into a river, smoke poured out of stacks, trash littered the ground; she knew this type of manufacturing pollution would never be allowed in the U.S., just a few hundred yards north. The workers and their children were sick; every single person's eyes were inflamed and red. It left an indelible mark.

The interweaving of cultures and societies that she lived in gave her a wholly different paradigm about the world than her white, American peers. And that visceral transparency into the invisible current that runs beneath our entire economy would become the inspiration for her planet-saving business.

After studying economics, political science, and communications in college, Davida went to law school with no desire to become a lawyer. Instead, she wanted to understand how the rules of society are written, and who writes them. Years later, when she was looking at the regulations around emissions, around who governs and is responsible for clean air and actually controlling climate-changing emissions, she realized the rules are not well written and are very outdated.

Facebook's first motto was "Move fast and break things." The idea, CEO Mark Zuckerberg told Business Insider, was that "[u]nless you are breaking stuff, you are not moving fast enough." Davida disagrees, and so do we. Our founders, like Davida, don't have safety nets to catch them when they fail. In order to launch Aclima, Davida's parents took out a mortgage on the family home and together the family maxed out their own credit cards, their life savings emptied. This business was deeply consequential, and there wasn't a lot of room for breaking things. She told us her motto is a little different: if you understand how the rules are written, you can actually rewrite them, especially when you're trying to work in service of larger public benefit.

In 2006, as Davida was a few years out of law school and defining what her role was going to be on this planet she felt so responsible for, she found herself watching *An Inconvenient Truth*.

As Davida watched Gore's film, her internal call to action found resonance. Her lifetime of exposure to supply chains and factories, and that connection between what we put into the world and how that affects us, was in her DNA. Human health was inextricably linked to planetary health.

She was frustrated by then that the focus of the climate movement had removed impacts on humans from the picture. All she saw was polar bears and melting glaciers. These impacts were profoundly tragic, but missed a critical point: those same emissions causing deep change in natural ecosystems at the global scale were also impacting people with every breath they took.

"We now know that pollution is impacting every single organ in the human body at every stage of life," she later told the *My Climate Journey* podcast. "Air pollution has been connected to diabetes, cognitive function, Alzheimer's disease, cancers, and fetal development, as well as asthma."

"We are what we breathe," Davida told us.

She identified this gap in understanding, that climate change was a really massive public health challenge. In order to drive change, she was convinced, the world needed data to better understand and connect the dots on that connection between human health and emissions. She was convinced that humanity needed new tools, and that was really about technology. But building a business takes more than great tech, and Davida knew she needed to develop a network of support to sustain her vision. When Al Gore, Citibank, and Rockefeller Philanthropy Advisors kicked off in the United States the Carbon Disclosure Project, a British-based program that requires members to publicly disclose data on their carbon emissions, she cold-called the Rockefeller advisors and asked for an invite. Soon she was in the room with Gore, Citibank leaders, and others, connecting with philanthropic and investment leaders interested in climate change.

At the time, there was tremendous interest in wearable tech, gadgets that could measure a person's blood pressure, body temperature, sleep hours, and more. Davida began talking to academics who were building similar sensing technologies, not for human bodies, but for quantifying the environment. A lawyer by trade, she licensed their intellectual property, from air quality sensors to programs that would connect their results to the Internet. By 2010, she had the licenses, and she had a plan, to map air quality, block by block, all over the planet. Now she had to find investors, customers, and builders. She was committed, and began tapping into the relationships she'd been building over the past few years.

A year later Davida had negotiated a significant contract with Google to deploy the world's largest indoor sensor network inside their headquarters buildings. The study was the largest and first of its kind, and among the rooms they were sniffing in Mountain View, California, were the offices of the Google Street View team. Davida pitched them on a bold idea she had been brewing for years—why not use the Street View vehicles as a roving sensor network for more than just images? Soon they were loading Aclima devices in Google's Street View vehicles, which are equipped with special cameras to take panoramic photographs as they drive down public streets. Now, with Aclima on board, those same cars could map the air quality in cities. The fixes could be simple, and quick: an intersection that is particularly polluted might need trees, or a change in the timing of its stoplights.

Aclima spent about six years in stealth mode, leaning on revenues from the contracts Davida had negotiated with Google, while figuring out their complex, multilayered business model. Finally, in 2017, they published a major study about the inequitable air quality that communities in West Oakland experience. The study proved that this radical new method of placing sensors on cars could deliver high-quality information about hyperlocal air quality that had never been available before. Davida recalled her childhood beehives when she deployed the software, hardware, ducts, pumps, inverters, meteorological equipment, and electrochemical and optical sensors to understand, at an urban scale, the human and environmental interactions that produced brown skies.

It was time to go beyond the long years of family mortgages and credit cards; she was ready to raise a round of capital, and she was looking for impact investors. She heard a lot of "not interested," but VCs at the Radicle Impact fund, which supports environmental and social impact tech startups, understood her mission and wrote a check. They also introduced her to us, and we wrote one as well.

THE BUSINESS OF PLANET HEALTH

In 2022, Aclima launched new results from their air pollution and greenhouse gas measurement network in the Bay Area—the first and largest of its kind in the world, spanning every public block of 101 cities, across 5,000 square miles and 8 million people. In doing so, they quantified the racist realities of air pollution in the Bay Area; people living in low-income neighborhoods, especially people of color, were breathing air that was far unhealthier than their white, wealthy peers did.

"Block-by-Block Data Shows Pollution's Stark Toll on People of Color," read the headline in the *Washington Post*.

For Davida, here was her vision, the evidence she'd been building toward. Until then, just a few dozen regulatory air-monitoring stations had been providing information in the entire Bay Area. Now anyone could type their address into a search box and find out the typical particulate matter, nitrogen dioxide, ozone, carbon monoxide, and carbon dioxide levels outside their front door—and compare those numbers to what the World Health Organization and the U.S. Environmental Protection Agency consider safe. They did the work in partnership with the Bay Area Air Quality Management District, who contracted Aclima to bring "an unprecedented level of access and visibility to air quality," combining Aclima's hyperlocal data with data from the Air District's existing stationary air-monitoring network.

By then Aclima had gathered hundreds of billions of data points in more than a dozen countries, which would lay the groundwork for growing Aclima into a global platform.

We spent a lot of time over many years discussing Davida's business model. A decade after launching, she opted to become a public benefit corporation (PBC), which is often confused with a B Corp, but they are dramatically different. B Corp is a certification by a nonprofit; a business must score a certain number of points on an assessment about their social and environmental practices, as well as adhering to a certain level of transparency. We don't have a lot of interest in B Corp certifications and similar ratings; we'll explain why in the final chapter of this book.

We do, however, often encourage our founders to become public benefit corporations as their companies are growing and they're bringing on new investors. Davida's Aclima and Donnel's BlocPower both saw the advantage. Becoming a PBC legally mandates companies to generate social and public good, to operate in a responsible and sustainable manner as well as to generate financial returns for shareholders. It allows them to push back on investors who want them to dial down the focus on impact since they are now chartered as a corporation with an official dual purpose of profit and impact. We knew that Davida, like all of our founders, was deeply mission driven. Here was a chance to let potential investors know that they would have to have aligned values, because they'd be writing a check to a company that would sometimes be making decisions in service of the long-term impact over short-term financial gains.

Davida knew those decisions would result in a stronger business, more revenue, more credibility, and bigger impact across the board. We strongly agreed with her decision to ensure that as Aclima grew, adding more sales leaders, expanding her board, and raising more money, the mission needed to be baked into their DNA, not just from a values perspective, but from a legal perspective as well.

"And what's so wonderful about that is that every dollar we make is literally a measure of our impact," she told listeners on the *Mission Driven* podcast. "They're not disconnected."

She opted against selling the technology itself, which were complex devices built in their San Francisco headquarters, the result of tapping into her father's global sourcing expertise for the various components. She told us that a single, stationary monitor simply doesn't tell the whole air story—which is why Aclima makes at least twenty passes at any given location with various cars and sensors, creating a multilayered data point backed by solid science and proven methodology.

Instead Aclima sells professional analytics software, and by 2022, customers were lining up: air quality regulators want to identify polluters, corporations want to clean up their emissions, communities want to target their climate change dollars.

She told us about a UC Berkeley professor, experimenting with what would become Aclima's technology, who ran an experiment at a Montessori preschool and found very high levels of pollution at the entrance. At the site, they found trucks idling every morning across the street. They had a conversation with the drivers, showed them their air quality data, and soon the trucks were no longer there. To us this seemed like a very simple fix that meant young children weren't chronically exposed to emissions, day after day. Like Davida, we were eager to seek the technology scaled up to impact people around the world.

GOOD FOR THE NEIGHBORHOOD

Davida hires people across the country, from the Bronx to Berkeley, to drive the company's sensor-equipped hybrid vehicles on preset routes. For workers it's a step up from gig work like driving for Uber; Aclima provides full benefits, paid vacation, and consistent hours to its so-called Aclimators. And at every rung of the company, they seek mission-driven employees.

A year into the pandemic, Andre, thirty-seven, landed a paid training position on the other side of the country, at Donnel's BlocPower Civilian Climate Corps. A father of a toddler, Andre had been incarcerated from age seventeen to thirty and was committed to turning his life around. He gave the Corps "two hundred percent" effort, because he hadn't been offered a lot of opportunities to grow and develop, he told the newspaper the *City*. He had plenty of qualities that employers would want, but when they saw his criminal record, he said they made all kinds of wrong assumptions; he'd been having a hard time finding good work. And he was ambitious. Now he was learning how to install heat and cooling pumps, solar panels, Wi-Fi systems. He helped install an efficient air-conditioning project at a Veterans of Foreign Wars post. Then a BlocPower manager suggested he consider working with their partner Aclima. Davida's cars were going to map the air quality of New York as Donnel decarbonized the buildings.

Andre began driving for Aclima at night, caring for his child by day.

"Prior to this, it's always been, I didn't know where my future was headed," he told the *City*. Now he could see promotions, opportunities.

On the other side of the country, another one of those drivers, Dave, was used to being questioned by community members when he cruised low-income neighborhoods in a white van that was so new to the fleet, it hadn't had the standard "I test air quality" Aclima paint job yet. Immigration agents, undercover cops, even bail bondsmen are pervasive and unwelcome on many streets in the Bay Area where he was driving.

As he described it, here's some random dude, with all this ghost-buster equipment in an unmarked van, driving around the same block again and again. People would ask him, "What the hell are you do-ing here?" He said he had to work to gain credibility on those streets, to earn the friendly waves.

"When you see me," he would tell community members, "it's a good thing, because I'm helping people around here. I'm measuring your air quality."

4

DIGNITY FOR ALL

PHAEDRA'S PROMISE

One spring morning the phone rang in a low-income housing complex in Louisville, Kentucky. An elderly woman, living on the brink of losing everything, answered, tentatively. Was this another threatening bill collector?

This time, however, the caller was Phaedra Ellis-Lamkins, CEO of a fast-growing tech startup, testing out a new service she'd launched to help water departments get their bills paid while supporting underserved residents.

"Hello, miss, I think we can help you with your water bill, but I'll need to ask three questions," said Phaedra, gently.

The woman was skeptical. There are so many scammers.

"Have you faced financial hardship in recent years?" asked Phaedra. "Have you had a job loss or reduced hours? How about additional expenses?"

Yes, yes, yes, the senior answered sadly. Times were extremely tough, and the pandemic made it worse. Her income was a few hundred dollars a month. She didn't have enough money to cover food, rent, and all of those unpaid bills.

"I'm so very sorry to hear that. But based on your answers, you do qualify for assistance. We'd like to start by wiping out your water bill today," said Phaedra. She explained that the account would clear in twenty-four hours. Billions of dollars of federal pandemic relief funds had been allocated toward energy debt. Now Phaedra was helping to spend those dollars, one senior citizen at a time.

There was a long pause.

"Thank you so much," the woman whispered softly, her voice breaking. Then she began to weep, and then sob, loudly. Phaedra listened and nodded. She recognized this woman's pain and relief.

Phaedra grew up relying on welfare, food stamps, and whatever other government support her family could find. Her single mom was a waitress, raising four kids, and as a family they found getting any assistance was a time-consuming, confusing, and humiliating experience.

Phaedra, as a child, tried to take charge. But she was reminded at every turn—by the school system, government offices, food pantries, and grocery stores—that her family was less important, less deserving, less dignified, because of their poverty. Those experiences shaped her and convinced her that no one, especially children, should be shamed over their circumstances. Nor should they be denied access to this support because of government bureaucracy and inefficiencies. Even when Congress writes laws that provide funds to close equity gaps, those funds often remain unspent, or the benefits are underutilized. That's not because people don't want support. It's because government programs, from health care to child care to job training, are usually designed inefficiently. Users' experiences can be perplexing, onerous, and demoralizing in large, bureaucratic systems. People become numbers, waiting in a line, as if they should be grateful for a handout. It's disrespectful and exhausting. Phaedra didn't want to see anyone suffer these indignities, but how could she change things?

FINDING HER FOOTING

Phaedra started college in Texas, at sixteen, but came home to California after a year; the campus was too far away and too expensive. She went to community college while raising her siblings, and then headed to California State University at Northridge. Like so many of the CEOs we've invested in, she brought a sibling to college; in Phaedra's case, it was her younger sister, who was still in high school. They shared a dorm room.

Before she even graduated, she launched her career as a labor organizer, hired as one of dozens of interns for "Union Summer" in Silicon Valley. At twenty, she drove thousands of miles throughout the Bay Area, door-knocking home health care workers and encouraging them to vote for a union and a contract. "I'm only here because I think people deserve to be treated like human beings," she told a local paper. Phaedra's commitment to the labor movement and unions came from her own lived experience. When her mother stopped waiting tables to take a position in a county government office that came with a union contract, Phaedra's family was finally able to begin moving up. Stepping out of the free lunch line and into the forty-cents lunch line is one of Phaedra's most joyful childhood memories.

After college, Phaedra rose quickly in the labor movement, and at age twenty-six was a "union boss," as the newspapers called her, leading what would become one of the most influential union offices in the U.S., the South Bay AFL-CIO Labor Council. "I think some people might say I'm too young, too Brown, too much of a woman," said Phaedra at the time. "But at the end of the day, we're measured by how well we do the job, and if I didn't feel I could do the job, I wouldn't be here."

The position was tough. Silicon Valley's big tech firms were booming, but marginalized populations, especially Black and Latinx families, were being left behind. Phaedra championed decency and respect for janitors and landscapers, trash haulers and grocery store clerks, the underpaid, unappreciated people whose work fueled the daily lives of newly minted millionaires at Google, Apple, and Facebook.

When tech firms were named "the best companies to work for," Phaedra called them out. The people serving food and scrubbing toilets in those same buildings deserved a share of that prosperity, she said. She battled publicly, at contentious meetings, boycotts, and marches. She was firm, bold, and strategic, demanding change in places where she was told there was nothing to be done.

She wasn't an entrepreneur yet, but she was already deploying the startup way of thinking—creativity, adaptability—to solve intractable problems. Phaedra's leadership at the Labor Council, representing more than one hundred unions and more than 110,000 workers, improved the lives of tens of thousands, winning them higher wages, better health benefits, and new housing and job security. Her wins rippled throughout the state and country, inspiring further activism. (We didn't know Phaedra back then, but we were working in tandem, pushing for all work to be valued equally—from house cleaners to home care workers—backing domestic workers as they organized, and helping undocumented women form co-ops so they could be employed.)

Phaedra also became what locals described as "a political heavyweight." An endorsement from her Labor Council could make or break a candidate's success at the polls. She did not shy away from the sharp elbows of Bay Area politics. Her advocacy pitted her against business leaders and political operatives, who saw her as a threat to their burgeoning wealth, but Phaedra was also a consensus builder, and when things got tense she'd been known to crack a self-deprecating joke, followed by loud, infectious laughter; it lowered the temperature. What struck her, repeatedly, was that in the U.S. today, if someone has money, it's assumed they'll be treated with respect. When people are poor, they face dire consequences and rigid systems, enduring distrust and harsh judgment at every step. There should be no shame in poverty, she insisted.

After more than a decade, Phaedra took her activism national, replacing longtime activist and television commentator Van Jones as the CEO of Green For All, an organization working to bring green energy jobs into low-income communities. At Green For All, Phaedra met lawyer-activist Diana Frappier, who had spent years as a criminal defense attorney, deeply concerned about the criminalization of mental illness and drug addiction. The two formed a strong, professional bond that would see them through a series of companies and jobs as working partners.

Green For All gave Phaedra a chance to take on the environmental justice disparities she had faced her whole life. Phaedra had grown up in Suisun City, California, between a crude oil refinery that occasionally spilled toxic waste into adjacent wetlands and a sugar mill that routinely violated its discharge permits, poisoning a nearby estuary. When she was a child, Suisun City was rated the worst place to live in the Bay Area, based on school test scores, housing prices, water and air conditions, and overall quality of life. Phaedra had asthma; most of her classmates did as well. Now she was a political powerhouse on Capitol Hill, demanding green energy legislation and briefing policy makers in President Obama's White House. She served on a national climate commission and led a federal government apprentice initiative, but her frontline work demanding improved water infrastructure, oil spill cleanups, and carbon taxes was what drew her so much attention as a Black woman in the largely white-led environmental movement.

"Today is the first day of the demise of the Keystone!" she shouted to reporters as she was led away in handcuffs from a pipeline protest at the White House in 2013. Also arrested that day: civil rights icon Julian Bond, Sierra Club executive director Michael Brune, and other leading environmentalists.

Like the chaotic home she was born into, the experience was shaping her, as an environmentalist, civil rights advocate, and social justice leader.

Phaedra remained close with Van Jones, who was in turn a close friend of Prince. Yes, that Prince. When the superstar musician and artist performed in Oakland, Van Jones introduced Phaedra, who asked Prince if he'd support her favorite nonprofit, the Tipping Point Community. When Prince suggested a charity concert, the organization had forty-eight hours to organize the event, raising a $700,000 windfall.

Prince, who died at fifty-seven in 2016, is known for his tremendous, groundbreaking musical talent. But his business battles also broke important new ground in the music industry. When he was a teen, he had signed contracts giving away most of his earnings and life rights to a record company. As he grew into his lucrative career, he launched a twenty-year legal battle to gain control of his songs, archives, and publishing and performance rights from Warner Bros. Records.

Phaedra, who had recently left Green For All to spend time with her children, became his business manager and fiercely fought for Prince, from boardrooms to courtrooms. She was there when he learned they had finally won ownership rights to his content. Van Jones would later write about Prince at that moment.

"The happiest day that I have ever seen him is the day that Phaedra Ellis-Lamkins got him his master recordings back. It was like someone being released from prison," he wrote. "After a two-decade struggle, his last manager, Phaedra, forced the powers that be to relent."

Phaedra was commanding Prince's finances and demanding those around him behave. Prince was grappling with fame, and not everyone in his circle had his best interests at heart. After all, there was money to be made and power to be gained. Prince trusted Phaedra completely, inspiring her with his fierce loyalty and faith.

Phaedra has said that working for Prince was tough, "because my job was to play bad cop." She wanted people to like her, but Prince felt that it only really mattered that people liked him. When Phaedra told Prince how much that upset her, he answered with wisdom she has shared in meetings, interviews, and conference stages: "If you want to play Madison Square Garden, you better get used to booing. If you don't like booing, then you should play in your backyard." In her own terms, it meant that if she wanted greatness, she'd have to get used to the haters.

Managing Prince was heady work with great pay, but as a former labor activist, she wasn't always sure she was a good fit. Growing up, she hadn't been a Prince superfan, and the entertainment industry's key mission wasn't about dignity and respect. Whirlwind tours and 3 a.m. parties left her exhausted. She talked about her mixed feelings with her friend and colleague from their days of activism, former NAACP CEO Ben Jealous, who'd joined Kapor Capital as an investor in 2014.

Ben talked to us about her intelligent and courageous work in the trenches of the labor rights and environmental justice battles. We invited her for a visit to Kapor offices and saw her greatness. That's when we introduced Phaedra to Honor.

DIGNITY FOR ALL

Founded in 2014, Honor was launched, with our backing, as an on-demand home health care provider, to provide care for elderly and disabled people who needed someone to help them in their home. One of its founders was Seth Sternberg, who was just coming off the successful sale of a messaging service to Google for around $100 million. During a visit with his mother on the East Coast, he had noticed that she wasn't driving as well as she used to. How in the world am I going to manage her care from across the country? he wondered.

Seth launched Honor, a service fueled with technology that allowed carefully screened caregivers to accept assignments and set their own schedule. Care recipients could decide what help they needed and when they wanted someone to come over. Seth encouraged Phaedra to bring her own expertise to Honor, and to follow her instincts, which were entirely focused on eliminating bias in the home health care system, where she knew, from her years in labor organizing, that all parties are vulnerable. Most caregivers are Black and Latinx women, often moms trying to make it on their own. And she knew that in traditional agencies, caregivers' assignments depend entirely on their relationship with the scheduler. Do they speak the same language? Are their kids in kindergarten together? Do they bake them cookies? Honor's technology took over scheduling, eliminating those potential biases. She also knew that rating caregivers based entirely on customer opinions could be unfair. Perhaps the seniors didn't like someone's look or their accent. Honor revamped the rating system, adding a caregiver's expertise, if they showed up on time, and how well they interacted with the app. Technology brought customization and scale to Honor. Did someone need a caregiver who spoke Mandarin and wasn't allergic to cats? Was a highly skilled caregiver only available certain days and on certain public transit routes? The technology could make these matches. It could also allow for a seamless handoff from an Honor caregiver to a family member.

A critically important part of what Honor's technology allowed was to charge seniors less and pay caregivers more. And that met Phaedra's life mission, to bring dignity to all, regardless of wealth. Phaedra upped wages and made caregivers fully benefited employees, not gig workers; Honor also offered them flexibility and dignity in the way they chose to work. The company boomed. Seth had hired Phaedra to recruit home health care workers, but soon she was responsible for revenue as well as hiring, and eventually helped to raise hundreds of millions of new investment dollars.

Honor also worked with families, helping them tap into available public dollars, from U.S. Department of Veterans Affairs benefits to cash programs that pay older people directly to cover some of their in-home care costs. Some programs, often untapped, even pay family members for caring for their own relatives. The applications can be daunting, but Honor offered support.

As the company grew, its offerings evolved—or, as we VCs like to say, it pivoted—taking over back-office tasks for local home health care agencies. Families desperate to keep mom and dad in their homes would turn to these agencies for caregivers. But those small firms, whose owners would have preferred to focus on providing loving senior care, were often overwhelmed with billing, recruiting, screening, staffing, and scheduling. Honor's newly honed technology standardized those operations, freeing up their clients to focus on what they really cared about.

At Honor, Phaedra also continued weaving Kapor Capital resources and talent into the multilayered portfolio it is today. She hired a young talent named Ruben Harris and gave him a daunting challenge: go to Southern California, launch Honor Los Angeles, and sign up ten new customers in a week or don't come back. Ruben came back, and Phaedra became his mentor. She was one of his first investors when he launched Career Karma, his startup, a few years later. So were we.

When Phaedra left her job with Prince, she had been struck by the fact that technology wasn't working for artists; streaming music had devalued their content. She had already seen that tech wasn't helping the labor movement, leaving fundamental workers behind. Environmentally, tech was contaminating the homes and communities of underrepresented people. Finally, at Honor, she saw tech that could close gaps, not widen them. With her friend and colleague Diana, she began thinking about what else tech could do for good.

TAKING ON CRIMINAL INJUSTICE

One night a friend called Phaedra in a panic—there were bounty hunters at the door. Phaedra hopped on the phone with the "wanted man." He said he had been arrested on a minor charge, paid bail to get out, and then misread a handwritten slip of paper handed to him by a clerk. He thought he was supposed to return June 28, but the date was June 26. When he showed up two days late, the clerk told him there was now a warrant out for his arrest, and advised him to leave. When someone doesn't show up for court, bail is immediately forfeited, an arrest warrant is issued, additional charges are filed, and bail agents hire bounty hunters to find and return the defendant.

"Now I'm on the run," he told Phaedra. "I work, I have to pay child support, what do I do?"

He was afraid of calling his public defender, because that could mean getting fired, arrested, additional chaos. Phaedra worked with him to call his attorney, who sorted it out with the courts.

Phaedra realized she had access to power that most people simply didn't have, and that shouldn't be the way it worked. It's a memory she drew on over and over while developing a company, an app, and technology that was aimed at getting people who had been arrested to their court hearings so they didn't end up sitting in jail, quite often innocent, awaiting trial.

Phaedra went to investors—including us—with her lived experience, not a Stanford University degree, and this pitch: More than 75 percent of people sitting in city and county jails are there because they can't afford bail, not because they've been convicted of a crime. So what happens while they're sitting there for a couple of weeks? They lose their job, she said. And if they lose their job, they're not paying rent, so now they lose their home. If they're homeless, they can quickly lose their kids. And as many as one out of five of those inmates are there for unpaid parking tickets. With some two million people behind bars at any given time, the U.S. has the highest incarceration rate in the world. Black men make up the largest group of those behind bars. Setting aside the human costs to those men, their families, their communities, and other social costs, this is a $180 billion a year cost to taxpayers.

Phaedra's company Promise sought to work with cities and counties to release people from jail while they await trial. An app would remind the accused individuals about court dates and mandated counseling, even giving directions for court-ordered drug tests and recovery counseling. Promise also introduced technologies that could make the entire criminal justice system more efficient. For example, Phaedra noticed that many jails were using outdated software to manage drug tests, which required a staff person to input paper results and fax them to jails. That process was taking many days, costing taxpayers money and inmates their livelihoods while they sat in jail awaiting the system's slow process. Her tech upgrade could get it done in seconds.

Turning out insights about how technology can dramatically improve the efficiency of systems is one of Silicon Valley's strengths.

Y Combinator launched in 2005 to accelerate technology startups by improving their products, getting more users, and providing more options for raising money. Participants who are selected receive $500,000 in funding and an eleven-week intensive in-house training that includes mentoring and collaboration from the other founders in your class, alumni, CEO speakers, and investors who all want to help chosen startups succeed. Y Combinator has launched thousands of tech startups, including Airbnb, DoorDash, Instacart, Reddit, and many others. Phaedra and Diana applied and were delighted to be tapped to participate. They laughed and laughed when they pulled up to the program in a minivan. Their first impression was that this was the youngest, whitest place they'd been in a long time.

Oh, we just changed the dynamic here, thought Phaedra. Probably a first in Y Combinator history, there was another Black woman founder in Phaedra and Diana's cohort—Lisa Gelobter, CEO and founder of tEQuitable. Like Phaedra, Lisa had an impressive track record across sectors—working on groundbreaking products as a technologist at Hulu and Shockwave, being an executive at BET, and working as part of the U.S. Digital Service. We describe Lisa's breakthrough company in our final chapter; suffice it to say she's managed to use tech to build human resources solutions we spent years working on.

The Y Combinator support and advice they received was tremendous, and both had years of experience with Honor. On their final day of the program, Promise was already launching. We were her first investor. Rapper Jay-Z soon joined us.

"We are increasingly alarmed by the injustice in our criminal justice system," said Jay-Z. "It's time for an innovative and progressive technology that offers sustainable solutions to tough problems."

It's not every day that a Kapor Capital portfolio company is featured in *Rolling Stone*, but Promise was something different.

Phaedra was raising millions, traveling the country, working hard, and helping her startup grow. Then everything came crashing down.

She took a meeting with a potentially lucrative customer at a county jail. Her pitch was simple: she showed them the "decarceration" app that could eliminate the cash bail system but still get defendants to show up for court.

The prison official began to laugh. Did she know how long he could keep people locked up on drug charges? People who weren't convicted of a crime? A very, very long time, and conditions are terrible, he said. If Promise got people out, he could put more in.

"I wouldn't let my dogs stay in these jails," he said.

Phaedra cringed; her body quaked. She imagined her own relatives behind bars, as she thought about what the prison official described, the system being used to institutionalize people in an incredibly inhumane way. How could she possibly be doing business with these people?

She asked for a short break, grabbed all her belongings, and walked out.

Pacing outside, she called Mitch. Aside from Diana Frappier, he was her only board member.

"I can't do this, Mitch," she said. "They're going to use Promise to put more people in jail, not less."

She had taken hefty checks from investors who took a chance on a Black, woman entrepreneur who promised to reform the criminal justice system. How had she gotten this so wrong? She was distraught, her voice urgent. Now she realized that by making the criminal justice system more efficient, it would mean that in some jurisdictions, officials would use it to lock up more Black and Latinx people, mostly men.

Promise had made a lot of sense to us when we'd made our initial investment, but now we all realized that what might work in the Bay

Area could backfire in other parts of the country. We were grateful she had figured this out early. The tool was a great idea, but it was too easy for it to be misused. Phaedra's visit with the county jail official exemplifies an important lesson: tech is often not inherently positive or negative, but a neutral tool that can be used to further gap-closing or gap-widening ends.

Other investors may have looked at Promise, seen it was going to make a lot of money, and encouraged Phaedra to put her concerns aside and keep moving forward. Instead, we asked her to regroup and come back to us with a new business model.

Phaedra still had some money in the bank. She offered to pay her investors back but no one left. We certainly stuck around.

KEEPING THE WATER ON

Phaedra began her next iteration with an experiment. If there were so many people in jail because of unpaid parking tickets, what if she paid those tickets and let people pay her back in installments? Cities could benefit by getting their money, and taxpayers would win by not having to pay for people in jail.

She selected three pilot cities—Oakland, Philadelphia, and Dallas—that had lots of paid parking spaces and high numbers of tickets. The cities were geographically diverse, and each represented broadly different socioeconomic populations. Promise placed digital ads offering to pay off parking tickets, recruiting 1,778 individuals who collectively owed $263,982 for leaving their car in the wrong place, or for too long. Here was a credible solution to their problems. Users were offered a no-interest loan from Promise and were asked to set up a repayment plan. They then received text reminders, notifications, and on-demand support to help them make those payments.

Borrowers living on fixed monthly incomes could choose to make incremental weekly payments before their bank accounts were empty. If someone needed an extension, all they had to do was ask. Soon she had evidence that the experiment was working. Almost everyone who signed up for her debt relief program, 96 percent, paid her back. She analyzed the 4 percent who didn't; they were all facing acute financial hardships. It turns out that most people want to pay their bills; they just need strong support, the kind of flexibility not often found in the public sector, and, importantly, empathy in the process.

Now Phaedra had new clarity for her mission: turn debt collection systems that are punitive in nature into payment systems that are rooting for people's success. She would start with water departments. Americans owe billions of dollars in water, electric, and sewage bill debt. Utilities often disconnect customers to pressure them to pay. Phaedra and her partner brought an ingenious solution.

Promise could help utilities reduce late payments and get bills paid while helping people pay off debt sooner and with fewer penalties. They never charge interest and allow for installment plans.

They also tap into stimulus and relief funds specifically aimed at assisting households to pay utility bills and avoid shutoffs. How much better off would people be if the funds allocated to them actually were used? Cities pay Promise to deploy its system, which is how it makes money. It's a good deal for the city because collections go way up using the Promise system; a small portion of those collections go to Promise.

SMARTER CITIES

Phaedra gathered with four other entrepreneurs at that Martha's Vineyard retreat we had arranged for CEOs in our portfolio to forge bonds, reduce stress, and share ideas. You've already met them: Jake and Irma were working to create tech jobs in underdog communities, Donnel was decarbonizing American cities, Davida was helping local governments clear the air, and Phaedra was bringing dignity to people with far too little of it. They talked, and laughed and cried, about their overlapping missions to build stronger communities and uplift underrepresented people. At 2 a.m. someone pulled out a whiteboard. By morning they had sketched out a set of opportunities they could go after jointly. They realized that together they could pitch themselves as a package, an alliance of their four tech companies bringing solutions to cities addressing disparities in job training, clean energy, air quality, and crushing debt. Billions of unspent federal funds grew to trillions during the pandemic; Congress and the White House repeatedly approved massive stimulus packages, but it was up to local governments to apply for, and spend, most of those funds. The Kapor companies knew how to apply for those funds on behalf of their customers, and in many cases were already doing so. Here were four mission-driven for-profits that leveraged public dollars, with track records far stronger than standard-issue government programs. Why not join forces?

In their first test pitch, a mayor from a major U.S. city agreed to stop by our Oakland office and hear what they had to offer. Each CEO walked through a slide deck, pointing out their proven strengths, offering their own stories. The mayor grew increasingly distracted, checking her phone, whispering to an aide. While she had some interest in our gap-closing companies, this was a fundraising trip and she was focused on getting to her next event. We were a little concerned, but then Phaedra got started.

She described a client, a water department in a large U.S. city. Thousands of people lost jobs during COVID and weren't paying their bills.

"So one thing you could do is just shut off everyone's water, and then turn them into collections," she said.

The mayor interrupted Phaedra. In her own city, citizens had been drowning in water department debt, penalties, and fines under the prior administration, she said. Black and Latinx families were disproportionately facing this burden. But under her new leadership, the city had ended water shutoffs, the mayor said. If someone didn't pay their bill, their water stayed on, with a payment plan option.

Phaedra listened thoughtfully, and when the mayor was done, Phaedra commended her for trying to bring respect and dignity to her community. But the problem in your city, said Phaedra, is that few people are participating. She held up her index finger, commanding attention: "We have a better plan."

The mayor looked up. "Please explain," she said sharply.

Phaedra was prepared.

The water department's debt forgiveness application required customers to upload check stubs, benefit award letters, unemployment documents, and many other personal documents to prove they were properly impoverished. If someone was self-employed, they needed to download a spreadsheet and input more than thirty-five pieces of information, from credit card processing fees to insurance costs. The application website allowed users just thirty minutes to finish, or else they'd have to start inputting their information all over again.

The application alone presented multiple barriers for access: someone already burdened with debt would need a computer, Internet service, and a scanner; they'd need to be literate and an English speaker. And this was just the beginning. If a customer made it through the approval process, they would receive a letter allowing them to enroll. After that, they'd have to pay a reduced water bill for twelve months. If they successfully made the payments, their water debt balance would be forgiven.

"Fewer than five percent of people carrying water debt in your city have enrolled," said Phaedra. "And even fewer have successfully paid their bills during their one-year period."

"I honestly didn't know that," said the mayor.

Phaedra held up her phone.

With Promise, she explained, the application was a few simple questions, answered on an app.

"We believe in something called self-attestation, which is to say, 'I qualify.' Instead of having to prove your poverty. We believe people's words matter. It's human dignity," she said.

Also, she said, Promise will never charge interest.

"Why would someone have to pay interest to the government?" she said, her voice rising.

Promise didn't mail any bills; it sent a reminder text. And customers could pay however they wanted, through a link in that text, using a debit card, Venmo, Cash App, whatever was easiest.

"And guess what?" said Phaedra. "In our pilot, more than ninety-five percent of the participants paid their bills."

The mayor leaned in toward Phaedra and the other Kapor Capital CEOs gathered at the table.

"Please come out and meet with my staff," she said. "We want to do business with all of you."

With water bills a proven success, Phaedra and her cofounder, Diana, soon expanded; even as she scrambled to hire a sales team, customers were lining up. Without asking for investments, VCs came knocking.

From Buffalo to San Francisco and dozens of cities in between, Promise began signing contracts. People can pay court fines, rather than land back in jail. Traffic and parking tickets can be broken down into monthly payments. Child support debt can slowly be recovered. Even unpaid taxes and other fees fit seamlessly into Promise's systems.

While many more privileged Americans have family and friends they can turn to in a financial emergency, Phaedra understands and supports members of the community who have no one they can turn to for a $5,000 loan. Promise taps into publicly available funds and platforms to help clients before they hit rock bottom. Sometimes it's a matter of adjusting the timing of payments or finding flexible payment plans. Other times there are government programs in place, but not being utilized, to cover costs. By proving their premise—that being poor is terribly expensive—Phaedra and Diana raised more than $50 million in three years, and the company's valuation soared to $500 million.

HOLDING FIRM TO YOUR VALUES

As a company, Promise had to become creative; it had, and pivoted to meet its goals. Phaedra has had to adjust, personally, as well. She's an extraordinary leader, tough as nails. She's just not touchy-feely; that is not who she is. As much as she cares about her customers, she's equally passionate about treating the people she hires with respect and dignity.

As a labor organizer, Phaedra didn't shy away from Silicon Valley's most powerful tech leaders. As she established herself as the CEO of a fast-growing tech startup, Phaedra used her position to hold her investors, and the broader Silicon Valley tech community, accountable. She did this privately and she did this publicly, fearlessly.

"When you've gone through really horrific things, you discover your inner strength," Phaedra says. So she didn't hesitate to respond when one of her most supportive investors published a shockingly racist tweet.

Unacceptable, Phaedra told him privately. What you said is racist, and we cannot be allies. She let him know she did not want him to invest in the next round of funding in her company even though he wanted to and had the right. Phaedra persisted. In the end, the VC did not invest and he deleted the tweet.

If there's one thing we've learned over the years, it's that every founder has strengths and inclinations toward things they love to do, and roles they'd rather not fill; no one can be all things to all people. Together we identify their strengths, whether it's Jake and Irma's business acumen, Donnel's visionary ideals, Davida's engineering prowess, or Phaedra's dedication to dignity. And we talk about who they should surround themselves with, including colleagues and investors, who can support them and also challenge them. We push our CEOs to adapt and even radically pivot, but never at the cost of losing their life-work passion.

We consistently support Phaedra's vision of building a company that can do good. And we remind her that what she's building is not easy, but extremely valuable. Phaedra embodies the belief that if you treat people with dignity and respect, there are enormous untapped business opportunities. She's taking friction out of government systems that treat both customers and workers badly. And by bringing both technology and a different mindset, she's unlocked an awful lot of savings for taxpayers.

Most customers sign up for Promise through the app. But the team regularly calls elderly people who have unpaid bills and might not be tech savvy. Although she has a big company to run, Phaedra takes time to make those calls now and then.

The calls are Phaedra's favorite part of her job.

On one call, a victim of domestic violence, home with her children, explained that her abuser had taken over her bank account and told the water department to shut off her water. On another call, it was a woman living on a fixed income of $510 a month whose dishwasher was leaking, sending her water bills soaring. Their relief is palpable when they realize their water isn't being shut off.

Phaedra's Promise is just getting started. With moral clarity and great ambition, Phaedra is on her way to bringing that same dignity and comfort to millions of people around the country.

5

BREAKING INTO TECH

RUBEN

It's a cliché in venture capital investing to say that when we're considering a new opportunity, we're really investing in people, not just the idea. But it's true: when it comes to writing that check, we're looking for great people who are solving challenges they personally faced, and a business that begins with the mission of serving underrepresented people. But what does it mean to invest in "great people"? All too often in VC land, it has meant investing in people of similar educational and socioeconomic backgrounds. It's meant investing in people who look the same and act the same, whose style and manners feel familiar and "safe." That's why the startup world, at least until recently, has been dominated by white men with Stanford or Harvard degrees. It's human nature: we are attracted to those who look and act like us. That's why breaking that pattern through unconventional, highly intentional efforts like ours is necessary and is starting to make a difference. And that's why when we look at the metrics for deciding whether to invest in a startup and its founder, we figure in a new concept, what we call "distance traveled." This is the measure of how far an entrepreneur has come in terms of personal circumstances, and the obstacles they have overcome on their path to Silicon Valley. In our experience, distance traveled is a far better predictor of long-term success than proxies like schools attended, "warm" introductions, or investments raised from friends and family.

Perhaps no one person better illustrates the concept of "distance traveled" than Ruben Harris, the cofounder of Career Karma, a startup launched in 2018 focused on helping outsiders break into the tech industry.

NO CLEAR PATH

Ruben graduated from a university most people had never heard of, with mediocre grades and degrees in music and business administration. As an accomplished professional cellist, he cared more about his performance onstage than his performance in school, which his grades reflected. At the time, most colleges had graduates competing for seats as new investment bankers or consultants, but nobody at Ruben's school had ever been an investment banker and he had no idea what an investment banker actually does. His cousin suggested he look into the career, thinking Ruben might be good at it. Ruben was interested.

In college, he had started the blog *A How To Guide . . .* with the firm belief that every goal is achievable—it's just a matter of figuring out what path to take. Years later, Ruben would launch Career Karma, which embodies that audacious belief, to help hundreds of thousands of underrepresented people get a foothold in technology careers. But he still had a lot of roads to travel along the way.

What Ruben didn't know at the time was that getting started in investment banking typically means getting accepted to a top-tier university, studying business and finance, and graduating at the top of your class. It means meeting global asset management recruiters in the quad during your freshman year, and mastering financial modeling. It means spending summers interning at global investment firms, and networking with bankers on LinkedIn a year before graduation.

So here was Ruben, a college graduate teaching cello to little kids. He had none of those prerequisites—he didn't even know those pathways existed. And, as we would learn much later in our relationship with Ruben, he also had a secret: Three days after his college graduation, after a night of drinking, Ruben had fallen asleep at the wheel of his parents' van, slammed into a power pole, and crushed the vehicle. He was saved by the air bag, walking away without a scratch. When he called the police for help, they arrested him for driving while intoxicated. Paramedics took one look at the van and told Ruben, "You must come from a praying family, because you should have died tonight."

Ruben came from a deeply religious and disciplined family. His parents were Seventh-day Adventists and medical professionals who observed the Sabbath and expected good manners. They were keen on giving their kids powers that no one could ever take away from them. That started with language and music education. His parents, originally from Cuba and Jamaica, spoke nothing but Spanish to Ruben, his brother, and his sister as they were growing up. The Harris kids arrived in kindergarten and baffled their teachers because they didn't speak English. They learned. Ruben and his siblings also began studying music when they were very young, picking up instruments at their Montessori school, where hands-on learning is prioritized. The hard work paid off. In addition to Ruben playing cello, his brother plays cello, guitar, and piano, his sister plays violin, and his father plays saxophone, guitar, and piano. His mother, who doesn't play an instrument, sat with him at every lesson all the way through high school, taking notes. He told his mom he wanted to quit, and she agreed, telling him that when he mastered his series of increasingly advanced cello instruction books he could walk away. But by the time Ruben completed that training when he was a teen, he was playing in Carnegie Hall, a professional musician brushing elbows with icons. Not a lot of Black men play the cello professionally, and he says working in those environments refined his approach and made him more polished. Ruben says the ability to be an extraordinary cellist is a by-product of all the life skills he learned by mastering the instrument, starting with the rewards of putting in all of those hours practicing. More importantly, he learned how to work really hard and make it look easy. He learned to take in feedback when he was doing something wrong and fix it. He learned to set goals that pushed him every single week.

Seventh-day Adventists don't drink or smoke. When Ruben came home after his arrest, his father took him aside.

"Ruben," he said, "you've been dodging death for too long." He'd been hanging around the wrong people, getting involved in Atlanta's club scene. Ruben nodded; his dad was right.

Hitting such a terrible moment didn't drag Ruben down. Indeed, it sparked a critical pivot. He stopped drinking, and with great energy and determination, he threw himself into becoming an investment banker. Like so many of the entrepreneurs we fund, the people they hire, and the communities they serve, who encounter inherently biased assumptions that could easily become roadblocks, Ruben was resilient and determined.

Ruben's first step was to write a blog that detailed why no one would hire him as an investment banker; he declared he was going to do it anyway. It's a quality we've seen from Ruben, too: he publicly declares he's going to undertake a new challenge, and then— with his community holding him accountable—he does it, whether it's running one thousand miles in a year or raising $10 million in a quarter (both of which he's done).

When it came to breaking into investment banking, he began contacting anyone he thought might have connections to the business. During college, he had organized dozens of events for nonprofits, athletes, and celebrities, including Tyrese, Kim Kardashian, and Jay-Z. He figured that in Atlanta, parents who had chosen to have their children study music might also be connected to the business world. He asked parents of his cello students for introductions, networked, met one person after another, followed leads, and finally landed his first, unpaid banking internship. Some of his steps were definitely old-school. He walked through the front doors of one investment bank after the next, whole blocks of them, and handed the surprised receptionists his resume. He figured that if they saw him in person, that would give him a chance to exercise his powers of persuasion.

"I wish you could've seen the expressions on their faces when it dawned on them that I was not there for the business meeting that was about to get started," he would later write.

He sent more than 1,900 unsolicited emails to strangers, watched a series of about 230 video lessons, and built more than sixty spreadsheets assigned by an online learning platform called Breaking Into Wall Street. This is important, because when Ruben came to us with his idea for a do-it-yourself tech skills training program, he already knew what motivated independent online learners to stay engaged and how to avoid burnout and loneliness. He'd been there.

The online learning taught Ruben the language of the world of finance, and the ins and outs of networking, interviews, and financial modeling. He cold-called senior bankers whose phone numbers he found online. He sent so many LinkedIn messages to complete strangers that the professional networking site warned him he was violating terms that ban users from inviting strangers to join their network. After more than twelve months of hustling, Ruben landed a position as a banking analyst. He also got a lawyer to reduce his potential DUI to reckless driving, a journey he shared publicly when he celebrated his tenth year of sobriety on the podcast *Roads to Recovery*. In sharing his mistakes and learning, as is typical, he showed a humility and fundamental desire to help others.

Ruben is driven by the belief that education, learning, and training can inherently change a person's position in life. It's a belief imbued by his parents, and the reason we backed him on his mission to build a billion-dollar business connecting millions of people to boot camps and other training programs for careers in tech. If it sounds impossible, it probably is. But Ruben figures out how to accomplish the impossible just about every day.

Early in his education, Ruben learned about research by Anders Ericsson and popularized by Malcolm Gladwell: the 10,000 Hour Rule, a concept that ten thousand hours of practice in any given field, be it playing violin or programming computers, will make someone an expert. Beginning a career in banking, Ruben wanted to learn as much about the business as quickly as he could. Ruben lives by goals, beliefs, and mottos, and as he moved to Chicago for his first professional job, he was focused on this one: learn in your twenties; earn in your thirties. He wanted to get an exponential learning curve going. That's why he worked eighty to one hundred hours a week for the next three years.

He also shared his progress on a blog, providing regular updates. It went viral.

At first, banking was grueling but fascinating, exactly what he was interested in. He was learning what makes or breaks a business, and the critical role communication and relationships play in growing equity. The networking paid off. After sixteen months he landed a better job back in his hometown, Atlanta. Ruben was realizing, as he reached the third year in this career, that "in the future, every industry would be driven by tech." His next step would likely need to be getting an MBA, but his interest in banking was waning. He was more excited by what he saw going on in Silicon Valley. Ruben had an epiphany. He wanted to work in tech. There he saw beauty and creativity, and a powerful way to help people.

So he was back to square one. Again, he lacked the prerequisites: he had no Stanford University diploma, no tech expertise, no money to get started, and no Silicon Valley network. He was going to have to reset his own assumptions and start learning again from another playbook. Investment bankers benefit from lots of data to make their decisions; all sorts of analytics exist to assess performance and gauge future prospects. But with tech startups, there is barely an idea, a little bit of code, and maybe some customer discovery activity. Operational data literally does not exist in tech startups, so investment banking approaches simply would not work. It's why we laugh when someone asks whether we look at five-year projections. If a startup pitch deck includes three-year and five-year revenue forecasts, we know they're naïve.

SILICON VALLEY BOUND

Ruben had developed great expertise in skills that no longer applied. Nonetheless, he did have experience in figuring out how to break into an entirely new field. He networked on LinkedIn and Twitter, studied, read, and watched tutorials, and one day tweeted that he was enthusiastic about "real world applications such as quantified self, MOOCs/edtech, Bitcoin, drones & 3D printing." In many worlds he might have been speaking a foreign language, but in Silicon Valley his message was met with delight. Here was a Black investment banker interested in systems that can measure heart rates, breathing, sleep hours, and more. He liked studying online and tech startups that improve learning opportunities. A well-connected venture capitalist retweeted Ruben's tweet.

"Naturally, I was not going to let this type of opportunity get away from me," Ruben said.

Ruben studied his retweeter's background and interests, and then continued posting about topics he was personally passionate about, but which were also relevant to the venture capitalist. There were more retweets, then direct messages, and soon other Silicon Valley venture capitalists were following Ruben on social media, asking questions about his background. Ruben followed their advice, read what they suggested, and studied their use of language to better understand the fundamentals of tech startups.

"Hey, we should get you into tech," the interested venture capitalist tweeted to him one day. It felt right. But none of this was going to work from Atlanta.

Ruben planned a feeler visit to California to coincide with a cousin's graduation from Stanford. Months in advance, he asked several VCs whom he'd been chatting with online if they could meet while he was in town; they put him on their calendars. He also began emailing people he considered key decision makers at tech startups, offering unsolicited suggestions of people he knew who might help them solve problems. He would send at least five a day. In order to start a tech business, you have to be creative, and you have to be willing to do a lot of work that ends up going nowhere. While these unsolicited outreaches may not have gotten his foot in the door, they were part of his process.

His motto, at this point, came from author and podcaster Timothy Ferriss: "Doing the unrealistic can be easier than the realistic." Ruben added his own twist: ". . . because there's less competition for the bigger goals."

Ruben is incredibly detail oriented without losing sight of his larger objectives. Before his trip west, he heard a radio report about the growing number of co-living spaces in San Francisco shared by tech entrepreneurs, musicians, and artists. He emailed one of these twenty-first-century communes and asked if he could spend a few days there. Why stay in a hotel when you can network?

Ruben had a heady week in California and returned to Atlanta full of ideas. Across the street from the bank where he worked was a place called Atlanta Tech Village, a startup community opened by an entrepreneur to fill a Deep South void. It was a vibrant place promoting faster connections between talent and capital. Ruben showed up for brown-bag lunches, made friends, and began building a new network with leading Black tech entrepreneurs and innovators like Paul Judge, who has invested in over sixty technology startups and has invented about thirty patented and patent-pending computer security technologies. He met some executives from BitPay, a bitcoin payment service provider, he organized a hackathon, helped a startup raise money, and took an online Stanford computer science course. He wasn't planning to build great software himself, but he did want to learn the language of technology.

He also identified the criteria he wanted for his first job in Silicon Valley: experienced founders, ethical culture, early stage with top-tier investors, solving a problem the CEO also has faced. Ruben also wanted a company addressing a challenge toward the bottom of Maslow's hierarchy of needs, a basic psychological theory that says physiological needs like food and clothing must be addressed before a person is able to really deal with love, emotions, and self-actualization. We hadn't met Ruben yet, although he already was following Mitch on Twitter, but our values aligned. We both believe lived experience helps entrepreneurs identify rapidly scalable, market-based solutions others have overlooked. We both believe in entrepreneurs from all backgrounds, especially people of color, women, and other groups that have been historically underrepresented.

Ruben packed his bags and flew west, reading on the flight a series of psychology blogs about gratitude and happiness. When he landed, he knew he was going to need a Silicon Valley support system. The next three weeks were an all-out sprint for Ruben, and that's saying a lot for someone who rises at 5 a.m. every day to exercise and get to work, without fail. He asked for meetings with tech leaders, investors, entrepreneurs, anyone who could introduce him to anyone else. One VC who took his call was Kanyi Maqubela, a Soweto, South Africa–born investor whose parents fled apartheid and arrived as refugees. The family lived in a homeless shelter for a while, but his parents—both educators—found work. Kanyi's dad, who had done all the research on his doctorate except the dissertation, was hired as an organic chemistry teacher at Phillips Academy Andover, an elite boarding school in Massachusetts. They lived on campus and Kanyi was a top student, going on to attend Stanford University. (Kanyi's dad, Temba Maqubela, was the head of a summer program called (MS)2, offering math and science for minority students at Andover. It was an inspiration for our own SMASH summer program.)

In 2014, Kanyi co-launched a fund to "solve the most important problems and vastly improve people's lives around the world." We often find ourselves in the same spaces as Kanyi and his partner. Kindred Ventures has raised more than $150 million and invested in more than one hundred companies, sometimes overlapping with our Kapor Capital investments.

With Kanyi's mentorship, Ruben was closer to networking directly with Silicon Valley's elite Stanford graduates, and Kanyi was happy to make the introductions. One person led Ruben to the next, and soon he was hired at AltSchool, a well-funded and highly hyped K–12 education startup. He had landed, ironically, at a tech startup we think underscores much of what's wrong about the Silicon Valley.

Ruben eventually found his way to starting Career Karma, which did align with his mission (and ours), but before we continue with his story, we need to explain our concerns about startups like AltSchool.

The idea behind AltSchool was to create private "micro" schools focused on individualized, personal learning. These would be educational laboratories where new learning systems could be tested, refined, and eventually packaged into software that could be widely sold. Founded by a former Googler, the company was initially a darling of Silicon Valley, attracting more than $170 million in venture capital in just a few years. "Is this the next generation of education?" asked CBS News. *Education Week* described it as "The Future of Big Data and Analytics in K–12 Education." Many early investors were just becoming parents, and worried that their kids might not get into the few elite San Francisco schools. Here was a new way to buy a slot for their children—that is, if a tuition bill of $26,000 a year in 2013 was in your budget.

AltSchool was a quintessential example of what's wrong with the larger ecosystem of mainstream tech and venture capital: its mission is to solve problems for the rich, and its players believe they're smarter than the experts. They figure they can easily use tech to solve a complex problem that has persisted for a long time. We're fed up with the broadly held but false assumption that the only people who need to be at the table, to design the solution, are those who are the best and brightest, as defined by various pedigrees attained through privilege. That's the distorted mindset in the Silicon Valley: all problems can be solved by tech, and if you put the smartest (or wealthiest) people in the room, they'll find a solution. Bill Gates, through his foundation in its early years, made the same mistake of believing that a silver bullet existed to fix K–12 public schools. His foundation spent billions in pursuit of "small schools" and failed completely, something they later acknowledged. Mark Zuckerberg's $100 million investment to reform Newark, New Jersey's schools similarly failed to hit its goals, in large part, researchers said, because stakeholders—including teachers, parents and students, and local nonprofits with deep experience—felt left out.

With AltSchool it's personal. We were asked to invest multiple times, but we always saw this model as gap-widening; we passed. The founder came back to us with what he thought was a brilliant idea: Why didn't our foundation fund a "charity" AltSchool in a low-income community? He would make money from our generous donation, while not putting up any of his own funds. Specifically, we would contribute cash to his company, and he could reap the revenues when it grew. When we challenged him about how his business model could help underrepresented children, he offered the equivalent of a "trickle-down" theory, telling us he would reinvent education with kids from wealthy families who could pay and then, once his teams had dialed in and proven a new and improved education model, Alt-School could scale up and get adopted everywhere, including neighborhoods with struggling schools. We were especially put off by his proposition that—unlike for-profit VC investors—we would contribute from our nonprofit and not receive an equity stake in AltSchool in return. Did he really want our foundation to subsidize an undertaking he wasn't interested in doing on his own, and also not offering to give us a share of potential profits? Particularly galling was the assumption that as impact investors, do-gooders if you will, we didn't want to build wealth.

None of this, however, tarnished Ruben's experience there. He was initially hired on a two-week contract, and immediately went to work proving he was so valuable that he needed to be brought on board.

Stepping out of his apartment as he was starting work, he recognized a man looking at him: it was Charles Hudson, one of the Silicon Valley's best-known Black VCs. Ruben had emailed Charles during his all-out networking campaign. Now Charles said Ruben looked familiar and they found out they were neighbors. They talked, became friends, and Ruben asked Charles if he'd mentor him. Ruben is very hard to resist.

Over the coming months, Ruben created a pipeline of more than one hundred philanthropists at AltSchool, resulting in sizable scholarships, to counter the criticism (not just from us) that the high tuition would create elite learning opportunities for privileged kids. He built ties with nonprofit organizations, mobilized racial equity in AltSchool internally, and inspired more women and people of color to apply for jobs and seats for their children in their classrooms. He even translated their information sessions into Spanish, drawing students to their experimental dual immersion program. Ruben became friends with a former teacher who was collaborating on a Startup Weekend focused on education, a remarkable visionary, Mandela Schumacher-Hodge Dixon. They connected on many levels, around their leadership styles, their values, and personal development. Over the years, they continued to collide in intentional and unintentional, spontaneous ways. Who knew that within a few years Mandela would work with us, and Ruben's own startup would be joining our portfolio?

A year into this job, AltSchool's CEO introduced Ruben to Seth Sternberg, the same Seth Sternberg who hired Phaedra at Honor to bring security to elderly and disabled people requiring care, and new dignity to their caregivers. Seth was so impressed with Ruben that he asked Phaedra to consider him for a sales and marketing position. Phaedra told us she thought Ruben was a little arrogant, but, she said, that's what tech does to people. She also saw something very special.

"I thought you were magical, and you were going to be amazing," she would later tell Ruben. She said she wanted to see his greatness manifest.

In Silicon Valley, the mythical ideal entrepreneur is gritty but not pushy, risk tolerant but not reckless, even-keeled and a smooth communicator. That's the kind of guy (and it's almost always a guy) the investors are looking for. But for everyone who believed that, they probably would have missed out on a lot of money with Ruben. His outsized, audacious personality and stop-at-nothing approach to life is at an extreme. Ruben broke the mold. He came from Atlanta, not the Silicon Valley, and when he did arrive the only people he knew were ones he'd met on Twitter. His family and friends weren't in tech, his college degree had nothing to do with computer science, and, when coming of age, he was hanging out in nightclubs, not coding and building apps.

Under Phaedra's guidance, which included what she describes as "strong feedback," Ruben became a top salesperson at Honor, building important relationships with hospitals, skilled nursing facilities, and assisted living communities. True to his nature of humbling himself to the task at hand, he also trained as a home care aide to experience, firsthand, what it felt like to do the work.

BE UNREALISTIC

Ruben didn't know how to launch a tech company, but he wanted to. To learn more, while working at Honor, he and his roommates—Ukrainian twins Artur and Timur Meyster, who also had pivoted from lucrative careers to dive into tech—launched a podcast called *Breaking Into Startups*. This gave Ruben and his partners the opportunity to learn, again firsthand, from the pros, who willingly shared the secrets of their success. Millions tuned in, and soon it was named a top podcast by *Entrepreneur* magazine and ranked number one in the category "Shows for People Switching Careers." CEOs and investors listened as well, to hear what their friends and partners had to say. Ruben was funny, curious, and very specific and detail oriented. People wanted to be on the show. Ruben Harris was getting to be a familiar name in Silicon Valley.

Years before we ever met, Ruben had attended our rooftop gatherings and networking events; he read our postings and watched us speak, and committed to working toward his mission through action as we did. He wanted to meet us, but he had assumed, correctly, that we are flooded with messages. He was reluctant to reach out, not wanting to waste our time with a "pick your brains" conversation. Instead he strategized and prepared, and when he was ready to launch a startup, he pitched *that* to us. Ruben initially asked Kapor Capital for $25,000 to help get Career Karma off the ground. He and his cofounders-roommates Artur and Timur wanted to move beyond their wildly popular podcast and actually create a pathway for people to break into tech, starting with boot camps. His passion for widening the path for a population that was usually overlooked by tech firms was evident, but he didn't have anything to show at that point, just promises from friends, and accrued revenue (meaning he'd sold something but hadn't been paid yet). Was this going to be an app, we asked? What were the details of the business model? We told him, if he could figure out a way to get more underrepresented people into tech, that's something we'd like to take a look at. But we weren't ready to invest.

Did that feel good? No, it did not, says Ruben. He also was turned down by Y Combinator, the tech incubator that launched Phaedra's Promise. He went to a mentor, Diishan Imira, a Black CEO who reminded him that the world of VC impact investing is small, and that nos can turn into yeses. Diishan's Oakland-based company, Mayvenn, had started out years earlier with a box of hair extensions in the trunk of his Toyota. He had been turned away countless times with his pitch to let Black stylists profit from the products they weave into client's hair, but had broken through nonetheless, and built a multimillion-dollar company. Diishan told Ruben, here's an opportunity to show us that when he says he's going to do something, he does it.

Ruben was pretty scared at this point. He had quit his job to go to Y Combinator full-time, and he didn't know what he was going to do to pay his rent. Y Combinator founder Michael Seibel, also a Black tech entrepreneur, told Ruben to calculate how much money he was going to need for the next stage of his startup, and raise it. In two weeks, Ruben had raised $200,000 from friends and family.

With his partners, Ruben reapplied to Y Combinator. This time, after refining their plans, they were accepted into the program. For three months they sharpened their goals, their business model, and their strategy. It was one of the most productive periods of his life, which is saying a lot. Y Combinator doesn't have a graduation; instead it has a Demo Day, when the founders pitch their now-existing companies to would-be investors. There were eighty-five companies on Ruben's Demo Day; Career Karma went first, and drew all the buzz. After all, even pre-pandemic in 2019, hundreds of millions of people were projected to change jobs in the coming years. Career Karma offered them free training, application support, and a spot at coding boot camps and other training programs. Boot camps, which would waive tuition in exchange for a share of graduates' early earnings, were lining up to pay Career Karma to enroll the highest-potential students.

Less than a year after his initial pitch, Ruben came back to us, raising a total of $1.5 million, and we were excited to be able to invest $300,000. Ruben remembers Mitch on that day, talking about all the places Career Karma could go. Mitch wasn't just an investor, thought Ruben. Most investors are followers; they listen to entrepreneurs and agree.

"Yeah, Mitch is very cool," Phaedra told Ruben. "But you've got to meet Freada, because she's the power."

We laughed when we heard that. Through his mother's example, Phaedra's mentorship, and Freada's lessons, Ruben has developed profound respect for women in technology. He's studied how Freada builds connections with love and passion, the way she understands the ecosystem and gets things done. When Ruben reached a point where he could choose his investors, he prioritized women and people of color, VCs he knew would trust his vision with transparency and wholehearted support.

An entrepreneur from his childhood, Ruben bought candy Blow Pops for a dime and sold them for a quarter. His distance traveled was the difference that gave him the unique insight, expertise, and empathy to solve the very challenges he overcame. As an adult, he figured out the many layers of lessons needed to become a successful CEO, and he put them all together to launch his tech startup.

Ruben believes passionately that entrepreneurs need to address the most basic human needs; he lives by a mission he learned from a CEO we invested in early, Justin Rosenstein, whose company Asana offers efficient project management software. Justin talks about being driven by helping humanity thrive. By focusing on solving basic problems for people—such as food and housing security—"Not only will you be making a big impact on community," says Ruben, who's adopted the philosophy, "but those are big industries and you will put yourself in a strong position financially."

GIVING POWER TO WORKERS

Career Karma originally acted like a college counselor for would-be programmers, largely from nontraditional and underrepresented communities, helping them figure out what kind of training they wanted, from web design to software engineering. It then helped them select and apply to programs from among the nation's hundreds of coding camps and other tech training programs. For many who have never been close to tech in any way, the challenges associated with even preparing for a boot camp can feel overwhelming. Career Karma offered study groups, peer support, and lessons on how to have a great job interview. All day, every day, users could log in to various, live coaching events largely led by alumni: Funding a Career Change, Side Hustling into Success, From Bootcamp to Capital One. Ruben has created the community of people, ideas, and learnings he sought on his own journey, as he was blazing his way into Silicon Valley.

"It's the product that we wish that we had when we were breaking into tech," Ruben told the Black Wall Street Times.

Some 90 percent of boot camp graduates land jobs. Career Karma starts users off explaining what boot camps are, and the difference between the careers they train for, from designers to software engineers.

Not only do members program themselves to work on coding every day, but they get in the habit of communicating with new people who are also learning to code or who've been there. Audio chats and support groups offered all day long provide registered users with community support and problem-solving. There are squads and mentors, success stories and pep talks available, too. Career Karma tries to match people who are on the same path or have a shared struggle. A mom, for example, might do better talking to other moms who understand their situation and can help them with their near-term goals. Ruben knows from his lived experience that focusing on the top of the mountain can be overwhelming, and that it's important to just put one foot in front of the other. Career Karma encourages its members, whether they're formerly incarcerated or unhoused, to turn around and pull someone else along.

When the pandemic hit, tens of millions of people lost their jobs in a matter of weeks; the unemployment rate jumped to levels not seen since the Great Depression. Then came the Great Resignation, as millions more quit their jobs. People didn't want to go back to impersonal or even dangerous work, and they didn't have money or time for a college degree. They were looking for training. In a matter of months, what had been tens of thousands grew to more than three million people a month logging into Career Karma, and 25,000 signing up for classes. Ruben and his partners saw the need, and quickly expanded their offerings beyond software development to a variety of tech skills, from cybersecurity to social media management. They set their sights even higher, to be the front end for all job training, from schools and universities to vocational centers. The company continued to focus on supporting a customer base of largely Black and Latinx people and women who know they want a better job but lack a clear path to get there.

By 2022, hundreds of thousands of Career Karma community members' lives had been changed by his company—people like a forty-one-year-old mother of two who had been out of work for nine years and out of school for more than twenty when she signed up.

"Nerves," she typed into an open chat at CareerKarma.com one morning. "I'm legit nervous. I know this is the way for me to level up. It's just so unknown and foreign." Within hours her fellow Career Karma participants were cheering her on, and within weeks her full-time tech training would be under way. Ruben's own brother landed a $150,000-a-year position after five months of training. A fifty-four-year-old formerly homeless man, who had worked in retail and as a driver before he was hospitalized for mental illness, was earning $75,000 a year after a twelve-week boot camp.

The next layer of Career Karma's future is packaging the service, and having companies offer it as part of its benefits package, just as they would with gym memberships or computer discounts. That was potentially going to scale up their already growing number of users, and it's why Ruben had more people wanting to invest than he needed. The other reason is that he started becoming very popular.

ENTREPRENEURIALLY EXTROVERTED

Part of Ruben's persona is being a human media machine. He started blogging in college and has either produced or been featured in hundreds of interviews, podcasts, tech talks, and inspirational videos. By 2022, he had hundreds of hours of airtime, tens of thousands of tweets, and a large Instagram following. He's happy to do mainstream interviews with tech media outlets like TechCrunch or *Forbes*, but he prioritizes publications focused on Black Americans, like *Black Enterprise*, AfroTech, and *Essence*. He also seeks out media where he can talk about things people normally don't talk about, spirituality and sobriety, to make the invisible visible. More than anyone we know, Ruben studies self-help books, tweets back, and memorizes inspirational quotes.

We watch from afar, sometimes beguiled, sometimes wondering if this is the best use of his time. For many entrepreneurs, we would suggest that frequent tweeting isn't great time management or is a case of misguided priorities. But this works for Ruben, and several of his investors have introduced him to their CEOs seeking advice on how to effectively use social media.

"If we don't empower ourselves with these tech skills, we are gonna continue to be digital cotton pickers forever," he told an interviewer who asked about his business.

"If you want advice, ask for money. If you want money, ask for advice," he told another.

Then, one day after he received a multimillion-dollar investment, a podcaster asked him about his life mission.

"Most people aren't doing what they like to do. I want to help people fulfill their potential and find their purpose," said Ruben.

A traditional tech startup mentor might advise Ruben to try conforming more closely to the "ideal founder type" in business dealings and argue that he'd be even more successful if he did. But we think that's wrong. Ruben's success came when he used his unique perspective with his creativity as a communicator. We've watched him make his difference become an asset, not a liability. By not conforming, he created a new path for those hoping to take the same journey he did. We're certain he wouldn't have been able to come up with this much-needed novel business had he not honored his difference—and the many people whose distance traveled also diverges. No one else could have founded Career Karma or helped it grow into a company that has lifted tens of thousands into new lives. We understand that Ruben, as an underrepresented entrepreneur, used his lived experiences to give him a competitive edge in identifying problems to be solved and markets to be accessed.

There's a lesson here for investors, too. Extrovert, introvert, subtle, or direct: these aren't personality traits that make or break a business. Instead, they're often a reflection of someone's community or culture. We look for grit, persistence, authenticity, and passion, but we've learned those qualities announce themselves in different ways in different people. And we never ask someone to leave themselves and their experiences at the door on the way in.

These days when Ruben comes to our events, he dazzles the newcomers. People stop him on the streets in San Francisco and ask for selfies. When someone with a nontraditional background asks for advice about breaking into tech, he's all in.

"If you really want to do this, I got your back one hundred thousand percent," he'll tell them. "Commit to start and finish it, and recognize that even after you break in, that's just the beginning, and you're at the bottom of a new hill."

Ruben says that most people he's seen building successful tech start-ups seem just like any other person, rich or poor. When he reads about them, they're famous, nearly mythical. And getting to know them, he's realized what makes them different is they have clarity on what they want to achieve and are willing to change their process to get there.

"If you're willing to commit to it, so am I," he tells students.

One important point: Ruben is an outlier. We don't want a world in which everyone has to be as exceptional as Ruben is to succeed. That's where the paradox begins. It's easy for us to talk about Ruben's success and have people conclude that with the right amount of drive and charisma, anyone can be a successful tech entrepreneur. But everyone, all of us, are extraordinary in our own way, just not necessarily in ways as visible as Ruben's specialness. What we need is a world in which women and people of color don't have to be exceptional—any more than white men need to be exceptional—to be afforded the same access to connections, education, and funding. Access doesn't confer automatic success but without it there's a very large barrier to entry. This can be hard to convey to VC investors, but we try. A white woman, a serial founder in our portfolio, once gave Freada a tote bag emblazoned with "Carry yourself with the confidence of a mediocre white man," aptly and perhaps cynically conveying this same paradoxical sentiment.

Freada once heard from a chief diversity officer at a major social media company about how frustrated she was that public schools in some of the poorest neighborhoods received funding to computerize, but then left hundreds of laptops and tablets unopened in their boxes for a decade, depriving students of opportunities to learn critical tech skills. School officials said they needed staff and training to use the gear, and that their Wi-Fi bandwidth was insufficient. What a waste. Freada offered to put this person in touch with a terrific company that was able to come in and get the school's technology up and running.

"Now those students can gain skills to work at places like your company," said Freada.

"That's not who we're interested in," the diversity chief responded. "We want to hire the kid who breaks into the school, unpacks the computers, and teaches himself to code."

We think this is the wrong approach, and yet it was exactly what her social media company was doing through its recruitment efforts. Notwithstanding the likelihood that a Black or Latinx kid would be thrown in jail if they broke into a school, her focus only on wanting "exceptional" kids means that the majority of Black and Latinx talent will be ignored. This particular diversity chief is Black, of Caribbean descent. She's a lawyer, who went to the world's most elite universities. Her experience informs her actions; no surprise that her reference points reflect her lived experience, too, in that she's most familiar with those rare, remarkable people who have found a way to break out of the grinding barriers many Black and Latinx people face. She may have traveled a great distance herself to achieve success, but it's easy for her to accept, then, that anyone who works hard can find a way on their own. Unlike the chief diversity officer, Ruben recognized that he didn't have to perform a solo act—that his failures and his successes could be a gift to others. By moving the spotlight on him to shine on those around him, he paves new pathways for others. As our partner Ulili Onovakpuri says, "When someone opens the door for you, you put down a door stopper and make sure others come in."

A RIGHTEOUS COLLABORATION

During the pandemic, Ruben launched a GoFundMe account to raise $50,000 for laptops for people who lost their jobs; he asked us to donate. That's not the right way, we told him. He needed to aim for

$500,000 and to do it in a way that allowed donors to get a tax deduction. We arranged for him to use our foundation as a fiscal sponsor. Companies and individuals could also donate cash or laptops to the new initiative, Reskill America. As donations and equipment came in, Career Karma distributed tech gear to low-income women, Black, Latinx, Indigenous, and disabled people as well as veterans who had lost a job or were furloughed due to COVID-19.

This was the right approach for a tech startup to collaborate with our nonprofit.

Ruben inspired us to believe that with a collective effort, we could help millions of Americans acquire new skills and prepare for the Great Rehiring. That's exactly what happened.

6

INVESTING IN MENTAL WELLNESS

MATTHEW AND PK

"I'm stepping down as CEO due to my mental health—and I want to talk about it."

Matthew Cooper, a soft-spoken, intensely driven startup founder, had been balancing his mental illness and exceptional career growth for more than twenty years. Now, in 2021, he was going public. He wrote about anxiety, depression, panic attacks, and suicidal ideation on an online business news website, Quartz. His words were moving and powerful, and for us deeply personal. We were investors in Matthew's high-growth company, EarnUp, which he had cofounded seven years earlier. Matthew and his cofounder Nadim Homsany's goals were incredibly ambitious, aiming for nothing short of helping 200 million Americans get out of $20 trillion of debt. We had known he was struggling, but we didn't know the extent of his problems.

Startups are hard. Change is the only constant. Living with un-predictability, with ambiguity, seeing millions in the bank one week and hundreds a few weeks later, can be terrifying for founders at high-growth startups, and even worse for many of the underrepresented founders we invest in. Severe angst and crippling desperation are common and frequent experiences for any entrepreneur, but they become even more pronounced for many of our CEOs whose lives continue to be impacted by the biology of adversity; experiencing or witnessing violence or any number of other traumatic events actually changes one's biology and impacts lifelong physical and mental health. Childhoods marked by hatred, harassment, racism, poverty, and food and housing insecurity have a long shadow. Think of how much talent our country loses to the trauma caused by systemic bias and the pressure to silence any talk of it.

DISRUPTING THE RISE-AND-GRIND CULTURE

Kapor Capital's founders and investors, who overcome considerable odds, aren't miraculously "fixed" when their companies become successful. Hardly. They ask each other, "So you think we've left our past behind?" And they answer, "Not so fast." We continue to see that emotional struggles don't evaporate when they launch tech startups for those whose childhoods included fear and trauma. Often the anxiety just ramps up. Matthew wasn't our first founder to step back because of struggles with mental illness and a desire to prioritize mental health. Sometimes their companies survive, and sometimes not. They're expected to be role models, glorified for making it against the odds. All too often our founders on those pedestals tell us they're lonely, scared, paying a very high price for the risky, fast-paced, goal-oriented process of launching a company.

Kapor Capital can't single-handedly eradicate these pressures, but we do encourage our founders to openly talk about mental health, and we work to support each other—that's definitely a different play-book.

"Being an entrepreneur requires this set of traits that maybe come with this dark side," said former venture capitalist and investment banker Stephen Hays, whose podcast, *Stigma*, builds on his own recovery from mental illness. "The environment you put yourself in creates a situation where you feel like you are the one that is treading the water, keeping everybody's head above water, keeping the ship afloat. And so when things get too hard, it feels like you can't reach out for help. Like, if you say, I need help, then what happens? Because you're the one keeping the ship afloat."

In the Silicon Valley boom and bust of the early 2000s, researchers studying the rapidly growing pool of startup founders—almost entirely white, privileged men—found alarmingly high rates of mental stress. The newly minted CEOs executing their vision and watching money roll in displayed major mood disorders, ADHD, anxiety, and depression. After seeing this firsthand in the first tech boom, we've watched the culture of tech startups just get worse. When more than half of the tech workers in a survey of Silicon Valley's top companies reported high job stress, some CEOs took it as a point of pride, as if stress equaled success.

Steve Jurvetson, a longtime Silicon Valley venture capitalist and investor in billionaire CEO Elon Musk, publicly congratulated the Tesla and SpaceX founder for having his teams report the most stress. "I think this is the root of success," tweeted Jurvetson, who was later accused of sexual harassment and asked to leave his firm. Musk responded, adding that high stress "goes with the territory."

So do mental health conditions.

That's why the startup world needs more people like Matthew Cooper to feel like they can come forward. He helped lift the taboo about talking about mental illness.

Matthew grew up in Vancouver, Canada, the son of a teacher and a minister. When he was around twelve, he says, he started having periods of extreme anxiety and, separately, periods of extreme depression. Seeking stability and control, he would starve himself, or purge. He began to feel another intense pressure, too, a need to win. His parents told him they were worried. You're working too hard, they said. You're not looking well. You need to slow down. Matthew figured they just didn't understand him. As an adult, when he sought help, Matthew realized his childhood behaviors were counterproductive tools he was using to try to soothe his mental anguish. At the time, however, he just plowed through, excelling in academics and sports, always craving to perform, putting immense strain on himself, to be better, go faster, and achieve that next thing, whatever it was.

He was drawn to prestige and started working at top consulting and investment firms after graduating from Princeton University. For years he hid his daily, pervasive dread, alleviated only by constant hustling, which brought affirmations for all of his achievements.

"I just lived off the high of the checklist, just getting things done," he said.

Matthew and Nadim Homsany met after graduating from college; they were both working in Dubai, first for a global management consulting company and then a private equity firm, sitting desk to desk. When the housing bubble burst around 2008, they began investing in U.S. real estate together, from the other side of the world. They grew close, later becoming housemates back in the States.

By the time he was thirty, Matthew was living in Los Angeles with what looked—on paper—like a great career and life. He had come out as gay a few years earlier and was looking to build strong relationships. But his mental health issues were getting in the way of his social interactions and making him physically sick as well. And so, for the first time, Matthew quit his private equity job to focus on his mental wellness. He hoped this simple act would help him feel better. It didn't. He sat on a beach, day after day, for two weeks, consumed with anxiety and depression. That's when he realized he was going to need more help. Like all endeavors, he went all in, with meditation, therapy, support groups, and more. He started to feel better, but there was still turbulence.

A few months into his recovery, Matthew was chatting with Nadim at their kitchen table about their parents' debt and the personal toll of those financial worries. Nadim's parents had fled the Middle East and pursued the American Dream. They bought their first home in 1986, with a thirty-year mortgage.

"Congratulations, Dad," Nadim told his father in 2016. "You did it. You own your home, you have three children, six grandchildren, you built a good life."

His father grew emotional. He loves the U.S. and tells everyone it's the best country in the world. However, his father said, we don't own this house. We won't own it until 2035. Nadim was shocked. How did a thirty-year mortgage become a forty-nine-year mortgage?

Meanwhile, Nadim had been paying down his own mortgage with an extra hundred dollars a month, figuring that would chip away at the principal to shorten the length of his loan and build equity more quickly. Now he took a closer look at his paperwork and found that the bank had been taking his extra payments and applying them toward future interest payments, not his principal. It just didn't make any sense.

Matthew and Nadim decided to start a tech company that could help home buyers pay their mortgages and other loans, while helping lenders mitigate risk. They researched and wrote a remarkable business model that piloted extremely well. Their plan would make it possible for people to stagger automatic bill payments to better align with their paychecks. After their initial friends-and-family $500,000 launch, Matthew and Nadim began seeking investors.

(We didn't realize it when we first met Matthew and Nadim, but we would come to learn that Mitch had already had what Nadim would later describe as "a massive personal impact" on him as a child. Nadim's father gave him a computer when he was ten and said that for every hour of games he played, he'd have to spend another hour using the Lotus 1–2–3 spreadsheet, documenting savings bonds. He mastered that software and, after Harvard Law School, found himself again using Lotus software in his early jobs.)

Now it was time for them to raise a lot of money.

Matthew is excellent at fundraising. He comes across as confident and calm; his keen intelligence and thoughtful answers are always impressively thorough. But privately, he has paid a cost. Like many founders, the ability to raise capital—or not—is very tied up with both the dream and vision, and also his own ego. Matthew still can't help but take rejections personally but understood that as a cofounder he needed to show up in person to represent the values and visions of the company. He also felt the weight of his earlier round of investors, who had put their faith (and their money) into their vision; he didn't want to disappoint them, either. Pitching and getting rejected took "a pound of flesh," he would say, and he later told us he had to set aside time to recover from his mental and physical reactions to the process.

Matthew and Nadim told us that as they made the VC rounds, walking into Kapor Center to pitch EarnUp was a completely different experience than the series of meetings they had been through with white straight men. At Kapor, we asked about their financials, but the three Black investors they met, including Brian Dixon, who would go on to lead the fund, also quizzed them about their venture's social impact. The tone of the conversations, the look and feel of everyone around them, even our offices with teens and dogs and laughter, were so radically different than the rest of the VC system they'd been interacting with.

During this frenzied launch period, Matthew later admitted to us that he was working all the time and binge eating, creating a weird equilibrium that he believed allowed him to be "super productive." He was able to achieve a huge amount, but the still-hidden costs were accumulating. There were plenty of low periods. He went on mental health retreats, got himself rested and stable, and came back to work, only to be overwhelmed again. Even when Matthew was checking all the boxes—rest, diet, exercise, therapy—he was still struggling. When he felt he needed to be in a safe place, he would be voluntarily admitted into a psychiatric hospital unit. Once he even held a board meeting in the hospital room.

During one nine-day stay in a psychiatric unit, Matthew had an epiphany.

"I'm not going to do this anymore," he said. "I'm stepping down from full-time executive work."

Matthew and Nadim talked about whether it would be wise to go public with his decision.

If someone is having mental health issues, are VCs going to give them millions of dollars to run their business? In recent years, we've seen some high-profile athletes and top celebrities—from tennis superstar Naomi Osaka to performer Britney Spears—speak out about their own mental struggles. They have a great deal to lose by sharing their problems but are using their fame to help dispel the notion that anxiety, depression, or any number of other mental illnesses are a sign of weakness or disgrace. In tech startups, where the percentage of CEOs struggling with mental disorders has been estimated as much as seven times higher than that of the general public, the discussion is barely broached. They would rather talk about term sheets and valuation, blitzscaling and risk.

Matthew was firm, and Nadim agreed that breaking the taboo of talking about mental health in corporate America could be incredibly transformative. For years after he posted about what he describes as his own neurodivergence, Matthew continued to get grateful messages from around the world. He had stoked a larger, important discussion.

THE PERILS OF TOXIC STRESS

We share Matthew's belief—there's so much more than term sheets and KPIs that needs to be talked about. Dr. Peolia Kansas Fonsworth III, or PK, is one of a handful of bilingual psychiatrists who specialize in treatment of addiction in Southern California, pulling patients, including entrepreneurs, back from their rock-bottom moments, providing a lifeline, and turning lives around. He's a brilliant and respected doctor, who had none of the easier paths of the privileged class but was offered opportunities—from the elderly woman who raised him to a local Safeway cashier who made sure he never went without food, and a Kapor Center scholarship that got him through college debt-free and with a supportive community.

Born in the Philippines and adopted by a Japanese American woman old enough to be his grandmother, PK moved to the U.S. when he was ten. They were extremely poor, taking shelter in a mouse-infested unheated garage, living with food insecurity and subsisting on meager Social Security payments. Sandy, a woman working at their local supermarket, once offered them a ride home and was so shocked by the conditions that she gave them food and helped support them in the ensuing years. She often drove PK to Kapor Center programs. PK says that without Sandy and her husband, Jim, whom he now considers family, he certainly would have starved. But with their support, he worked hard in school, graduated with honors, and was accepted into UC Berkeley, where our tuition support and peer group programs were already in place to help him. Just one month into classes, PK's "grandmother" died. He called Freada, wondering if she thought UC Berkeley would allow him to stay in the dorms for the holidays. No, said Freada, you're coming home with us.

Like many families, we talk about gratitude on Thanksgiving before digging in to turkey and potatoes. We went around the table, thankful for family, for love. PK said he was thankful for the food on the table, to have enough to eat, because that was not always the case. Mitch teared up. It was one thing to hear about hunger in the abstract. It was another to have somebody he has a relationship with sharing their life experience. We talked. PK shared his ambitions, and they were big. He told us he wanted to go to medical school, to be a doctor, to help people like his grandmother. We could see ourselves in his shoes, and we knew that one way to have people gain traction and move forward in their lives includes a sustained investment. Like our CEOs who defy the odds and make their own paths, we were honored to be able to make that investment in PK. We helped get his education paid for, and offered mentorship. When he called Freada during a semester abroad, feeling lonely and isolated, she flew to Spain for a visit so he could share his adventure. He's our family as well.

Now, after decades, we turn to PK for his expertise. We've talked to him about how, at their core, many of our founders live with fear, believing they have to do everything themselves or their company will fall apart. That's a large burden, and very isolating. They talk about feeling alone, the classic "lonely at the top" cliché. We get it. While they may be surrounded by people, their own power and leadership can create a distance between them and their teams. They have immense responsibilities, but few friends or colleagues who have a shared experience and whom they can turn to for support. And they're expected to fly solo, handle everything. We're also often dealing with people in a very early stage of their own development, young and maybe naïve in some ways. They often don't have the life experience or a support network to survive the stress of starting something.

For many of our founders, the startup stress comes on top of pain and worry that begins when a child grows up poor, Black, or Latinx in America. Literally thousands of studies over decades of research have found that early experiences, positive and negative, leave their mark in our bodies and brains. Strong, safe, stable, bonded relationships are critical for children, promoting healthy brain architecture and well-functioning immune and cardiovascular systems. Facing tolerable levels of stress can even build resilience.

Many of our founders, their employees, even their clients and customers, haven't been so fortunate. As children, they lived in a state of constant chaos, dealing with any number of impediments to what experts consider early determinants of academic success and long-term health. Factors that can cause persistent problems include neglect and abuse, mentally ill family members, addiction, divorce, and having relatives sent to jail. Some were so disrupted as children that they lived in shelters or foster homes.

Compounding that trauma is direct or indirect exposure to bias, verbal abuse, harassment, or discrimination. Very real and personal pain is inflicted every time another video emerges of a white police officer shooting a Black man, every time a pipeline is laid through Indigenous land, every time a shopkeeper shouts "Go back home" to a Latinx family.

When people feel threatened, their hearts pound, their blood pressure shoots up, adrenaline rushes to their fingertips; it's "fight or flight" time. We certainly know how that feels. But white, privileged people are often able to have that feeling leave their bodies as soon as the threat is gone. That's not the case for many of our founders and investors who endured persistent turmoil when they were young and vulnerable. That state of being chronically stressed-out disrupts brain circuits, making it harder to focus and self-soothe, and increases the risk of heart disease, diabetes, and mental illness as an adult.

Pediatrician and researcher Dr. Dayna Long, a member of our own extended Kapor family, doesn't mince words about this when she trains clinicians to screen their young patients' mental welfare during routine visits. "Racism causes structural inequities and poor health outcomes across the life span," she said in one 2022 lesson. She not only created a pediatric life-events screening tool; she also got the state of California to reimburse providers every time they use it.

Our founders, along with those they work with and serve, often expect that when they finally have money, their anxiety and depression will fade away. It's frustrating when financial stability doesn't solve their emotional problems. They tell us they still wake up in the middle of the night fearing the pounding on the door because they're getting evicted again. PK's patients include entrepreneurs who are first-generation college graduates who grew up in economically deprived and forgotten neighborhoods. It makes sense that some of these people don't automatically feel safe, he said. He's found that people who are running companies are more than tech savvy—they're visionaries, often incredibly organized with the potential for pushing the boundaries of technology to better the lives of those around them.

He advises his clients, whose relentless schedules keep them focused from one task to the next, to put explicit breaks into their own calendars to nourish themselves. And he asks them to consider using the tools they've developed as entrepreneurs, like the ability to connect with people, to open up with their friends and family about their struggles.

"Bring the skills that have strengthened your company into your personal life. Seek the right consultants appropriately," he said. "That will pay dividends."

In therapy, PK bears witness to their own transformation as they move forward to more rewarding and connected lives. If there's friction in a CEO's startup relationships, PK explains, there's probably friction in other places, possibly in their own identities and their own relationships. He encourages founders to work with psychiatrists and therapists, as well as peers and mentors, to help them integrate their often-difficult pasts into the present.

"To be able to come to the table and do the work, be vulnerable with a good psychiatrist or therapist, that can be an important tool to unlocking what success means and having more fluidity when difficulties arise," he told us.

When we've worked with founders to navigate their mental wellness, we've learned that healing doesn't happen overnight. We tell them this is another kind of long-term investment they must make in themselves, and we will support them through their process. We continue to encourage all of our founders to have open and meaningful discussions about mental health.

A year after Matthew's blog post about his mental health, well-known VC Andy Johns was crying on his couch. Until then, he had hidden the "war zone" that was his first ten years of life, a period of massive trauma, behind his public persona as a young, hoodie-wearing, confident, and successful techie, advising and investing in more than $1 billion worth of startups. In his moment of crisis, he opened up in a series of tweets, posting about his own suffering, his buried pain, and what had helped.

"I wasn't sure how people would react since I had never spoken about mental health before," he said a year later. "I'm a 'growth guy' so I was supposed to stay in my lane and only talk startups and growth. That was my internal narrative, at least. But I resisted the fear, went with what my gut was begging me to do, and posted the tweet anyway." More than one hundred people sent him private direct messages expressing their silent suffering as well.

The door was slowly opening. Another year passed and Andy Dunn, the former CEO of online clothing site Bonobos, chronicled his own bipolar journey in his book *Burn Rate: Launching a Startup and Losing My Mind*.

Andy cofounded Bonobos in 2007 with a Stanford Business School classmate. Ten years later they sold it to Walmart for $310 million. Now Andy described manic episodes, delusions, and hospitalizations, even an arrest, all while raising tens of millions of dollars for a company that was growing incredibly quickly. The hypomanic state brought on by his bipolar disorder served as jet fuel for the entrepreneurial drive, he said, but it came with great costs. "If there was not a profound stigma around mental illness, this book would not be necessary," he wrote. "Mental illness is one of the final taboos."

A KINDER APPROACH

Mitch learned about mental wellness before he even entered tech, working as a counselor in the psychiatric unit of a community hospital. It was a place where people who had long-term, serious psychiatric issues could come to keep themselves from boiling over. In the best cases, they would get calmed down and put back together so they could go out and function again. But for others, it was just a revolving door. A key takeaway was that until we understand the roots of mental illness well enough to develop cures, we have to employ a multifaceted approach to support individuals with mental health challenges.

Here's our approach: invest in mental wellness, lead by example, and be truly founder friendly.

At Kapor Center, we've expanded health benefits and encourage time off. Our staff are paid to volunteer with underrepresented communities, especially in organizations that are meaningful in their own lives. And we offer assistance for student loan repayment. Student debt can be crushing; it is one of the starkest differences between the circumstances of privileged kids and kids from low-income backgrounds entering the workforce. The debt keeps them from helping their families, joining their colleagues eating out or going on trips, or saving to buy a house and is a constant source of stress. Mental health care is available 24/7, and dogs are usually around, offering a friendly, low-stakes snuggle. We encourage founders to seek therapy and executive coaching before the excitement becomes anxiety. And we listen. Our go-to conversation opener can open a floodgate: "What's keeping you up at night?"

When founders pitch tech startups to support mental wellness, we pay attention. Karan Singh came to us in 2011 and said a friend's suicide had sparked his commitment to changing the way mental health care is provided around the world. He named his company Ginger because, when he was a child, his mother brewed him ginger tea when she felt he might be getting sick. He wanted mental health providers to look like the people they serve. We invested. Over ten years, the company went from an idea to a powerhouse, with more than five hundred companies paying Ginger to provide their employees emotional support. Coaches, therapists, and psychiatrists are available via text 24/7. During the pandemic, Ginger became an essential support, seeing revenues triple as stress levels soared and people were told to stay home. By 2022, the company had received more than $200 million in investments, and over 10 million people in over forty countries were accessing support through their phone. Singh is also accomplishing Ginger's equity and inclusion mission: half of Ginger's coaches, therapists, and psychiatrists identify as people of color, more than three times the proportion found in the membership of the American Psychological Association. In fall of 2021, Ginger closed a merger with Headspace, an online meditation, sleep, and wellness company, creating a $3 billion mental health company.

We also appreciate that during the pitch process, founders' stress levels have never been higher. They've quit their jobs, often fairly high-paying, high-profile positions, to put their life and energy into a mission-driven business. Often they haven't been paying themselves, and are living off credit card debt, many without a safety net. They're working more than two full-time jobs when they're both running their companies and fundraising. And they're in the midst of a rejection cycle, an emotionally draining process that can feel deeply personal.

That's why we've doubled down on a term thrown around by investors: "founder friendly." For many venture capital firms, those words are often a pernicious form of happy talk. More than one of our founders recounts being jolted by 2 a.m. calls from investors, telling them they're running the business all wrong. Another example we've seen repeatedly: so-called founder-friendly VCs routinely tell values-focused entrepreneurs to take impact and diversity out of their pitch deck, because impact and diversity goals, for most investors, are still seen as obstacles. But that directly ignores an entrepreneur's reason for wanting to launch a business. That's not friendly at all. That's demeaning and demoralizing. We affirm and celebrate the missions of founders who are risking everything to solve a struggle they faced themselves, often an issue that brought pain to their entire family. That's inspiring and motivating.

We certainly don't take entrepreneurs aside and say, "All of those other VCs are going to lie to you." But we do have very frank conversations about how they aren't always presenting the full picture of reality. We try to help founders become educated, so they can make good choices for themselves. We remind entrepreneurs that most investors' ultimate loyalty is to their limited partners, the people who invested in their funds. That means, above all else, that they will be driven by their goal to maximize returns for those limited partners, no matter what.

Some VCs will claim they want to be an entrepreneur's best friend. We remind founders who come to us about how the game is typically played, and then we share our experiences and our approach to prepare them for what's to come, particularly if they're from outside the system. For example, when Mitch once launched a startup, he found himself being exploited because of "information asymmetry." The investors and their lawyer had negotiated this type of deal hundreds of times, and they didn't point out to Mitch pieces of the agreement that worked against him; terms were included in the deal that Mitch had never explicitly agreed to that were very unfavorable. It damaged the relationship but taught us an important lesson about how to treat founders when they bring us ideas and ask for investment. We do have self-interest, of course, and sometimes it can be in conflict with what a founder wants. Where we differ is that we practice transparency and try to surface the hidden factors that might be driving a deal or creating competing interests.

For us, sometimes being founder friendly means looking like we're leaving something on the table, giving the founder the advantage in a deal, but it ends up that it benefits us the most in the long run. When it comes to our founders, at every intersection, we defer to their vision. We believe in them and we share in their success.

Like all venture capital investors, we scrutinize our potential investments. Will there be litigation? Are there environmental issues? What licenses and permits will they need? But we believe that as investors in underrepresented founders with gap-closing companies, we also need to understand their life experiences and not just project our own onto them. What worked for us as investors, Mitch as a tech entrepreneur, or Freada as an impact entrepreneur and researcher, is not necessarily going to work for them. And we consider it our responsibility—not theirs—to educate ourselves and then apply what we've learned; it's on us to make sure they don't feel like they have to check themselves at the door. Whether it's coming to our office for a meeting, or offering an expert to provide advice, having an intersectional lens is crucial in any of the resources that we offer to founders.

GATHERING FOR STRENGTH

Finally, one of the most important things we do to support mental well-being is bring together amazing groups of investors and entrepreneurs who look different than their tech startup peers. They all want the same thing: equity, opportunity, connection. Sometimes there's a weeklong retreat, or a Q&A with an investor. Other times it's just lunch on our rooftop, where conversations can and do quickly become personal: How much are you raising? How much are you charging? How fast and big do you want to grow? Then they go deeper: Did that investor brush us off in a very uncomfortable way? Did that panel feel really awkward?

We make safe spaces, without saying safe spaces. Our partners and founders describe them as magical moments, when they can get in a room that's not traditional and then make it a new tradition.

"When we are able to gather with our founders, it just feels like there's a glow in the room," our partner Ulili Onovakpuri told us. "These are the folks who are in the trenches, building with you. They like you, they understand you, we are in the struggle together."

One entrepreneur said he'd "always been the only one in the room," whether it was a tech startup conference room or a major corporate boardroom, before joining us at a gathering.

"It's not just being in a room of people of color," he said. "I think it's going back to the distance traveled, the economic journeys that a lot of us have gone through. You can just feel that." He added that, when Kapor founders talk about growing up with a single mom, there's a deep understanding of what that experience was like. They talk about having imposter syndrome and feeling like they're not enough, all the time; the feeling that they're always failing because they don't know all the things.

"But then when we're together we realize that nobody knows all the things, either, and we're just figuring it out as we go. I walk away from that feeling so proud of all of us, because I know the journey they've been on. I've been on that journey, too," he said. "It gives me a little gusto in my step."

LOGGING OFF

Every day, for decades, we'll walk our dog, or dogs, depending on who we are lucky enough to be living with. When we lived in San Francisco, we'd wander off to our favorite bookstore. In Oakland, we head for the waterfront, across the bay from San Francisco's lit-up skyscrapers. We walk dogs on the beach and in the hills. Over the years, our dogs have brought us comfort and laughter.

Mitch can meditate while he walks, spending hours on winding trails in redwood forests, contemplating life and solving conundrums. Freada works with designers, creating one-of-a-kind fabrics that become colorful, natural, and comfortable clothes. But we also struggle. We get overwhelmed. We get stressed out. And here's one thing we are very clear about: we log off. Sometimes it's for the day, sometimes a week, but when the world of tech is moving too quickly, we find we can replenish ourselves by simply unplugging. We realize this is a privilege, but we do hope everyone can find a space for solace, whether it's in a quiet church or during a gentle bus ride to work.

Because we are so available so often, we're careful not to just disappear, ghosting everyone we are accountable to. We're thoughtful about our out-of-office memo. The key thing is to validate why it's important to take time to disconnect, and also provide other contact people so that work can go on.

In 2021, Freada had this auto response:

Subject line: Woof—napping & chasing my tail this week

Thanks for reaching out. My young dog is teaching her old person a new trick—taking time off. If your message is urgent, put WOOF in the Subj. line. Otherwise, please resend next week or wait patiently in dog years as I work thru my Inbox.

She mentioned who to reach out to in our absence. Then we put our phones away.

As the World Health Organization says, "The relationship between mental health and human rights is an integral and interdependent one."

7

THE PRICE OF LOYALTY

UBER

Every day, millions of us catch a ride in an Uber. The ubiquitous global personal transportation service is hailed—by app—everywhere from small-town U.S. to the largest cities in the world. Far more convenient than taxis, and typically cleaner and more pleasant, Uber has changed the way we get around and, for better and for worse, has been foundational to the gig economy. The roller-coaster ride of the company itself is the stuff of bestsellers and streaming television.

For more than a decade, we had a ringside seat as original angel investors. We were users of the service in its earliest days, and were occasional advisers, mentors, and trainers. Here's what we came to understand: if Uber had stuck to playing by the rules by seeking permission to operate, the service would never have been allowed to get off the ground. It was necessary to bet the company, by going up against the taxi and livery industry, as well as the municipal authorities those services had in their pocket. But in Uber's case, the aggressive team of battle-waging employees fighting the system gave rise to a toxic culture that nearly killed the company.

We've come to learn that it's exceedingly difficult to foster a culture where employees are hired and rewarded for breaking external rules to build a business—in this case defy the stranglehold of the taxi regulations—and expect those same employees to leave their tendencies toward risk taking and writing their own rules at the door when they come to the office. As we often told Uber executives, the company needed clear guardrails to delineate acceptable from unacceptable behavior.

Those early years were notoriously scrappy. When we'd fly into a city and request an Uber, the car would come, along with a message asking us to join the voices petitioning local regulators to allow the service. When taxi drivers in Paris slashed Ubers' tires, Uber called them a "taxi cartel." Battles over where Ubers could pick up passengers at airports, one of the most profitable places for taxis and limos, were the norm.

As Uber CEO Travis Kalanick continued his nationwide, sweeping rebellion against the status quo, one city at a time, he was the epitome of a brash, cocky, arrogant founder. He sent Uber staffers into competitor Lyft cars to try to recruit drivers. He talked back to potential investors, tweeted rudely at city officials.

"It's hard to be a disrupter and not be an asshole," said an early investor. During job interviews, potential staff were jarred by Travis's blunt or even rude questions, but that was deliberate. Travis wanted to recruit colleagues willing to confront the standards.

Inevitably, internal culture became a natural extension of growing external turbulence. In 2013, Travis sent a memo to Uber's then four hundred staffers before a Miami party advising them not to throw beer kegs off tall buildings and warning of a two-hundred-dollar "puke charge." Later there were reports that an Uber manager had groped a female colleague at a different company retreat while another had threatened to beat an employee's head in with a baseball bat. Lawsuits were filed alleging sexual harassment and verbal abuse.

We were sadly not surprised at the scandals. We were among the very earliest Uber investors, and when the series of scandals began making headlines, we had been trying to counter the jaw-dropping levels of unprofessionalism and harassment for years.

Our relationship with Uber dates back to a more innocent time of the web, 2007, when a fellow angel investor brought Garrett Camp, fresh from graduate school in computer science in Canada, to meet Mitch and raise money for his startup StumbleUpon. The core idea was charming: A user told StumbleUpon what topics they were interested in and it would show you web pages that corresponded to those interests. As a user gave StumbleUpon more feedback, it got better and better, often delighting Mitch with its serendipity. In that more innocent, pre-Google era of the web, we immediately sensed its appeal. Just fifteen minutes into the meeting, Mitch short-circuited the normal pitch process and said, "I'm in." Not a calculated business decision, but sometimes going with our gut is exactly the right move.

It ended up being a good bet. StumbleUpon's star rose quickly, becoming one of *Time* magazine's "Best 50 Websites," and before there was any business model, much less any revenue, Garrett sold it to eBay for $75 million within a year for a 6x return. eBay didn't find a way to take advantage of the asset, and a few years later the online auction site sold StumbleUpon back to Garrett for next to nothing. We were ready to jump back in, but some of Garrett's other new investors, who were Mitch's former partners at Accel, didn't want us involved. Garrett said it was because they perceived Mitch had a conflict with another project he was working on, but we weren't so sure. It might just have been payback for quitting the firm.

Garrett was apologetic but there was nothing he could do about the veto. Undeterred, Mitch asked him if he was working on anything else we might get involved with. Very much on Mitch's mind was the fact he had recently missed an opportunity to invest with Evan Williams in Twitter, precisely because he didn't do this kind of follow-up. That's when Garrett first told Mitch about the idea for Uber, "but I'm a year off from starting it."

Mitch responded: "You have to let me in when the time comes." Garrett assured Mitch he would.

There was silence for a year, but then an email arrived: Garrett and his partners were closing a round of financing within days. We should wire $75,000. That's how we got into Uber in July 2010. This was before we had established our Kapor Capital fund or had articulated our specific investment criteria. Nonetheless, we believed in much of Uber's mission. Here was a company that could bring financial stability to just about anyone with a car, allowing them to drive when they wanted, setting their own schedule around family and other work and priorities. And it offered a safe ride for anyone who was not near public transportation or didn't feel it was safe, or was unable to flag a taxi as they exited their shift at 2 a.m. Flagging a cab while Black, in New York City and many other places, even in a business suit and tie and carrying a briefcase, was notoriously difficult.

When we invested, let's be clear, Uber was an idea, not yet a service. It did have a very creative founder in Garrett, who could build stuff. At this point Travis Kalanick, a friend of Garrett's, was simply an angel investor in Uber like Mitch. There were so many possible pitfalls: the features on which Uber relied, like widely available, high-speed mobile Internet, reliable GPS, and complete and accurate city maps, to name just three, were immature and unevenly available. Mitch thought, I don't know if this is really going to work or how big it might get, but it's worth seeing how it develops. Trust us, nobody knew it was going to be a big thing. Nobody knew it was going to reinvent transportation.

But even in its earliest days when the app was rough and barely worked, the magic shone through. The old way of arranging for a car service was laborious, inefficient, and frustrating. We never knew if the car was going to show up on time and in the right place. It was often impossible to get through by phone to a dispatcher, which was the only way to reserve a car or find out its whereabouts. With Uber we could track the black dot moving on the map as it came closer to us, and our confidence that the car was going to show up grew by the moment. And then the car just appeared. We hopped in and off we went. Like we said, magic.

Travis helped recruit their first full-time employee with Craigslist and Twitter help-wanted posts. Ryan Graves, a tall, buff surfer, tweeted back: "here's a tip. email me:) graves.ryan@gmail.com." This was a gamble that would make Ryan a billionaire; Travis and Garrett brought him in and made him CEO. But within a year it was clear that Ryan didn't have the leadership and management experience to handle a rapidly growing company, so he stepped back into a management role where he stayed until 2017 when Uber went public. Travis replaced him, heading up the company. We didn't know him well and didn't see the red flags.

For the next few years, as Travis built one of Silicon Valley's giants, bro culture, with its attendant biases, harassment, and exclusionary practices, was flourishing at Uber. Travis would hold what he called jam sessions, loose and open conversations with staff that veered wildly off course. He was caught on video yelling at an Uber driver he caught a ride with to "grow up." He joked, to *GQ* magazine, about a women-on-demand service called "Boob-er." Senior executives left. Others came to us, confidentially, for advice.

As angel investors, we didn't have a board seat, and we were neither expected nor invited to be very involved. Nonetheless, we tried to help, with one-on-one meetings, mentoring discussions, and suggestions. In keeping with Silicon Valley etiquette, we had been publicly supportive throughout Uber's early growing pains, and offered constructive criticism only in private. Freada came to executives with specific strategies to combat racism and sexism in the company, including hiring outside of their own networks, removing names and schools from applicants' resumes, and rewarding employees working with nonprofits to develop underrepresented talent. She coached Ryan as he struggled to lead, and he conceded they were not doing very well when it came to diversity and inclusion as they quickly hired engineers and marketers. Top managers told Freada they agreed it was important to get equity right, and that Uber, as a leader in its field, should be a leader on diversity. The obvious demographic differences between drivers and employees was a constant reminder that talent was out there if you knew where to look.

In 2015, Freada was invited to Uber's San Francisco headquarters and gave a presentation about how hidden bias operates in tech startup culture. She was careful, as always, to not put everyone into a defensive crouch, but instead she spoke simply and transparently, trying to broaden their viewpoint. Questions and challenges were explicitly welcomed. On a regular basis, senior execs facing issues of bias or sexism would call Mitch's mobile phone, often on the weekend, and ask to speak to "his wife," an ironic example of at least some of the C-suite's view of women.

Over the years, Freada consulted on surveys for Uber, and during her training she shared the company's data with executives and employees. Trained as a researcher, Freada often designs customized surveys. For the Uber team she presented aggregate tech startup data alongside Uber's own findings. In general, 81 percent of the staff at Uber said they believed that diverse teams in the workplace are better at innovating and problem-solving than teams without diverse members. But 2 percent did not, and another 13 percent said it depends more on the team. The survey also showed that 39 percent of Uber's men, compared with 23 percent of women, agreed that "fit" was more important during hiring than diversity. So what did Uber's staff identify as "not a culture fit"? Not "fierce" or "super pumped," a favorite Travis term.

Freada also brought broader, evidence-based findings. In study after study, she told Uber's leaders, white-sounding names were offered jobs off identical resumes compared to Black-sounding names. Matching startup pitches from men were funded almost twice as often as those from women. For whites, having an own-race manager significantly reduced the probability that "dissatisfaction with supervisor" was given as the reason for quitting. She strongly encouraged Uber's leaders to measure competencies, not proxies.

Any time we hopped in an Uber, we were researching. Freada would ask the driver about their work and their life. Often they were driving to supplement their income or meet a financial goal, like adding a room on to their house, paying for college, or getting out of debt. Sometimes the drivers were SMASH parents, sharing their pride and appreciation while dropping us off at Kapor Center. We learned that driving Uber was a great second job, but a terrible "only" job without benefits, insurance, or other support. It's very hard to make a living on gig work. After listening to our drivers, we would go back to Uber's headquarters and urge them to provide programs for drivers' kids and other support. But that's not how the gig economy has been evolving. Uber, Lyft, Airbnb, and other gig platforms don't hire their workers; they're just creating marketplaces, with no regard for the conditions the workers face at their jobs.

Even as we were trying to help, the situation devolved, and things only kept getting worse.

STEPPING INTO A DEBACLE

In 2016, Bernard Coleman was working on Hillary Clinton's campaign, making history as the first chief diversity and human resources officer of a presidential campaign. He assumed Hillary would win, and that he'd take a position in her administration. But he also had a family to support, a house payment, and there are no guarantees in politics. So as Election Day neared, he more deeply considered a Plan B.

Bernard's wife noticed in 2016 that Uber's Global Diversity and Inclusion lead was leaving. Bernard made a clandestine, unsolicited pitch to replace him, reaching out to an Uber recruiter on LinkedIn. It was a long hiring process, about six months and eight interviews. That's okay, thought Bernard. It's a big role and Uber is going to be super deliberative on who should take the position.

At the time, Bernard had heard the rumors about Uber's troubled reputation. But he never could have foreseen the crucible he was stepping into.

Uber had already big-footed its way into city after city, challenging longtime bureaucracies that had been set up for taxi services. The company showed little regard for the taxi drivers whose medallions were now worthless and who fell into huge debt or bankruptcy in the wake of Uber's arrival.

More than 35,000 drivers had filed a class action lawsuit in 2013 demanding classification as contractors, not freelancers, in order to receive health insurance, paid sick leave, and other benefits. By 2016, when Bernard was interviewing, the class had grown to 385,000 drivers and a federal judge had rejected Uber's offer to settle for around $100 million.

Travis's own larger-than-life personality was also raising eyebrows. And there came an uncomfortable moment in Bernard's own job interview with Travis. When Bernard explained that he had attended

Hampton University, one of 106 U.S. historically Black colleges and universities, or HBCUs, Travis was stymied.

"Why didn't you choose a normal school?" Travis asked Bernard.

We're going to take a moment here to explain why that question was so very off base.

After the Civil War, more than one hundred institutions opened around the United States—mostly in the South—to serve Black students who were banned from many colleges and universities. Just 3 percent of universities in the U.S. are HBCUs, yet 20 percent of Black Americans with a college degree attended one of them. There's more support for first-generation college students, the average cost of attending an HBCU is more affordable than comparable predominantly white institutions (PWIs), and they provide a deeply committed alumni network for graduates.

Our first SMASH high school summer program to open outside of California was at Morehouse College, a HBCU in Atlanta that was Dr. Martin Luther King Jr.'s alma mater. We've since expanded into Spelman College, another HBCU in Atlanta, where former minority leader of the Georgia House of Representatives Stacey Abrams got her degree. Bernard's own parents as well as his wife and sister are proud HBCU graduates.

"Oooofff," Bernard said, recalling Travis's question. He said he thought he knew what Travis meant, but his phrasing sure made it sound as if attending an HBCU was abnormal. Bernard is patient, and optimistic about bringing about change. He saw this as a teachable moment, and explained what the school meant to him, why he felt he was supported by the community, and that every student is different in terms of what they need when they go to college.

Bernard left the interview thinking he could do this job, and he planned to work with Travis, help him with his word choice. He hoped he understood the CEO's intentions.

There were numerous consequences at Uber because of the election of President Donald Trump, but for Bernard it was very personal. Just around election time, Uber offered him the job. And with Hillary Clinton's White House no longer an option, he made the move with his wife and daughters from Virginia to California. Bernard anticipated higher prices, a different West Coast culture, and an introduction to Silicon Valley. But the Uber crisis caught him by surprise.

Later, Business Insider would describe 2017, Bernard's first year as the head of Global Diversity and Inclusion, as "Uber's no-good, very bad year." It was a time when "Uber and President Donald Trump often seemed to be in competition for scandal of the day," said Vox's Recode.

Troubles started in January 2017, when Trump announced a so-called Muslim ban, shocking communities and sparking immediate lawsuits and protests. In response, New York taxi drivers called for a one-hour strike at John F. Kennedy International Airport. Uber's New York managers, who didn't want to be seen as price-gouging scores of protesters, humanitarian attorneys, and advocates racing to JFK, tweeted that surge pricing, which increases fares when there's high demand for rides, had been turned off. This backfired. Uber's move was immediately seen as an effort to undermine the striking taxi drivers, and soon #deleteUber was trending on Twitter, along with some very specific hate. Some 400,000 people deleted their Uber apps and the company lost millions. Bernard was just being introduced at headquarters; his wife was packing boxes back at home.

Just a few days later, new fury arose when it emerged that Travis was still serving on Trump's business advisory council even after the Muslim ban. He quickly stepped down, emphasizing that his role had not reflected an Uber endorsement of Trump and his emerging, racist immigration policies.

"Families are being separated, people are stranded overseas and there's a growing fear the U.S. is no longer a place that welcomes immigrants," wrote Travis in an email to staff. "Immigration and openness to refugees is an important part of our country's success and quite honestly to Uber's."

It was a lot for Bernard as he set up his new office, but he was firmly committed—new house, new job, new schools—and he figured, here was a good challenge.

He flew back to the East Coast for the family's final going-away party (also Bernard's middle daughter's birthday party). Friends gathered to cheer the family off on their new West Coast adventure. Bernard glanced down at his phone and saw that his new Uber inbox was flooded. Something was going on. He took a closer look. Engineer Susan Fowler, who had left Uber just weeks earlier, had decided it was time to come clean about a series of terrible experiences she had there.

"I've gotten a lot of questions over the past couple of months about why I left and what my time at Uber was like," read Susan's blog post that was blowing up online. She wrote how her first Uber manager, on her first day with her team, messaged her that he was looking for women at work to have sex with. She went straight to HR, who told her it was an innocent mistake, the manager was a high performer, this was his first offense. Over weeks and months her situation devolved, as she faced more harassment and learned from the handful of other female engineers that they were dealing with the same issues. "Such a strange experience," she wrote. "Such a strange year."

By the time Bernard returned to California, people were looking at him sideways. Folks who were, weeks before, congratulatory now sought to distance themselves from him and Uber. On the positive side, all of this was pushing Bernard in our direction.

A TIPPING POINT

Susan Fowler's blog was so detailed, specific, and really a blow to us after the efforts we had put in as investors, behind the scenes, to shift

Uber's culture. It was also the tipping point in public awareness about Uber's toxic culture.

In the aftermath of its publication we received a series of increasingly urgent evening and weekend calls from Travis's right-hand man on how to handle the crisis. Freada patiently spent hours walking him through all the steps they could and should take. They followed through on exactly none of them.

Having exhausted all other alternatives and seeing no hope the company would address these issues on its own, we felt we had to act. Freada reminded Mitch, "Ultimately, it's our reputation on the line, too."

We published our own open letter.

"We are concerned that the company will try to manage its way past this crisis and then go back to business as usual," we wrote. "As investors, we certainly want to see Uber succeed, but success must be measured in more than just financial returns. . . . The stakes are too high not to get it right."

We called out the whisper culture of Silicon Valley, pointing out that investors in high-growth, financially successful companies rarely, if ever, expose and criticize inexcusable behavior from founders or C-suite executives. We said we were speaking out publicly, because we believed Uber's investors and board would rightly be judged by their action or inaction. As always, we offered to help, "if the company is indeed serious about a fundamental analysis and potential overhaul of every aspect of its policies, practices, complaint systems, training, upward communication systems, sentiment analysis and commitment from the top." And we warned them: "Current, past and prospective employees will be watching, as will drivers and entrepreneurs and countless others, including these investors."

The *New York Times* tech columnist, Farhad Manjoo, interviewed Freada and wrote a column on whether the Uber situation could be "a watershed for women in tech." Manjoo supported our optimism, recognizing that Uber's ambitions could easily include a turnaround and become the best tech employer for diversity. Nonetheless, our blog was an earth-shattering move in the insular world of VC, a huge betrayal for an investor to say anything critical about a company they have a stake in. And we heard about it.

One angel investor told NPR that as shareholders and stakeholders, we should speak with one voice and work together on the problem. Our action now meant Uber had to solve the problem and respond to our open letter. Other major Uber investors, from Goldman Sachs to Jeff Bezos, remained silent. Clearly we had completely broken the unwritten rule that underscores relationships in Silicon Valley. And then things got worse.

Some Uber investors, venture capitalists themselves, began trying to poach our Kapor Capital startups. First there were rumors, but then we heard from our founders that some VCs were offering to buy out our positions in their startups in order to box us out. It was dirty business, and Freada learned about it live, in person, onstage at a conference when an entrepreneur asked her how she felt about this. That entrepreneur had been told "Kapor Capital will turn on you, too," just as we had "turned" on Uber by exhorting them to get serious about toxic company culture.

Of course, we hadn't turned on anyone: we'd stood firm and consistent on clear principles. When you spend your days being asked for money and free advice, you have to make hard decisions and have thick skin. And if you want to make a real difference, you have to risk rubbing people the wrong way.

BRINGING THE CHANGE

Bernard Coleman was weeks into his job as Uber's head of Global Diversity and Inclusion when our open letter hit.

"Go deal with Freada and Mitch," Uber leaders told him. They said we were being unreasonable, unhelpful. Expect an adversarial encounter, a dustup, maybe some accusations or finger-pointing. And so he came to us, in his mind a sacrificial lamb.

We met at the Kapor Center that winter day in early 2017 and shared a Oaxacan-style Mexican meal in the ground-floor restaurant. We didn't know what to expect, having never met Bernard before, but suffice it to say we were, mutually, delightfully surprised and immediately struck up a friendship. Bernard has a presence, a beautiful smile, and a warmth that we were immediately drawn to. He's humble and smart, strategic and transparent. He respected our knowledge and experience in the diversity, equity, and inclusion space, and the world of venture capital and social impact. We invited him to join us for one-on-one meetings every couple of weeks at the Kapor Center and he said "yes please."

Bernard appreciated that we legitimately wanted to help, as partners committed to seeing Uber turn around its culture. We never pressured him; it was merely an offer and advice: read this study, look at this blog, talk to this person.

His first immediate challenge was that Travis wouldn't share staff diversity data, not publicly, not even with Bernard. This was a big mistake, we told Bernard, and he knew it. In 2014, Rev. Jesse Jackson came to Google's headquarters and launched an advocacy campaign to pressure big tech companies to release federal data on diversity in Silicon Valley's largest companies. By 2017, when Bernard arrived in California, most of the biggies, including Apple, Google, Twitter, and Netflix, had acquiesced, revealing abysmal numbers of Black, Latinx, and women in their workforces, but also making Uber look like a holdout. Although Google released their numbers in May 2014, it was only after years of suing to fight a Freedom of Information Act request filed by a *San Jose Mercury News* journalist. They claimed their embarrassing data were "trade secrets." How was Bernard, leading diversity and engagement, supposed to do his job without knowing where the gaps were? We validated his concerns, and encouraged him to focus first on community engagement, talking to people he could reach, since the data was a nonstarter.

Within weeks, however, under growing pressure, Travis had an about-face and Bernard had a new task: write Uber's first-ever public diversity report. Now we all saw Uber's diversity data, not all that different from comparable tech giants but disappointing nonetheless: 36 percent of its staff, but just 15 percent of its engineers and computer scientists, were women; 8.8 percent of its staff, yet only 1 percent of its technical staff, were Black; and 5.6 percent of its staff, but just 2.1 percent of its technical staff, were Latinx. Uber committed to spending $3 million over the next three years to support organizations focused on underrepresented people of color and women in tech, a task Bernard was ready for. The report also noted that Uber didn't have specific diversity goals in place, but again, Bernard at least now had a baseline.

From his first days at Uber Bernard was eager to sort out the organizational crisis under way, and get proactive about making Uber more diverse and inclusive. But from the start, those goals went unsupported, and he often faced outright difficult pushback.

"I'm the brains, you're the face," a manager once told him. The manager was white, he was Black.

When Bernard said Travis's written response to the Muslim ban was weak and needed to be more resolute, he was met with disagreement. Managers and colleagues declined to join him in advocating for diversity data and he was told Uber didn't need an ombuds to handle complaints of bias, harassment, and bullying as a third-party neutral and confidentially. Bernard told us he had been asked to write a diversity plan and a budget, without access to any figures of what he might be able to spend. Then, when he asked for more money and staff, he was told he didn't need it, pointing to those invented numbers. When Bernard received a Diversity Award, he was asked what it was for, and told he hadn't done anything yet. One day, when Travis asked him what he needed, Bernard asked for a communications assistant. Travis agreed, but the next day he was warned that he had stepped out of his lane with the request and management would "undo that." Even worse, Bernard had no one to turn to even if he did want to be a whistleblower, because people above him at Uber were the people assigned to hear those complaints.

We were also talking to his managers. Again and again, in the executive ranks at Uber, we found people tasked with equity and inclusion were actually exacerbating the problem and were divisive on diversity issues instead of unifying. They were manipulative, perplexing, and sometimes prone to tears. And so we encouraged Bernard to define his strategy, and set specific, reachable goals. Bernard took action. He put his effort into growing the community of employee resource groups, known as ERGs. At their best, ERGs are employee-led groups of underrepresented staffers who can network, problem-solve, and improve the work environment, fostering innovation from within. Bernard set measurable objectives, asking his ERGs to have ten recruiting gatherings per quarter. He funded their events, organized, and mobilized them, making Uber one of the first companies to give cash bonuses to ERG leaders. He also created a Diversity Advisory Council, including Freada and other external and internal experts on inclusion and equity, to make sure they left no stone unturned in thinking about what he was trying to do at Uber. At quarterly meetings, Bernard would battle-test his plans, and share our approval. If his managers didn't trust him, they'd have to trust the council, some of the most credible leaders in the field. He launched Why Diversity Matters, Uber's first diversity training. More than four thousand staffers around the world showed up for the nonmandatory training in its first year. He turned the fifth floor of Uber's headquarters into an "Inclusion Gallery," with more than fifty "action cards" generated by ERG members hanging on the walls. Bernard called them "micro inclusions," a tactile representation of the opposite of microaggressions, simple steps anyone could take, from saying hello in a hall to shifting a gathering from a bar, where some people might not be comfortable, to a café. The change at Uber has been palpable. Bernard invited the Phenomenal Woman Action Campaign into Uber, an organization that supports women's causes and hosts fireside chats to highlight Black women in leadership. He backed a Black Women's Equal Pay Day, and Black Women's Power Lunch. Uber gave grants to our own SMASH program, along with Girls Who Code, organizations that could use the funds to enable science and engineering development among underrepresented students. There were hundreds of small initiatives, and enough of them stuck that they started to shift the culture and the diversity demographics. By 2021, the diversity report showed that women and people of color had much higher representation company-wide and in engineering in particular.

In our twice-monthly meetings, we tapped into our Lotus lessons that we had tested and teased out decades earlier to help Bernard and his colleagues make Uber a great place to go to work. At times he came to us with crises of confidence. We would tell him, your plans are right. That's solid. Make this tweak, make that tweak.

While Bernard was trying to blast a fire hose of equity and inclusion initiatives at Uber, the company itself did take one strong action in response to Susan Fowler's scathing blog post: Uber immediately brought in former U.S. attorney general Eric Holder to conduct a thorough and objective review, not only of Fowler's allegations, but of diversity and inclusion. Arianna Huffington, an Uber board member, would oversee the investigation. Four months and two hundred interviews later, Holder's recommendations were released. Notably, Bernard was singled out by name: Uber should elevate Bernard, add support to his team, and promote him to a new position called Chief Diversity and Inclusion Officer, reporting directly to Uber's top leaders. Bernard was on Capitol Hill the day the recommendations were released, and a call came in from Uber's general counsel. Eagerly he answered.

The message was crushing. Contrary to Holder's recommendations, Uber was not going to promote him, and instead they would begin an external search.

Bernard came to us. He couldn't complain publicly without jeopardizing his position, and what would that help? They moved the goalpost, we told him. Keep pushing. Stick to your strategy. Bernard lasted at Uber a tumultuous three years, leaving a tremendous legacy.

He left to take a position as chief diversity and engagement officer at Gusto, a Kapor Capital portfolio company that manages human resources for medium-sized businesses. For Bernard, Gusto was revelatory, by far the best company he'd ever worked for. People collaborate to support each other. Leadership's goals aligned with his own. We continued meeting up every two weeks.

FOCUSED ON THE GOAL

Watching the fiascos unfold from within was a confident and dapper Uber engineering manager, Luis Madrigal, who became Bernard's ally at Uber. Luis led teams of engineers, attended C-suite meetings, and managed to hold his own team together amid the turmoil, protecting his engineers from the bias and toxic culture that was bleeding into other parts of the company. We only learned much later that he had crossed paths with us.

Luis's journey began when President Ronald Reagan's so-called crackdown on the border granted amnesty to anyone who had entered the United States before 1982. Luis's Mexican parents made it under that bar, although they often returned to Mexico. His mother wasn't ready to leave her home in Guadalajara and Luis was born there. This meant that when they entered the U.S. as a family, his parents had legal documents, but baby Luis did not. For five years they used a U.S.-born cousin's paperwork to sneak him in, but eventually Luis couldn't pass as his cousin. He remembers the night a coyote smuggled them over the border, one last time.

His dad hired a white American man to take them into the U.S., and at six, Luis was warned that if he heard a helicopter or horses, he should throw himself on the ground and cover himself with dirt. He cried during that dark hike, and his father told him he could go back and stay with his grandmother.

"No, no, no, let's go," he told his father. And so they did.

The Madrigal family settled in South San Francisco, where his father became a chef and Luis became a citizen, along with the rest of the family. After high school, with few resources and little experience, Luis was one of thousands to be taken in by false promises at a for-profit institution that inflated job placement rates and preyed on low-income immigrant students. Luis borrowed some $25,000 for an eighteen-month associate's degree in computer technology, and, in hindsight, he says they conned him into borrowing even more to get a second associate's degree in network technology.

Luis's younger brother Kevin, ten years behind him, was a gifted student who could well have followed the same path to large debt and no four-year degree. But in high school Kevin applied to become a SMASH scholar, spending three summers at UC Berkeley. He became one of our stars and went on to Stanford University on a scholarship.

The for-profit university was sued by then California attorney general Kamala Harris. It shut down and eventually its owners were slapped with a $1.1 billion judgment. This did nothing for Luis, who had an overwhelming amount of debt to carry as he entered the workforce without a university diploma. The one benefit of that education is that the school had required students to wear a suit and tie. Luis learned to dress for success, and he says he's grateful for that, if nothing else.

Undaunted, he threw himself into a series of jobs, each better paid and more tech oriented than the last. Initially, he screened airport luggage for the Transportation Security Administration. He moved to Best Buy's Geek Squad, where he cleaned viruses off personal computers for a fee. He also took a job at Canon, servicing $100,000 copy machines at the offices of a global engineering firm, Arup, whose notable projects include the Sydney Opera House, San Francisco's de Young Museum, and Beijing's National Stadium. He brought a tremendous work ethic to every position, respecting and uplifting his colleagues.

One evening, as the staff was leaving for happy hour, an Arup IT manager asked him why he was rushing to repair a printing device rather than joining them. Luis, in his requisite sharp suit, explained he had to get to his evening gig, fixing personal computers.

"Hey, that's information technology. What the hell are you doing fixing copy machines?" said the manager. Luis explained that without a bachelor's degree and the right experience, he couldn't get into an IT interview.

Six months later the manager called him with a job offer. "I love your professionalism," he said. "I'll pay you more than what you're making in two jobs."

Over seven years Luis went from replacing monitors and keyboards at Arup to reporting to the chief information officer and leading mobile architecture. It was a big journey, but he was still on an hourly wage. In 2014, a friend told him he was undervalued.

"Silicon Valley is dying for people like you," said his friend. Luis wasn't so sure, and like so many of our own founders, he was plagued with self-doubt. All of these companies want a bachelor's degree, he thought.

That evening, he updated his very outdated LinkedIn profile.

Luis woke up the next morning with a dozen recruiter messages, and as more poured in over the next few weeks, he spotted one from Uber. They liked his experience at a prestigious global engineering firm, and saw he had the skill set they needed. Also, the recruiter said he liked his swagger, that cocky hat, the sharp suit and tie.

In 2014, Luis joined the frenzy as an engineering manager at Uber, which was growing exponentially. He was about the seventy-fifth engineer at the time. When he left in 2021, there were some three thousand engineers. But it wasn't Luis's engineering that brought us together. It was his advocacy.

In his early days at Uber, Luis focused on keeping his team in a safe and supported bubble, separate from larger issues he saw happening around his company. When an engineer on his team founded an employee resource group for Black engineers, Luis attended as an ally. He would later tell us he had his doubts about the entire concept. He wondered how separating people who identify as a minority, whether by race, ethnicity, gender identity, or anything else, could help bring them together.

As Luis sought to inspire and uplift his team, he discovered the power of community, and the power of sharing thoughts, opinions, experiences, and brainstorming in a place of psychological safety. Within months of attending the Black engineering ERG, Luis was asked by Uber's Latinx ERG, Los Ubers, to help lead the group. He knew he had the ear of top management, including Travis. If I can use my voice for good, Luis thought, I should do that.

As Luis was coming around on ERGs, Bernard called for the

first-ever Uber ERG Summit and invited Freada to speak. Bernard says Uber, at this point, was "in all the shit." It was all bad. Nothing good was happening. There were lawsuits bubbling up, and rumors of raunchy parties, sexism in meetings. Luis had seen colleagues struggling, burning out. Freada talked about how employee resource groups build diverse and welcoming work environments. She talked about biases and barriers from pre-K to tech careers and described how advocates could become advisers to senior management and help retain and recruit talent. If not you, then who? she asked. She told them she believed in them, that they could be the change.

"You all can do it," she said.

"Freada came and gave us that rah-rah. She lit the fire that day," recalls Bernard.

After her talk, Luis introduced himself. He told Freada that SMASH had changed his family, since his little brother was a SMASH scholar; he thanked her. Freada looked at Luis's badge, noting his last name, and asked, "Is your little brother Kevin?" In the earlier years, it was possible to know most of the scholars.

"I firmly believe your program is what got him the upper edge," he said.

Freada, being Freada, asked if she could give Luis a hug. When we realized he was one of the ERG leaders at Uber, we asked to keep in touch. And so began Luis's mentorship. He would come to us with challenges. Freada would try to talk him through the situation and advise. We were able to learn more about the inside workings at Uber, and Luis says he awakened to broader issues of racism and bias.

Uber's diversity reports were a disappointment to leaders throughout the company; they showed that most Black and Latinx employees were working in low-level jobs at Uber's Centers of Excellence, basically customer support centers for critical incidents that required immediate attention. Throughout their shifts, these team members would answer calls, far from the fabulous Silicon Valley headquarters, in places like Phoenix and Chicago, and offshore in the Philippines and Costa Rica.

On a visit to the Chicago center, Luis met up with an ERG group and was surprised to learn that many of these people doing entry-level hourly work had not only bachelor's degrees, but graduate degrees as well. Uber's leaders were telling the world they had a hard time finding diverse candidates for corporate roles, and here were these Uber centers filled with Black and Latinx staff who, much like Luis, took any job they could get at a respected company to try to climb the ladder.

Luis emailed the head of human resources, telling her how frustrated he was, literally moved to tears, by the narrative that leadership painted about not having diverse pipelines when this highly educated, untapped pool of talent—already on Uber's payroll—was answering calls.

Uber's leadership listened and put together a "Path Finder" program, which Luis oversaw, taking high-performing hourly staff from the call centers, training them in analytics, and pairing them with a mentor and an executive sponsor. Luis would often run into people who graduated from those cohorts and got placed at Uber's corporate headquarters; they would stop him in the hallways and thank him for his advocacy. Luis later told us he had been inspired by our discussions to be to be fierce, to call out leadership, hold them accountable, and bring plans and ideas to the table.

Luis says he was often at the right place at the right time, and he thinks about how most people have untapped potential; he tells us that one of these doors opening can change a person's trajectory in life.

We saw that Luis was thrilled with the speed and excitement of working at Uber, and despite cultural challenges there he was among the rare managers cultivating inclusive teams. When Susan Fowler posted her blog, his staff stood up and thanked him for shielding them from that type of workplace experience.

But as his awareness was raised, he came to us with new concerns. He was being passed up for promotions only to see Stanford or Massachusetts Institute of Technology alumni get positions he was better experienced for. We affirmed that this is part of a pattern and talked about implicit bias. Solving these inequities was the hard work he was doing with the ERGs. Luis also bristled at Uber's stack ranking requirements, which made him, as a manager, identify the lowest two performers on a team and often force them out. We agreed that this Silicon Valley management practice diminishes teamwork and collaboration.

One day, at a meeting for Uber engineers, Luis was the fourth speaker in a lineup. There were about seven hundred colleagues in the room, several thousand more online. The first few speakers, all white men and women, ran long in their talks. As he stepped onto the stage, a particularly offensive executive began to heckle him to hurry up. Shaken, Luis launched into his slides. "Hurry up! Finish up!" the executive shouted. Luis began to stutter. People in the front row were turning around, looking at the executive. What's wrong with this guy? wondered Luis. He managed to make it through the presentation but was deeply shaken and tried to report it. Then came what Luis described as "an emailed, half-assed non-apology." We talked with Luis. He was never going to change this man. But what he could do was leverage his influence, get more resources toward diversity and inclusion efforts in engineering. In the end, this executive's behavior, including sexism and anti-inclusion, led to his departure at Uber. Luis outlasted him.

Luis's experience and advocacy mirror our own belief that talent is everywhere but pathways and opportunities are not. We're humbled that by acting on our principles and values we inspired Luis to do the same. We hope that many of those for whom Luis opened the door have in turn helped others. As many who are underrepresented in one circumstance or another believe, you may be the first, but make sure you're not the last.

LOYALTY TO VALUES

In the end, our open letter did just what we had hoped. Yes, it landed hard. Yes, we upset people and were seen as stirring up even more problems. But Travis was pressured to resign as Uber's CEO in 2017 and left the board of directors two years later.

His replacement, Dara Khosrowshahi, committed to a new direction, new culture, new governance. And Dara asked us to help. He did this in a very public way, an implicit acknowledgment that when we called Uber out, we were pushing for positive change. We joined the new CEO in his office to tell him how we thought Uber was doing. We were invited onstage at an event with Uber's top management, in New York, and were invited to speak to senior managers of the Asia Pacific region in Singapore, continuing to believe in its value as a global company.

We believe in Loyalty, with a capital *L*. But we also believe that being loyal to a set of values is more important than loyalty to any particular company. Further, it's key to building a culture of transparency and trust. Employees should be able to see their immediate managers and the C-suite make day-to-day decisions that reflect the stated values. We always knew that when Uber was at its worst, its extreme problems weren't all that different from those facing most large tech firms. And loyalty can be used as an excuse to allow senior, visible people in the larger tech ecosystem to condone or even reward the reprehensible behavior of some individuals. We've seen a pattern of bad actors being promoted, moving to new companies or even launching their own. This so-called loyalty holds the entire sector back.

There's also a prominent belief in startups that the best hires are those whom the founders have worked with previously. While knowing how team members perform is important, this path leads to an insular club where most people have no way of breaking in, regardless of their talents and potential. Loyalty to values trumps loyalty to individuals when their behavior veers off course. As the talent shortage, especially in tech, intensifies, employees are choosing employers on many factors. It's not just the job or the compensation; it's also the company culture. Clear values, transparency, opportunities to raise concerns without fear of retaliation—all characterize employers who will be better able to attract and retain talent, especially those who are currently underrepresented.

Uber went public in 2019. Its market capitalization by 2022 was north of $60 billion. Most Americans with a 401(k) or a mutual fund probably are investors whether they know it or not. We think our moment of putting principles over loyalty to the Silicon Valley code of silence was one of many voices that helped tip the needle at a company so many of us are involved with, moving Uber today toward a place of growing diversity, inclusive culture, and a climate commitment.

8

FORK IN THE ROAD

MANDELA AND THE CHANGEMAKERS

INTERVIEWER: What kind of grade would you give the Valley over the last two years at improving diversity in venture capital?

FREADA: At improving diversity? (Her voice rises sharply.)

INTERVIEWER: Yes.

FREADA: Writ large: flunk.

INTERVIEWER: Flunk?

FREADA (LEANING IN, LOUDER): Failing. Failing grade.

Long pause.

We know change is possible, but we also know it's hard. There's no playbook to consult, no formula to apply or algorithm that computes the right thing to do for every founder or investor reckoning with global racism and disparity. Founders will hit crises, like Phaedra realizing her app might put more people in jail, or Jake worrying he's going to run out of money. Tech leaders will call us looking for quick fixes when they've been accused of racist or sexist comments. There are moments when an investor, founder, or company hits a fork in the road. Those moments take a lot of one-on-one work, questioning, prodding, listening, and empathizing. Honesty, even when it hurts, is critical. We try to help them choose the better path, but sometimes it's clearly too late to have a good outcome. At that point we tell them there are lessons learned, to be applied next time, or to prevent the problem in the first place. And we've had our own lessons learned; sometimes we make the wrong call and things go very, very wrong. Sometimes the founder doesn't take our advice and it works for them anyway.

In 2018, Silicon Valley had acknowledged, albeit briefly, that there was a huge imbalance of male-female representation at every level. In the past decade, $355 billion in wealth had been created by the top ten IPOs, and 92 percent of that wealth went to men, mostly white men. As this was recognized and amplified from boardrooms to collaborative workspaces, we dubbed it "the summer of Silicon Valley's discontent." A year later, and Silicon Valley was patting itself on the back for adding about a dozen women VC partners to investment firms since the #MeToo movement blazed through Hollywood, college campuses, Wall Street, and venture capital. A journalist interviewing Freada for Vox's Recode said he'd been writing about how well the venture capital industry has done at improving diversity, bringing on new female investors with the power to write checks. We saw things differently.

"If those women partners are white and Asian, and went to the same schools as their male counterparts, and grew up in the same zip codes as those male counterparts, and now live in the same zip codes as their male counterparts, that doesn't get me very far on diversity," said Freada.

The process of counting women—and not breaking out the number of Black and Latinx women in a separate category—is an ongoing challenge as the tech sector struggles to be more equitable. White women in this country lean conservative; a majority of them voted for Donald Trump in 2016 and again in 2020. All too often, white women tell us that our SMASH summer program—which serves underrepresented high school students of color from low-income backgrounds—makes it harder for their own, privileged kids to get into college. Exactly where on their children's birth certificates is the stamp admitting them to an elite university? We rarely see inherent positive social impact when these same white women join VC firms or found companies. Indeed, we're often approached by women founders pitching products or services aimed solely at wealthy consumers. When we explain that we won't be funding them, as we consider their company to be gap-widening, they are often angry and push back with something like "I thought you cared about diversity," signaling that they remain clueless. We patiently explain that if you offer college coaching for three hundred dollars per hour, you are making it harder for smart kids without those kind of resources, but who've done everything right, to get into college. Their essays won't be as polished, they won't have padded their applications with "community service" trips to Vietnam that supposedly gave them an epiphany about their life's goals, all while costing tens of thousands of dollars.

FALSE STARTS

This issue came to the forefront when most of Silicon Valley's top female venture capitalists launched a nonprofit called All Raise in 2018. The founders were almost all white or Asian, and their stated mission was "to accelerate the success of female funders and founders." The goals were specific: double the percentage of female partners from 9 percent to 18 percent at U.S. tech venture firms in ten years, and increase the percentage of venture funding going to companies with a female founder from 15 percent to 25 percent in five years. It was an easily trackable metric, but they were completely ignoring the intersectionality between class, race, and gender.

The All Raise team had dropped their VC due diligence skills when they launched; basic research would have shown them that they needed a different group of women at the table to diversify tech. Our own surveys showed, for example, that Black and Latinx female founders were far more likely than their white counterparts to hear unwanted comments or jokes about race, and ten times as likely to experience nonconsensual touching while pitching VCs. If a white female entrepreneur is mentoring, or interviewing, a potential female founder of color, a lot of important nuances could go unaddressed. Our own Kapor Center study, "What's It Like to Be a Female Tech Entrepreneur?" documented that some Black and Latinx female entrepreneurs' most difficult and biased encounters while raising startup money came from white female investors. When All Raise started office hours for female founders, their criterion for being a mentor was how much money she'd raised. This was another troubling oversight— requiring a certain dollar amount actually ignores systemic racism in the investment process. Given that only a handful of Black women had raised over $1 million when this program started, the requirement of $2 million was completely tone deaf. Based on their actions, not their words, All Raise seemed to care only about the gender in the seats, not who or what got invested in, nor who benefited from the investments. Intent barely matters. Impact does.

Freada called them out publicly.

"When Black and Brown women entrepreneurs, Black and Brown women VCs, investors, walk into that gathering, do they feel welcomed? Do they see themselves? Do they feel like this group has my back?" she asked during an interview.

But she also was working with All Raise privately, as various partners reached out and asked her for help and advice through many back-channel calls. We later learned that some founders of All Raise were unnerved by our unflinching demand that anyone and everyone who wants to come into tech ought to have a pathway. Some were ready to listen and wanted to know why we thought they were misguided. Others wanted to know how to collect demographic data for their firms and companies. We were happy to respond. Little by little, we nudged the founders to think beyond the male-female archetype of equality. What does diversity really look like? we asked. What is an inclusive workplace?

Change is possible, and we began to see it.

All Raise started an inclusion working group to hold itself more accountable. And their first full-time CEO acknowledged within weeks of her appointment that they weren't doing enough on building diversity across the spectrum, including race, age, and sexual orientation. We remained concerned, however, as All Raise grew across the country, supporting thousands of female founders and funders. The number of women writing checks slowly rose, but who the checks went to didn't change much. The flow of capital to female founders remained a dribble. Far worse, there had been no improvements for women of color when the CEO stepped down three years later.

All Raise cofounder and board member Jess Lee asked Freada for advice about the nonprofit and its mission. A few years earlier, Jess had made headlines when she was the first female and one of the youngest investing partners hired by Sequoia Capital, a leading Silicon Valley venture capital firm. She has remained grounded and collaborates with a real lack of entitlement, despite the power she wields in the tech startup ecosystem. Freada and Jess talked, for more than an hour, at an elite, invitation-only tech conference in Southern California, going over Freada's litany of problems with All Raise's approach. A Stanford graduate who had paid her dues at Google and spent nine years as, she says, "head down" as a successful startup entrepreneur, Jess was new and open to concepts of distance traveled, pattern matching, and intersectionality. She simply hadn't considered that being a woman, and Black, was a double whammy when it came to access to opportunities and capital. Jess explained that All Raise's founders, who included just one Black woman, were really just a group of friends who, at a dinner party, decided to launch an advocacy group for female entrepreneurs. You have to be very deliberate and purposeful, said Freada. A photo of a bunch of white and Asian women and one Black women in *Forbes* magazine means something. No one wants to be the "only," said Freada. This resonated. Jess had often been the "only" as she broke into tech and launched a business.

"Wow, we messed up," said Jess. "We have to back up and start over."

Freada was stunned. In the unwritten code of VCs, no one openly admits they're wrong. Sure, failure is embraced in Silicon Valley, but those failures are blamed on someone or something, a confluence of events.

Freada told Jess that starting over sounded like a good idea. "How can I help?" she asked.

Jess later thanked Freada for the impactful teaching moment.

We like to say that anyone can be the change. That pretty much describes Mandela Schumacher-Hodge Dixon, who became All Raise's next CEO.

"We knew we needed a leader that possessed both a nuanced understanding of the VC-backed tech ecosystem, as well as a deep empathy for what it is like to be marginalized and excluded," wrote Jess in announcing Mandela's appointment.

Mandela likes to say she's operating at the intersection of hustle and high consciousness. The daughter of two civil rights attorneys, she grew up in Pittsburgh, where, all too early, a boy told her, "I don't play with Black people." She was seven. Her dad was Black, her mom was white, and Mandela grew up talking about social justice, power, and truth. They had a loving home where fairness and justice were valued, and empathy and equity were expected.

After college, Mandela began her career as a sixth-grade teacher in Los Angeles through the nonprofit Teach For America, inspiring students both in the classroom and outside. She once coached a group of low-income first-generation middle schoolers to run—and complete—the Los Angeles Marathon. From the classroom, Mandela saw firsthand how systemic problems in our country's schools fail children. During staff cutbacks, hundreds were laid off, mostly based solely on their seniority. Mandela wondered why talent in the classroom, measurable teaching skills, and student achievement weren't factors for deciding whom to retain. In her next teaching job she was also tasked with hiring an educator, and realized how archaic and broken the screening process was. She wished she could virtually preview candidates giving lessons in classrooms before bringing them in person to demonstrate their teaching abilities. Those ideas for a more robust and intentional screening process became her first startup, Tioki, an online professional network for educators and a job search platform connecting great educators with great schools in search of each other—kind of like a LinkedIn for teachers. We invested in 2012 and three years later asked Mandela if she would be willing to join us as our portfolio services director, a newly created position to operationalize the support we offered our growing portfolio of companies, including how to build their own inclusive and diverse cultures.

Years earlier, when two more Black men were shot and killed by white police officers in a single week, Freada had reflexively checked in on Mandela. We knew this was a troubling time for our country, and exceptionally painful for many Black people.

Mandela surprised us with a powerful and poetic post that immediately went viral:

> A White person.
> Better yet, my boss.
> At work.
> Initiated a conversation with me about racial injustice in America.
> She expressed disgust and outrage.
> She asked if I was OK.
> She offered to speak out.
> She planned to take action.
> How many of my Black brothers and sisters—especially in tech—
> can say that their White colleagues acknowledge the current state of
> racial injustice in America?

Mandela would go on to launch a successful startup, Founder Gym, tapping into the expertise of Silicon Valley's accelerator directors, angel investors, venture capitalists, startup lawyers, and funded founders to train underrepresented entrepreneurs on how to raise money to scale their tech startups. She'd been named one of Forbes 30 Under 30, Top 100 Powerful Women by *Entrepreneur* magazine, and LinkedIn's Top 10 Voices in Venture Capital and Startups when All Raise asked her to join them.

By 2022, All Raise's board of directors had recognized their shortcomings and shifted their commitment. They were ready to truly build and support inclusive tech workplaces. It took four years at All Raise with some efforts along the way, but change is possible, and it happened.

Freada hadn't attended All Raise's inaugural summit in 2018. She hadn't been asked to speak. The only Black woman onstage that year was asked to lead a diversity panel; she's a partner at a very successful venture firm investing in EdTech startups. She was the only Black woman on the All Raise founding team. As if All Raise hadn't shown their cluelessness enough, the tipping point came when the event was held at a high-end San Francisco hotel where the hotel's workers were on strike. Crossing a picket line of mostly women, all people of color and many immigrants, didn't seem to faze All Raise and its supporters. Those workers apparently weren't the women these female investment leaders cared about. When Freada thought of that picket line, all she saw were the moms and aunts of our SMASH scholars who were working two or three jobs to try to support their families. One Latinx woman investor who felt she couldn't pass up the opportunity to attend the summit later told us that walking past those strikers was devastating—her own mother was a house cleaner, scrubbing white people's toilets for a living.

Four years later, in 2022, not long after becoming All Raise's CEO, Mandela asked Freada to speak at their next conference. She told us that because we had recognized her potential and given her a chance when she was a sixth-grade teacher with no tech startup experience, she understood that as CEO of All Raise she had the responsibility to continue that mission of access and opportunity, seeing beyond pedigree and all the resume items that don't account for the whole person or what they're capable of. This time Freada was happy to go, especially because she would share the stage with our colleague and partner Ulili.

Mandela emphasized that we are a rarity: VCs that truly walk the talk with respect to diversifying our investment team. Her impact on All Raise at the 2022 summit was palpable. Women of color were involved in every way—as speakers, moderators, panelists, and attendees. Mandela's opening remarks included powerful challenges—in her tactful and inspirational, non-guilt-inducing way—to all participants to figure out what actions they were going to take about issues of concern to them. As the first day progressed, everyone anxiously checked their phones as the horrifying Uvalde, Texas, school massacre of nineteen students and two teachers unfolded. Tech and business summits are meticulously orchestrated events; their agendas take months of planning and there's no room for change, no matter what's going on in the world.

Mandela saw things differently and met the moment. The next morning, as participants were processing their anger and grief, she took the stage and spoke poignantly and vulnerably about the impact of the attack on her, as a mother. She talked about the people who were murdered, and the shattered communities left behind. She was prepared with vetted places where summit attendees could donate—to Uvalde community organizers and families, and supporters of several other devastating mass shootings that had taken place in recent weeks in Buffalo, New York, and Laguna Woods, California. All Raise started as a call to action, and Mandela encouraged everyone to remain committed to transforming upset into action and use our collective power to create positive change. Mandela knew her people couldn't just get back to business as usual. On this day they needed a rallying cry.

STORIES WE TELL

The venture capital community believes that Silicon Valley is a perfect meritocracy, and that anyone from any background can succeed if they have superior talent, innovative ideas, and relentless drive. That doesn't describe the reality, but over the years we've seen business models, CEOs, and investors challenge the myth, reach the fork in the road, and choose the right path. We know it's possible.

One critical issue we've repeatedly pressed Silicon Valley's investors and tech founders on is to challenge their belief they made it entirely on their own. That's a difficult concept for people who attribute their success as entrepreneurs or VCs entirely to their incredible hard work, intelligence, and grit. It's important for them to understand, in great detail, that the CEOs we invest in face challenges that are exponentially more difficult, whether it's watching a loved one being taken away by the police or being immediately dismissed by a VC because they didn't go to Stanford.

We try to create an environment where we can gently challenge their assumption, where we can say, "Wait a second, I assume your heart is in the right place, but you stuck your foot in your mouth, and let's talk about why what you said or did is exclusionary."

We've gone through this very specifically with Jason Calacanis, an entrepreneur, investor, podcaster, and author, a self-described "person with power" who wrote a book about turning $100,000 into $100 million by investing in tech startups. He's a complicated, influential, and sometimes polarizing figure. Once, at a tech conference, Jason asked a panel that included Freada how he could diversify judges at tech startup competitions, which are *Shark Tank*–like gatherings where entrepreneurs pitch their business ideas to win cash or investors. Jason said he already gave scholarships to help people attend his founder training classes, and he'd added a "Diversity in Tech" panel at his popular conferences, giving free tickets to women. "Should I lower the standards for judges?" he asked.

Freada jumped in. "I find that the expression 'lowering standards,' or 'we're only looking for qualified candidates,' I find those to be offensive. Well-meaning, but offensive," she said. "What counts a lot is the distance traveled, not just getting to the finish line."

She tried a sports analogy: "We continue to reward people who start on third base and swing the bat and think they hit a home run." She asked Jason, why did he think he needed someone with twenty years of tech experience. "Whatever you were doing twenty years ago is irrelevant to tech today," she said.

Jason nodded. Her words were profound, he said. He thought about it. And he changed his criteria.

That same year, after selling a tech blog to AOL for more than $25 million, Jason sparked a heated debate with just a few obnoxious tweets that described the tech space as "largely post-race. Pure meritocracy . . . Page views rule."

We knew he was only going public with what many others said behind closed doors, and it opened us up to many conversations with him.

So we were pleased when, almost ten years later at a Kapor Center gathering, he conceded to a group of Black and Latinx entrepreneurs that his understanding of meritocracy in the tech industry has evolved: "Does everybody have an equal shot in Silicon Valley? The answer is no," he said, especially when it came to taking a chance on startups with unproven founders. He grew up cleaning his dad's Brooklyn bar on weekends, and paid his way through college, taking classes at night while working three or four jobs at a time. He figured no one had it harder than him. "I learned that my personal experience of 'I had it hard' is not contextually correct," he told us. "Others had it harder." Jason is still wrong when he says our diversity principles and impact requirements limit our moneymaking potential, but he's right about this: our criterion isn't just about dollars, it's making change in the world. And he's interested in learning how to do that.

Longtime tech investor Bryce Roberts reflected on a blog post that for years he too had told himself a story that his success was a result of his hustle. After all, he worked his way through college and lived on a thousand dollars a month when he launched his startup. But Bryce is a listener and a thinker, and over the years he recognized his privilege. There's no doubt he hustled. But he also grew up comfortable, never wanting for food or much of anything. His parents gave him a used car, helped with tuition, paid his rent for a year when he launched.

"I could not have taken those risks, or reaped the subsequent rewards, were it not for my family's financial support," he wrote. "So, that story that I've been telling myself all these years has holes that need filling. Safety nets that require recognition. And privilege that deserves acknowledgment."

Bryce also spent a lot of time thinking about a discussion we had with him before investing in his VC fund. We felt like we had a good connection and were close to writing a check. But Freada was concerned. Bryce was an active Mormon, and Freada knew that Mormons traditionally encouraged women to work as mothers and caretakers inside the home. She had helped prominent workplaces work with Mormons in leadership positions who were conflicted about mentoring and promoting women into senior positions. We asked, directly and without judgment, if his faith would implicitly or explicitly keep him from funding female founders. We weren't confronting; we just needed to know.

Bryce would later say that the thought had never crossed his mind. But he also said we had raised his self-awareness. More than a decade later, he said he still thought about our question, and urged others in tech and VC to do the same.

We invested. In hindsight, Bryce says the impact of any dollar amount we committed to his fund pales in comparison to the impact of that question. We're glad we asked.

THE DISTANCE TRAVELED

Adding new partners is a tricky business, and VC firms are very careful and deliberate about how and when they bring someone on board. Typically, the searches are private, meaning there's no way at all for an outsider to even be considered if they can't tap an existing partner's former tech colleagues, business school classmates, or other personal networks. First Round Capital, a San Francisco–based, seed-stage investment firm, was no exception for its first sixteen years. Their recruiting process was, as they described it, opportunistic, using their existing networks.

In 2020—amid the national reckoning on race brought about by the murder of George Floyd—First Round's partners realized that it wasn't a coincidence their team was all white and all male. They hadn't done the necessary work to build a diverse senior investment team. Inspired by a blog post from our Kapor Capital partner Brian Dixon, in 2021 they posted a position, accepting resumes and applications from all prospects for the first time.

Soon there was news: "Meka Asonye joins First Round as its first Black investment partner after the firm conducted a rare open search for the role," said *Forbes*. It was that easy.

Meka, the son of Nigerian immigrants, was an experienced tech investor and leader, who built startups and had become a top manager at large firms like online payment company Stripe and investment firm Bain Capital. In their announcement, First Round noted that Meka was "an immediate culture add" to their team. In his own words, Meka talks about the distance traveled, not only his own journey from Princeton University and minor-league baseball, but that of his parents and grandparents, who were entrepreneurs.

"There's nothing I love more than a founder who's been underestimated," he said after joining First Round. "Talent is evenly distributed, but opportunity isn't." He may not have realized it, but he was quoting something Mitch had been saying for a decade.

Like VCs, which have to institute changes in order to diversify, our portfolio companies always have to be flexible, take new approaches, and try new paths when their business models aren't moving them toward their goals.

Just before the pandemic, we were backing entrepreneur and CEO Roberto Ortiz and his cofounders, who were launching an online marketplace called Gather Wholesale, connecting farmers, wholesalers, and restaurants. A chef could hop on their website, order ten cases of avocados, and boom, there they were, on time, ready for guacamole. Suddenly, as the country locked down, there weren't any restaurants open for business. No need for avocado deliveries. No dining out with freshly made guacamole. Then a fire broke out in the apartment where they'd been running their business. Everything was in ruins.

Quickly, on the back of an envelope, Roberto and his cofounders took a look at the rapidly changing world and pandemic projections and came up with an entirely new idea: Welcome, an online event hosting platform that bumps up quality and ease, a system that makes high-production meetings, lessons, and events. A core value was to open doors, create space for diversity of people and thoughts.

"When we look like the world, we build the world," they said.

We liked his plan and encouraged him to go for it. Now it was time to buckle up. How did a wholesale food company become an event host overnight?

Roberto's own distance traveled had taught him to be willing to change, even if that means stepping into the unknown. Raised in Philadelphia's inner city, one of five kids struggling with their single mom, Roberto fell in love with technology. But most of the tech at his high school was in the metal detectors he walked through every morning on his way to class. Roberto's path took a new direction when Lockheed Martin announced the launch of the state's first registered information technology apprenticeship. A few dozen high school students tapped for the three-year program would leave their traditional schools and attend their program instead, graduating as Information Technology Technicians, equivalent to an associate-level college degree. Better yet, successful graduates would be offered a full-time position with Lockheed Martin. A high school counselor spotted Roberto, a self-described nerdy teen interested in computers, and asked him if he'd like to apply. Thus began a decades-long path for Roberto, through Lockheed Martin, Google, and even a fantasy sports startup acquired by Yahoo. When we first met him, social justice and gap-closing missions weren't front and center for him. But as he pitched and refined his business model, he shifted his priorities and embraced the clear framework of making a positive impact. Now he was at a crossroads: his startup was funded and staffed, but their business model was completely new.

Over the next months, Roberto, his investors, and cofounders listened and refined Welcome, first as a next-generation virtual events platform, then, after listening to customers, moving its focus to internal company events and help with employee engagement. His team of designers, engineers, and technologists were growing both weary and wary about being asked, at high speed, to dump a lot of what they had done, experiment quickly, and shift their focus.

Roberto told them change was important, that startups are risky and that this new idea was brilliant. VCs were knocking on his door, and he was proud his investors included Kapor Capital. But people depend on their jobs, for mortgages, health insurance, security, and Roberto also knew he had to reassure his staff. From his own experience, he knew startups are a roller coaster, but some of his team hadn't been through those types of ups and downs. He told them they had to pivot, bob and weave, be super agile.

"It's not all rainbows and butterflies," he said. "Sometimes you've got to get your hands dirty."

Roberto asked us for advice, and we said to stick to his message. He asked us to speak at a company all-hands meeting. Maybe we could bolster his case?

After introductions, Roberto asked us to talk to his entire staff about the startup journey.

"Bumps in the road are the norm on the path to success. That doesn't mean anybody has done anything wrong," said Mitch. "Out of this adversity and the need to change, here was a golden opportunity to do something bigger."

"And more inclusive," added Freada.

Roberto smiled and nodded.

"It's one thing just to say it yourself," he said after the meeting. "It's another thing to bring people that have been there, done that, and seen the patterns of these startup journeys lead to phenomenal companies."

As for his team? They were finally assured that they didn't have to go find another job. They were motivated, all in.

Roberto's virtual events platform, Welcome, features production and engagement tools that turn boring online employee meetings into highly engaging experiences. Before anyone could declare the pandemic over, Roberto had already raised $12 million. And as new hybrid and remote workplace practices took hold, he and his team were perfectly positioned.

GLAD WE ASKED

While some companies shift to entirely new business models as they grow, others have found themselves soaring financially but flailing on diversity. These forks in the road can be more nuanced.

We were early investors in Jeff Lawson's Twilio, before we locked in our gap-closing commitment. It's been a wildly successful company, making billions in revenue through a platform that unifies communication between phones and computers, from online customer support chats to messaging an Uber driver.

We had no doubts that this was a platform that would become essential to online businesses very rapidly, and it did. We worried about whether Twilio would become yet another typical Silicon Valley company, dominated by white, male engineers and managers, tone deaf to racial injustice, and rife with gender disparity. Over years we nudged Jeff, inviting him to diversity-related events, introducing him to our SMASH scholars, bringing him to our founders meetings. We warned him against using costly and counterproductive diversity programs. He later told us he was getting a little annoyed with us for deluging him with this stuff. He figured he was killing it with his business and he had added some important leadership programs. At some point, yeah, he'd get this diversity piece right, but now he had a business to build. He later told us that after some of our conversations he'd reflect, was he waiting for Twilio to hit one thousand white, male engineers before he took action?

When the national Black Lives Matter movement erupted in 2020, Jeff acknowledged that he knew Twilio wasn't doing enough. There was no ignoring the fact that his staff was 5 percent Black. He'd been asking himself for years, when would it be a good time to prioritize diversity? He had reached the fork in his road.

He told us he had decided to go all in and commit to becoming an antiracist company. That's not something CEOs of publicly traded companies ever say. This was a very important decision. We suggested he bring in a diversity, equity, and inclusion officer to report directly to him, develop a company-wide strategy, and, most importantly, have a very honest—if challenging—meeting with his staff. Freada suggested he tell his Twilions they need a culture that supports the growth of people and the growth of business. Those have to go together.

"You helped me find my right voice for the moment," he later told Freada.

Jeff got busy after that. Twilio set new priorities and measurables, launched RiseUp, a cohort-based leadership program for new Black and Latinx colleagues, offered coaching and career planning to employees of color, expanded its apprenticeship program, and gave candidates interview preparation. The company has curricula to build a common language around inclusion and mitigate biases, and a hiring process that includes a neutral interviewer. We could go on, but the point is that when Jeff said Twilio would be antiracist, he took action.

"Twilio does not pretend that it has all the answers. We will make mistakes. We have made mistakes. But we will examine our imperfections in an effort to reduce them," said Twilio's chief diversity officer, Lybra S. Clemons, and Jeff when launching their 2020 Diversity, Equity & Inclusion report.

Twilio's software is not inherently gap-closing or gap-widening. Twilio.org—their impact arm—has prioritized helping nonprofits around the world use Twilio products for good. Jeff's commitment to being an antiracist company is a model of excellence for anyone who ever says they simply cannot identify competent employees, companies, or colleagues of color.

RED FLAGS AND FALLING HARD

Not all of our changes end so well. Impact investing is complex and challenging, in no small part because "impact" has come to mean all things to all people. We've seen some remarkably positive pivots, but sometimes our founders, and yes, sometimes the two of us, make the wrong decision when we come to a fork in the road, leading to some of our worst situations.

We once fell hard for a charismatic Black founder, whose exciting plan was to build a new private, online university that would be both affordable and accessible, allowing low-income students to get a college degree. This founder countered the same false narrative we were at war with, the notion that intelligence is a fixed, innate trait apportioned unequally among individuals and groups. Wrong, he said. We agreed, wrote the check, and invited him to run his startup in our Kapor Center. But there were problems with the plan. He was using out-of-date Web 1.0 style marketing. He acquired a struggling for-profit university. And then there was the founder himself. We liked his resume, and we liked the history he offered, as a serial education entrepreneur who had launched several startups. His pitches were full of buzzwords: All we had to do was "turn on the spigot" and money would be pouring out. We'd see immediate "positive unit economics," making more off a customer than it cost us to get one. He was "creating a flywheel," shorthand for a business strategy where a founder can deliver huge results with an early, big push.

The first red flag came when Freada, responding to rumors, conducted a customized anonymous confidential survey of his entire team. She had done this at Wall Street firms, international law firms, the United Nations, the World Bank, and more, sometimes in reaction to corporate crises and PR scandals, other times to help diversify staff. The results were the worst, by far, she had ever seen in all her decades. Employees were incredibly unhappy, didn't trust management, couldn't figure out the mission, and felt very off track in their careers. Here was the moment where choices needed to be made, and there were two obvious possibilities. Well, said Freada, it's obviously time to replace the founder. But Mitch, and other investors, were taken by his promise and his personality, and kept him on, throwing good money after bad. We didn't realize until it was too late that the companies he had started before had lost money, been dogged with problems, and in some cases engaged in questionable business practices. We also didn't make the necessary calls to people who later told us, candidly, that he was unreliable.

It was painful. Ultimately the CEO was fired. Though his board-picked successor made Herculean efforts to turn the company around, it was too late. We ultimately lost our entire investment.

We had chosen the wrong path. And there were learnings to make a better pivot next time. It's better to cut your losses rather than continue to pump money and hope someone is going to pull a rabbit out of a hat or hope that they will change their management style. When someone says they've launched startups, there's no excuse for not getting the full story on what happened to those companies. When a survey—hard data, research—says there's a bad apple, don't be swayed by charm. Believe the objective numbers. And call former associates and ask what we've honed to be the single most important personal reference question: *If you could hire this person again today, would you?* If you don't get a very enthusiastic and immediate "yes," walk away.

Another fork-in-the-road moment came from a husband-and-wife team we invested in who had way too many investors and a business idea that wasn't working. We told them, "You are never going to make money on this. Please walk away. Your lesson is not a failure. We'll back you in your next startup." But they couldn't hear it; they couldn't change. Although they were in their fifties, they poured in all of their retirement money. They continued to lose cash and ask us for more. We wired them emergency funds out of our own pocket to help them make payroll. Twice. But the second time we told them, we're not doing this again. We're done.

These founders, who were in a major midwestern city far from Silicon Valley's "fail big" culture, literally couldn't live with themselves if the company tanked. They didn't feel they could face friends and family, and so they gave away a large piece of the company and their own upside in exchange for a last-ditch-effort investment to save it. The cash infusion enabled the company to survive the crisis, but the investor, not the founder, was now positioned to reap the financial returns in the coming years. At least the company is having a positive, gap-closing impact. But a truly founder-friendly, impact-focused investor wouldn't exploit a difficult situation in this way.

Going forward, we have become much more definitive: we tell our founders how much we will invest, and then set specific targets they have to hit, with deadlines, before investing further.

This isn't to imply there aren't gray areas.

We still question whether we made the right call when we decided not to invest in a company because they weren't willing to put people on their board and management who came from the same communities they aimed to serve. The two white women founders had won a business school competition with a plan to provide healthy lunches to disadvantaged and charter school students—a gap-closing mission. It concerned us, however, that the company's board and management team were white, mostly women, while most students in U.S. public schools are of color, and so are most cafeteria workers. Over more than a decade, they became the poster company for early-impact startups, providing nutritious food to children from low-income families. They didn't put a Black person on their board until their tenth year in operation. We still wonder if we shouldn't have written that check and been a constant thorn in their side. Perhaps that would have led to a more diverse board of directors and in turn, many other changes at the company?

Through our experience, we've come to embrace the dirty secret Mitch learned early in tech: when push comes to shove (as it often does), most investors don't care about the entrepreneurs they "support." Not really. A high valuation at any stage can backfire badly because it creates expectations that are impossible to fulfill. And too many investors with too much cash can be a death knell for a startup, or its mission. No doubt, startups crash if they are starved for cash, but we've seen them choke to death on having too much.

A startup founder we admired and supported had moved to the U.S. as a baby and watched her family slowly work their way out of poverty. She was intelligent and persistent, underserved by her public schools. She launched her first company while still in college, helping her fellow students get loans to cover their tuition.

In 2012, at twenty-five, she came to us with her next big plan, a new iteration of that college-launched business that would help refinance loans for people whose credit or payment history might otherwise force them into higher interest rates. We were excited to invest, bringing our advice, our cash, and our shared values. It wasn't long before she shifted her business plan: she told us she wanted to focus more on helping students across the board with college affordability, not just loans, and we agreed that seemed like a sound idea. Even more, her passion and lived experience were palpable and we believed in her.

Soon other VCs were noticing her promise, and she caught the eye of a billionaire Silicon Valley investor, a former executive from a major tech company whose top partners once quit en masse because they were so frustrated with his controlling strategy and demands. We can't—and wouldn't want to—tell an entrepreneur whom to take money from. But we did suggest she talk to other founders this abrasive VC had invested in. By reputation he was a great salesperson, charming and warm, but once he invested, founders said he could be unpleasant and demanding.

Nonetheless, she made her decision and took a substantial investment from him. While we invest to back both the business and its founder, this newly added VC was ready to throw her focus on college affordability out the window. Together they came up with a completely new business: a service for "underserved geniuses."

The founder knew all too well that high achievers, especially in science and engineering, often aren't challenged at schools where spending on essential equipment is anemic, classrooms are overcrowded, and services are scarce. Overworked teachers are simply too busy helping underserved kids learn the basics. Top students get bored and drop out. The founder's new business model would identify these gifted kids and tap into universities to find them mentors and tutors. The twist was the way she would identify at-risk, talented participants: by having them compete online, solving ever more complicated problems, and gaining points for their achievements.

The site took off, but it didn't work the way it had been pitched to us. The company made no effort to reach out to students in low-income communities of color in the U.S. Instead, the site reached out to a global community, including drawing many wealthy, privileged college-bound students around the world to win prizes and attention. Our target population was lost in the shuffle. We understand better than most that as companies grow, they must change. But this founder was changing her business model. When faced with two clear directions, she chose to go in the direction of widening gaps, not closing them.

The founder understood our concerns, and we had multiple conversations about whether she could pivot. She was sincere and thoughtful, but she was keenly listening to the other VC, who sat on her board enjoying the swift growth of her company. When her company had developed a substantial user base and was ready to scale even larger, more investors lined up to buy shares. Ultimately, she wasn't going to change the model.

We had a tough decision to make. We knew that exiting meant walking away from a bunch of money; we thought the company would grow substantially and it has. In the end, we asked to be bought out and go separate ways. We had believed deeply in the mission underlying the original online education company and some of its iterations. This difficult shift taught us to ask an additional set of questions from the beginning as part of considering an investment: What was a particular founder likely to do in such a case? Was their gap-closing incidental or bone-deep? Could we rely on them to stay with their commitment?

The need to change business models is a commonplace of start-ups. At first a founder has just a hypothesis, so she builds, she tests, she iterates. That's the way of entrepreneurs. They always adjust, but sometimes they find out that their initial idea was really wrong, or circumstances shift. This has been a recurring challenge for us. We would invest in something gap-closing, and then it became clear that the first business model wasn't going to work, so now what? Sometimes the entrepreneur's new idea was not gap-closing, but neutral or gap-widening. Sometimes they would be pushed by other investors to dump impact out the window. We realized we needed to anticipate this possibility when we invested, but how? We needed to consider what any particular founder was likely to do in such a case.

Unlike typical venture capital investors, during pitches we would ask entrepreneurs about what motivated them to launch their startup. It often became clear that a painful life experience was at the root of their ambition. The reason they were building this product was so others wouldn't have that same experience. In other words, there would be no reason to do the business if it didn't aspire to that goal. We learned to look for a basis of that commitment in their life story and experience, their values, passion, and character, not just their brilliance or charisma. If a founder hasn't experienced the problem their company seeks to solve, firsthand, or otherwise lacks a basis for passionate commitment to the gap-closing element of the business, we're unlikely to invest.

In 2015, at a meeting of founders following a tour of our SMASH program, our CEOs reached their own fork in their roads when it came to hiring. Startups have to staff up quickly, and they knew they could take the easy way, onboarding friends and people they knew. But they wanted to be intentional about building a workforce that resembles the customers they serve. They said that in order to attract top candidates they would appreciate some type of branding—something like a stamp of approval—that could identify them as

Kapor companies, meaning they're genuinely committed to having a diverse workforce and inclusive culture. They came up with the idea of a Founders' Commitment.

We thought it was a terrific idea. We knew that locking in diversity, equity, and inclusion in a company's culture from day one would be foundational to building a diverse workforce as they grew. The CEOs developed our Founders' Commitment, launched in January 2016. Ever since, before Kapor Capital invests, CEOs must commit to establishing diversity goals and investing in resources that mitigate bias, organize volunteer opportunities for employees to engage with underrepresented communities, and participate in sessions hosted by Kapor Capital to learn about what works and what doesn't.

Existing companies in our portfolio reached out asking if they, too, could sign on, and most of them did.

These commitments were completely different than anything found in venture capital investing, which is exactly how we operate.

That commitment, and our principles, give our founders some ethical and moral codes to turn to when they come to us after they hit a fork in the road. We share what we've seen, and talk about trade-offs or different approaches. We try to prepare them, encouraging them to work with values-aligned investors and supportive board members. But at the end of the day, founders and investors have to make their own decisions and live through the tough times. We should know. We've been there ourselves.

9

PARTNERSHIP

ULILI AND BRIAN

Uriridiakoghene "Ulili" Onovakpuri is one of the handful of Black female VCs in America in 2022 with more than $100 million at her disposal to invest in promising tech startups. Her gentleness and warmth have made her a favorite among founders and nieces alike. But we've known Ulili's strength since her early days in college, and as the CEOs whose companies she funds have warned, it would be a grave miscalculation to underestimate her.

Ulili likes to say that she's a formerly poor person, and that is her truth. Her father is Nigerian, her mother from the U.S., and she was one of seven children. Life for their family, neighbors, and community was challenged by many of the same struggles the CEOs she now invests in had to face: insecurity, trauma, debt. In 2022, Ulili's home was a short fifteen miles across the sparkling bay from where she spent her childhood in San Francisco's Hunters Point. But the former naval shipyard, with a toxic legacy so extreme the Environmental Protection Agency declared it a Superfund site, might as well be in another country. Industrial fires from "The Yard" at Hunters Point would fill Ulili's largely Black, working-class neighborhood with heavy smoke, and the AIDS epidemic ravaged her community. Ulili recalls gang violence, asthma among her peers, and cancer rates the highest in the city. She told her parents she wanted to be a doctor.

When we met her as a high school senior, Ulili told us she wanted a different life for herself, her family, and her community. She wasn't sure how to do that, but she knew how to work really hard. She was a gifted student and an avid reader who paged through dictionaries for fun. She excelled in school, taking advantage of opportunities like 826 Valencia, a nonprofit learning center founded by bestselling author Dave Eggers that helps under-resourced students develop their writing skills. By the end of high school, she had several college offers, including UC Berkeley, and enough scholarships to become the first person in her family to attend university.

All college-bound students have a few weeks of their lives when they have to decide which offer to take. What Ulili didn't know was that during those weeks, her application was being reviewed by Freada and her team at the IDEAL Scholarship program. IDEAL, or the Initiative for Diversity in Education and Leadership, was a program that invested in high-caliber, underrepresented students, providing resources and support to maximize their educational experiences and leadership opportunities during college and beyond. The scholarships sought to provide some support after California's 1996 law Proposition 209 forbade race-based affirmative action for college admissions; with IDEAL, we were hoping to begin to close the gaps caused by that harmful policy. While she was still mulling her options, IDEAL Scholars invited Ulili and students like her to a reception to learn about who we were, what we provided, and to meet other IDEAL Scholars who had traveled her same path.

Ulili didn't want to go to UC Berkeley. Going there felt like a Bay

Area cliché, and she had a writing scholarship for a special program at the University of California, Santa Barbara, where warm beaches beckoned. I'll go to the interview, she thought, and get the free dinner, but I'm not going to UC Berkeley.

That evening she changed her mind. Yes, she had made it into college, but here was a team intent on making sure she succeeded. Ulili learned that IDEAL would help her obtain a college degree with a no-strings-attached stipend—meaning she wouldn't need student loans and a work/study obligation. She would also gain access to a community of fellow students, a mentoring program, a computer, tutors, an annual retreat, and summer internship support. Perhaps for the first time in her life, Ulili could be surrounded by people from communities like hers, who shared her drive, her interests, and her ambitions. This is my tribe, she thought. Freada had deliberately made community a centerpiece of the scholarship program, a place where peers could talk about how it feels to be "othered" or to address the noxious effects of the "myth of the model minority." Freada had developed layers of support aimed at overcoming barriers to success that affect women and underrepresented students of color in higher education. And so Ulili, at nineteen, packed up and went to UC Berkeley. Next door? Candase Chambers, eighteen, raising her baby Kyle. Ten years later, both were working within our organization: Ulili was a leading Kapor Capital investor and Chambers was head of digital media and marketing for the whole Kapor family of organizations.

Initially, Ulili was a little confused by our investment in her. These people are millionaires, she thought. Why were we spending all of this time with a bunch of kids? Didn't we have better stuff to do? Over time, her thinking changed. We chose to be with Ulili and her peers because we wanted to support their aspirations. We could do that by opening doors and making connections, but their visions for the future? Those were entirely up to them. The feeling that grew for Ulili, she told us, wasn't dependence. It was freedom.

Ulili was beginning a new journey and sought out any opportunities offered at Berkeley. She spent a semester at sea, and a study-abroad year in the United Kingdom. Before college she had thought about medical school, but when she shadowed an ob-gyn, she realized that the day-to-day work seemed to be doing paperwork and arguing with insurance companies rather than delivering babies and diagnosing cervical cancer. Ulili turned her attention to health care technologies. After college, for a time she worked at a tech startup, which was inspiring and frustrating—she saw that tech could improve the lives in the community she came from on a very large scale, but the company culture wasn't always a great fit.

As the startup was struggling, we asked Ulili to work at our non-profit, then called the Level Playing Field Institute. Ulili's job was to try to convince tech companies to allow us to bring free diversity training into their workforce. Even with no price tag it was a hard sell, but her colleagues were supportive and the mission was clear. And here was a new type of workplace for Ulili. Freada's dogs bounced around, and Ulili could bring baby siblings and nieces into the office to play. Her youngest brother, then three, would ride Dudley, our beautiful and goofy one-hundred-pound labradoodle, through the halls of the Kapor Center.

Freada invited Ulili into meetings unrelated to her own position, and appreciated her perspective and ability to frame and contextualize complex issues. One day Mitch asked her to sit in on a pitch from Sherita Ceasar, a Comcast senior vice president and the highest-ranking Black woman in cable telecommunications. Sherita and her brother were developing a math app for an iPhone.

Mitch turned to Ulili and said, "I'd love to get your feedback since you're using these things currently." Ulili was always helping one of the young children in her life with homework, and was familiar with which online tutorials worked, and which ones were just a waste of time. She was honest, asked great questions, and soon took over the meeting. Why did you build the software this way? What about kids who get confused with this part? How does a user feel successful?

Mitch was impressed. She had a talent for getting to the heart of things. After the meeting we talked. Mitch said that if Ulili was interested, he'd like to have more of her time on the investment side of Kapor. Ulili was interested. She'd spent time at a startup and recognized the potential. She went to work as a Kapor Capital analyst, reviewing new investment opportunities, supporting the execution of deals, diving into market research, and improving our reach in the local startup ecosystem.

Several years in, Ulili realized she wanted to sharpen her business acumen beyond what she was learning on the job. She chose Duke University's Fuqua School of Business, where she graduated with an MBA with a focus on health care. Partway through the two-year program, she won a highly competitive pitch contest that came with a cash prize. She was sorely tempted to drop out and launch a company immediately, but she knew she wanted that degree. After graduation, we were ready to welcome her back, but Ulili was eager to branch out on her own.

She launched her own company, LifeKit, aiming to improve access to health care in the most rural regions of the world. She also went to work directing global programs at Village Capital, the largest organization in the world supporting seed-stage, impact-driven startups. The firm, which supported more than 1,200 entrepreneurs, was backed by CEOs including Jeff Bezos, Bill Gates, and Mark Zuckerberg. Now as an entrepreneur, businesswoman, investor, and mentor, Ulili had a view of tech startup investing from all sides, which gave her broad insight into what worked. She was beginning to define her own place in the ecosystem.

She was frequently recruited by venture capital firms, and soon opted to join Fresco Capital, which was closer to home and prioritized health care, education, and work—issues she was passionate about. She also joined several startup boards, where her contributions on strategy were welcomed.

In 2022, even as Ulili had risen to the top of her field, as one of the few Black, female VCs in the U.S., she kept seeing a troubling pattern: ideas are everywhere, but opportunities are not. She had seen firsthand that if Black and Latinx people were given the same access to investment capital and networks as white, male entrepreneurs, they would grow and uplift themselves.

In an industry dominated by white men, she realized that even a small number of Black or Latinx venture capitalists or the CEOs they funded could exponentially shift the demographics.

She was also keenly aware that others were watching and judging her, and she felt the weight of her responsibility. It's not just managing other people's money; it's also being among the first generation of Black women partners in VC. She's been in the industry long enough that would-be startup CEOs know who she is and what her interests are, although it's common at tech conferences for people to mistake her for the few other Black female investors (who look nothing like her). Also common: having everyone from the registration desk to the people hooking up her microphone assume her young, white male intern is the speaker. Typical Silicon Valley fashion might be jeans and a T-shirt, but Ulili dresses more formally. Otherwise, even when she is presenting at a high-profile conference, she is often stopped at the door and told, "Oh, you're not allowed here." Typically she only goes to conferences where she's going to speak; she's fearless onstage, calling out her own VC peers.

"You measure what matters, and thus far VCs haven't been held accountable for creating diverse portfolios," she said when asked to address racial equity at Kaiser Permanente's Institute for Health Policy. "It can't be just us alone, though."

Once the crowd recognizes her stature, the pitches start rolling in. She's been approached inside bathroom stalls, in hallways, and over the phone. She looks for founders whose intentions and goals aren't about making a lot of money. She wants founders who are building something based on their lived experiences, that can change people's lives, solve problems, and scale into a big business.

A coach once told Ulili that to be a successful venture capitalist she would need to behave and make decisions more like a traditional VC. Is that true? she thought.

She decided that she was going to come up with an authentic way of doing venture capital investing.

Ulili once met LL Cool J. He described, early on, sending demos to every record company, and getting rejected so many times that he was ready to give up. His mother took her entire six-hundred-dollar tax refund to buy him a proper drum machine, and he recorded a new demo that landed him with Def Jam.

"You know how we are with our tax refunds," said LL Cool J.

Yep, thought Ulili, for most people she knew growing up, the tax refund was the only windfall they would get every year. If it hadn't been for his mom investing that check in her son, we might not have LL Cool J today.

It made Ulili wonder, how many great ideas are we missing out on today, because someone doesn't have a parent, or uncle, or cousin with deep pockets willing to take a chance on them?

Ulili found her home at Kapor Capital and her insights have been invaluable. She started a Summer Associates program for would-be investors to support more Black and Latinx entrepreneurs and investors. Her first hire: a bright and motivated student named Brian Dixon.

INVESTING IN PEOPLE

The son of immigrants, Brian jokes that his parents moved from Jamaica to Jamaica, but that's exactly what they did, immigrating from the Caribbean island nation to the Jamaica section of Queens, New York. When he was still a toddler, the Dixons settled on Long Island, where they hoped their children could attend better schools and have more opportunities.

Over the years, Brian and his brothers watched their parents build lives from scratch in their chosen country. His father drove a taxi; his mother worked in an assisted living facility. They worked and they studied. Ultimately his dad became an engineer, his mother a nurse. Brian's parents wanted their kids to be well educated, and to know their world beyond Long Island. Every year they would take a family vacation, even if it meant driving from New York to Florida.

As a teen, Brian gravitated toward computers. Also sneakers. He loved sneakers, but his parents could only afford to buy their four boys one pair of shoes a year. Brian launched his first company, Blak-Out Sneakers, at fifteen, buying sneakers in stores and custom-painting them. First he sold them all over the Internet; then he found eBay and moved his business there. He sold a lot of shoes, hundreds, buying them retail for about $100 a pair, and then using Photoshop to design them. He would send the designs to customers, and with their approval, he'd paint the shoes and ship them for $200 a pair. Among his customers was professional basketball player LeBron James. "Peak. Peak. Peak," says Brian, remembering that order. Today anyone who can afford it can click onto any number of custom sneaker shops. Want a green midsole? Click. An iridescent swoosh? Click. But in 2000, this option was barely conceivable, and Brian was enthralled. This new World Wide Web offered him a connection to the world. He could access global markets from his AOL dial-up. Once he had a taste of building a business online, he was hooked.

Growing up, Brian's older brother learned alongside his parents all the ins and outs of the college application process. They learned by trial and error rather than already having that institutional knowledge embedded in their psyches and their community. When Brian was ready to apply, he counted himself lucky that some people in his family had already gone through the process; he had support with federal aid applications, college essays, SAT prep, and the vast network of scholarships. His oldest brother started at a Long Island community college, following their parents' path. By the time his younger brother, seven years Brian's junior, was applying, the family's understanding of the process had evolved. That brother went to private, elite Brown University, a member of the Ivy League, for undergraduate and a master's degree. Today when Brian visits our SMASH scholars he understands the paths they're on, and the step-by-step lessons they need.

Brian attended Northeastern University, paying his way with a mix of scholarships, loans taken out by his two working parents, his own student loans, and summer jobs. He liked coding, building stuff, and studied computer science but wasn't sure exactly how he wanted to use it. He tried working on a computer support help desk but wasn't thrilled being on call to fix broken things. He wanted to build things, change things. He tried a government job, but as he says, "That wasn't for me." When he wasn't working or studying, Brian was building a startup called ProfileLinker, which he founded with several college friends. The idea was to link profiles across multiple social networks. Senior year they finished second place in a competition, winning Brian his first angel investment, and more importantly a chance to talk to some VCs. He hadn't understood what venture capital was at that point, assuming that startups were self-funded or bootstrapped. It planted a seed, this experience pitching an idea to the VCs. Maybe down the line I could actually be a VC, he thought.

After college, Brian went to work paying off his student loans as a software engineer with an IT team for Citibank municipal bond analysts. It wasn't thrilling work, but he was taking care of his financial responsibilities, following a path that many of Kapor-backed founders must take. He was also moving forward as CEO and building a team at ProfileLinker.

When ProfileLinker ran out of money and went out of business, the experience taught Brian deep empathy toward founders whose companies don't work out, which is more times than not.

In the next six years, Brian moved from one tech position to the next, building websites, living in Canada for a bit, working for a firm that was sold, and then sold again, eventually working for Disney. Brian's interest in entrepreneurship and venture capital only grew, so he got his MBA at Babson College's F.W. Olin Graduate School of Business. Like Ulili, Brian participated in a program during graduate school called Management Leadership for Tomorrow, which steers Black, Latinx, and Native American talent into high-level careers. Kapor Capital had an internship partnership with that graduate program, and Brian was in the first class of that summer internship.

He remembers landing for his first time on the West Coast and marveling at the fact that he was in Silicon Valley. He couldn't figure out where this promised land of tech and innovation began or ended, but there was something special about being in the birthplace of Google, Apple, Facebook, and so many more. As we do with all of our interns—and because venture capital is an apprentice-based business—Brian regularly attended pitch sessions with the rest of the investing team, and then we'd sit together afterward and talk about what just happened and why. That might not seem like a revolutionary approach. But especially for people from communities who haven't had access to the world of investing and startups, that kind of inclusion is a golden opportunity to learn what questions to ask and to develop judgment and good instincts about people, business models, risk, and so forth.

In 2013, Mitch and Brian sat down for a pitch meeting with one of the most remarkable entrepreneurs we'd ever met, Frederick Hutson. Frederick was pitching a tech company called Pigeonly, to help incarcerated people communicate with their families. Interesting idea, we thought. But then Frederick told us how he began dealing marijuana in his late teens, and was sentenced to four years in federal prison at age twenty-three. An entrepreneur at heart, Frederick had found an untapped market of incarcerated people whose families couldn't afford to be in touch, and in some cases couldn't even find their loved ones as they were moved from one facility to the next.

Frederick told Brian and Mitch about how he was housed at eight different facilities in fifty-one months, and how hard it was to communicate with his family because of restricted points of contact, and no cell phones or Internet service. Commissary payments from his sister, and letters from his brother, sustained him, he said, but he saw men around him growing increasingly isolated and depressed without any outside contact. He told us he wanted to solve this problem in a way that was equitable and affordable, starting with a service that, with just a few clicks of a button, would print photos off cell phones and mail them to incarcerated people.

For months we'd been talking with Brian about how it's critical for our founders to have lived experience with the challenges they are trying to solve. Here Brian saw the perfect example. It was clear that Frederick, who was also building a team of formerly incarcerated people, understood how to use technology to tap into a huge market currently dominated by private companies that prey on families of millions of incarcerated people. It was one of those rare pitch sessions where Mitch and Brian were ready to invest before Frederick even left the room.

Over the years, Pigeonly would grow into a multimillion-dollar company that makes it easier for friends and families to find incarcerated people, place funds in their prepaid phone accounts, lower call rates by 80 percent, and send cards, letters, and news articles. Brian has kept up on the research and has talked to us about how this isn't just good business; studies consistently show that close family contact is instrumental in reducing reincarceration and successful transitions outside of prison.

From early on, we could see Brian had the makings of a great investor. He had foresight to realize that this underappreciated idea could actually turn into a real business. We liked how methodical he was, in his due diligence and his communication with everyone he works with. He's constantly learning and always curious. Because many in the VC community think their race makes them outliers, Brian and Ulili are constantly being scrutinized and doubted; they've had to be tough, self-confident. But here's what both Brian's and Ulili's LinkedIn profiles, resumes, and portfolios don't reflect: they're both patient, funny, and thoughtful. They don't rush would-be entrepreneurs when they stumble during pitches; instead they help them. If they believe in an idea, a person, or a company, they will fight for it fiercely. They lead by example, building a workplace culture through their own, kind examples.

BREAKING NEW GROUND

A decade after launching our first fully committed gap-closing fund, we were ready to move on to new projects and hand the reins over to a new generation of investors. We were confident that our partners

Ulili and Brian were ready to take over Kapor Capital. They agreed. For us, it was a celebration. For the Silicon Valley, this was groundbreaking. Years earlier, they'd been among the first Black investors to become partners at a Silicon Valley venture capital firm. Now they're running it, as the new managing partners of Kapor Capital.

We have seen that technology can solve some of the world's toughest problems. Brian and Ulili are ready to help tech solve America's longest-standing problem: systemic racism. And they are living proof that distance traveled and lived experience are two valuable metrics for evaluating potential. They're ready to close the gaps in our society and exchange greed-first investing for a system that truly builds equity. Ulili and Brian weren't interested in making dramatic changes when we left. But Ulili did suggest they broaden the portfolio to international companies. Impact in Nigeria or India is as important to them as impact in the U.S. They also saw that entrepreneurs in other countries, facing major problems, were coming up with brilliant solutions. For example, in the U.S., the estimated national maternal mortality rate is about three times higher for Black women compared to their white counterparts. Ulili, who had worked in global VC at another firm, was watching Kenya solve this problem, dropping their maternal mortality rate in half over two decades. Were there technologies or ideas at play that could solve problems here? That was one of the questions they hoped to answer as she and Brian embarked as the new leaders of the fund.

Their first big step was to raise money for a new fund, which meant pitching their investing philosophy to potential investors. Notably, this was the first time Kapor Capital had sought outside money. Until then, we had been investing our own capital. We anchored the new fund with our own 25 percent investment, and we offered introductions to our network of VCs and advisers. But the hard work was up to Brian and Ulili and they were eager to get started.

They faced the typical challenges: skepticism and doubt. But they also confronted racist systems of exclusion; the pushback they got was sometimes flat-out shocking.

"Don't you think that the only reason you're partners at Kapor Capital is because Mitch and Freada like you? You wouldn't be partners at any other venture firm now, would you?" asked one potential investor.

"No," said Ulili, who along with Brian was frequently recruited by other firms. "I don't think that's true." In her mind, she was compiling their growing list of successful investments. At least she knew who she was dealing—or not dealing—with now.

At that time, investment firms were increasingly responding to their lack of diversity by launching funds specifically for Black fund managers, a double-edged sword for Brian and Ulili. On one hand, they wanted more investments going to a growing pool of Black fund managers in the entire universe of VC. On the other, they were being limited by that categorization.

"Oh, we're out of our Black money," a VC told them one day.

"We'll take green money, too," said Ulili, trying to make a joke of it.

Ulili and Brian were often asked how they differed from the dozens of newly minted Black fund managers, brought into firms in the new rush to diversity.

They would shake their heads. They explained that they were seasoned investors; they had founded companies, sat on startup boards, and successfully climbed the venture capital ladder from junior analyst to the seniormost partners in a firm. They were seeking investment in Kapor Capital's third fund, worth $125 million. They would point out that the previous two funds had delivered higher returns than their peers. How did they differ from the new investors? Normally, Ulili and Brian knew how to roll with the punches, but it was hard not to be insulted by this line of questioning—as if all Black investors could be lumped into one category.

Even investment firms that they had coached on how to diversify their own teams turned them down when they pitched their fund. No one is ever obligated to give anyone funding, but they do deserve to be treated with respect, and in all too many cases, that didn't happen. And they still faced great skepticism about their gap-closing, impact investing strategy, even after we'd been proving the model worked for the last decade. Brian and Ulili made their case again and again, showing VCs that they could get returns and do good for the world. VC benchmarks are published, and they could show that Kapor Capital was beating comparable non-impact funds.

There was also just plain old rudeness. We had set up a meeting with a white woman managing a multibillion-dollar fund. This investor had already seen Brian and Ulili's pitch deck, which included their names and pictures. It was a Zoom call, and Ulili was the last to join. Her window popped open, and there she was, her beautiful and powerful name in the corner of her window: Uriridiakoghene Onovakpuri.

"Who is this?" the investor yelled, really, at the top of her lungs. "Someone with an unpronounceable name just joined!"

We stared at each other in silence. It was so completely inappropriate.

It took a few months and dozens of meetings longer than it should have, but once they were fully funded, Ulili and Brian didn't hesitate with their investments. And while investors may have hesitated, their reputation as venture capitalists, and Kapor Capital's fundamental commitment to founders, worked in their favor.

CHANCES WORTH TAKING

One of their first major investments in 2021 was CareCar, a company supporting seniors living independently by connecting them with a reliable network of vetted caregivers, transportation, and other in-home care benefits. For caregivers, the $28-an-hour, flexible sched-ule work removes high broker fees. For elderly community members, CareCar works with health plans to cover costs. Founder Joshua Itano saw a problem when he was working at a health care startup—transportation was a barrier to care. He studied successful companies that made things more accessible, like Airbnb and Uber. As Ulili said, "It's the right product set, market, and team at the right time." In less than a year, CareCar was in the process of being acquired, a win for Joshua and a win for Kapor Capital.

During any given week, Brian and Ulili work with as many as five newly minted CEOs, raising funds to grow their startup. Of-ten it's the CEO's first company. Brian will run through their pitch deck, talk about their list of potential investors, help them practice their story, and make introductions. One CEO described Brian as "the kindest venture investor I know." Having been through their own ordeal getting funded, they tell their entrepreneurs that they're never going to be declined for overtly racist reasons. As Brian says, "You never get it directly, but there are a hundred other reasons they can give you that won't get them in trouble."

If an investor does decline, Ulili will meet with the CEO to figure out what happened. They keep a finger on the pulse of their entire portfolio, reading investor updates and offering Kapor's suite of ser-vices to the portfolio companies.

Founders who work with them say they are consistently kind and respectful. But they're also tough, tougher than we were, be-cause they are under such scrutiny, both from the limited partners who invested in their fund and from the broader VC community, many of whom still seem dubious or uncomfortable with their race, whether consciously or unconsciously, and explicitly skeptical of impact investing. They are tough, too, because they know what's at stake: vulnerable people, underrepresented communities, society as a whole.

"Many investors can be purposefully abrasive, but with Brian and Ulili there's zero posturing," said Sebastian Seiguer, CEO of emocha Health, a Kapor Capital firm. His company's mission is simple: make sure economically disadvantaged, marginalized patients take their prescribed medicines without fail. Seeing a health care provider and getting some pills is never a cure, but taking the medicines as prescribed can actually eliminate diseases like tuberculosis and hepatitis, and control conditions like asthma and high blood pressure.

"I can breathe now," said one laughing boy during a video visit, after emocha was brought in to manage his care.

Kapor was Sebastian's first institutional investor in 2017, after Brian thoroughly vetted his business model, reviewed his vast experience, and understood his science-based approach and his financials, which included federal grants. Brian liked those. National Institutes of Health funds—they were nondilutive, meaning the company gets money without giving up equity. It became a running joke: "Nondilutive funding!" Brian would cheerfully call out to Sebastian when they ran into each other at conferences.

Early on, Ulili took a look at emocha's marketing materials featuring stock photographs of kids and caregivers. "Hey, Sebastian," she said, "you're serving Black kids in West Baltimore. Why don't you put some Black kids on your front page?"

It was eye-opening for Sebastian. He had never thought about it.

Sebastian's inbox was flooded with investors as emocha Health rapidly became a hot startup. When he sought a $5 million round, investors pushed him to take $10 million. Ulili urged him to be cautious about bringing difficult personalities to his board just to get more cash. Sebastian had a harmonious board, including Ulili, who had an observer's seat. Bringing in abrasive or difficult investors would complicate emocha's culture and jeopardize its growth, she said. This happened several times, and each time Sebastian declined investments, Kapor came in with more funds.

bethanye McKinney Blount, CEO of Compaas, a Kapor Capital portfolio company, says that with Brian and Ulili, she never has to put on a good face. Ulili understands and accepts there are great days and not-so-great days, bringing a unique combination of empathy and pragmatism. She has no interest in the Silicon Valley culture of "always crushing it," said bethanye, but she warns: don't underestimate Ulili. Entrepreneurs pitching impactful companies to Kapor Capital have told bethanye that because Ulili is a Black woman with an impact investment fund, she'll easily write the check.

"Don't expect a cake walk," bethanye once warned a startup founder. "This is not how this goes."

Ulili combs through pitches and business models, demanding fundamentals that are believable and measurable both for impact and revenues. If she can't understand every detail offered in a pitch, it might be a good idea, but Ulili is going to pass.

ACTION, NOT SLOGANS

In the immediate days following the murder of George Floyd, we were deluged by well-meaning tech investors frustrated and ashamed by the lack of diversity in their portfolios and in their own firms. As months passed, the urgent calls kept coming.

One venture capitalist gathered twenty-five major players, some of the biggest investors in the country, for a diversity initiative. He had buzzwords to "lay a technical foundation for 'barrier reduction.'" He suggested that they could, "for the first time," generate accurate statistics about investing in Black and Latinx communities. (In reality, we and other experts have been doing that for years.) He had the requisite social media campaign in mind, and some big announcements.

This is what we call performative nonsense.

We told him his initiative was implicitly counterproductive. Also forget the announcements, the Twitter and Facebook plans. And the hour-long meeting he asked for with us wasn't going to be enough. "We are concerned that those who show up will see themselves as enlightened exceptions who are going to save the ecosystem, not as part of the problem," we wrote back.

If it sounds like we were a little harsh, we had reason to be. Across all three of our organizations in our Uptown Oakland center—Kapor Capital, Kapor Center, and SMASH (which are all Black-led)—we get asked for free advice all the time and then watch, in dismay, as it's usually ignored. We've spent countless hours in meetings and sessions and proposing programs and initiatives, mostly to no avail. And that's exhausting.

Nonetheless, as we have with hundreds of other similar requests, we said we'd try. We would offer a framework, an annotated version of our investment principles. And we'd take some questions. Just one thing before we schedule this, we said.

"It would be great if everyone would send demographics for their organizations; specifically, how many Black and Latinx men and women in investing roles, in C-suite positions. Our view is that those who haven't made significant progress in their own organizations can only speak theoretically about how to do better and are therefore not in a position to architect solutions," we wrote back.

They agreed to try. At least six months later there was a meeting, but it was composed of very few of the original intended attendees. Almost none of them turned in their demographics. If you don't know where you're starting, how do you know if you've made any progress? Those who showed up were earnest, mostly Black and Latinx women and men, and several white women.

As one of the first Black partners in a venture capital firm, Brian too was being overwhelmed by firms asking how to get more Black CEOs into their portfolios.

No one would overtly admit to racism. But founders of color are historically underfunded. It's obvious to all of us that there's a higher bar for what Black and Latinx CEOs need to accomplish to raise the equivalent dollars of their white male counterparts. And they don't raise as big of rounds historically, so they typically have to do more with less.

Brian decided to try to answer all of the queries he was getting at once.

"So you want to fund Black founders?" he wrote on a Medium blog, challenging Silicon Valley's crescendo of diversity pledges.

Brian kept it simple:

- HIRE BLACK INVESTORS. *Diverse investors have access to diverse founders. Investing in talent today means investing in the leadership of tomorrow. And publicize the jobs. At Kapor Capital, our diversity is by design, our inclusion is intentional, and it starts with publicly posting available job openings.*

- FUND BLACK FOUNDERS, AND DON'T WASTE THEIR TIME WITH SUPERFICIAL MEETINGS. *If you're not seriously interested in writing checks to Black founders, then save the lip service and skip the PR stunts. If you are serious, put your money where your mouth is.*

- HOLD YOUR FIRM ACCOUNTABLE. *Your public commitment does not have to look like ours, but it does need to be something you are serious about being held accountable to. State your goals, measure your progress, and publish your results.*

"Tech has figured out some of the world's hardest problems and prides itself on being the 'special' ones, who can solve anything it chooses to. How about this time, tech chooses to solve America's longest-standing problem: systemic racism. How about this time, tech starts by fixing itself."

The impact was swift. Two prominent VC firms—First Round Capital on the East Coast and Initialized Capital on the West Coast—publicly credited the blog post for their decisions to post their open positions and hire their first Black partners. It was really so simple.

Ulili describes this time as "our redemption tour."

VCs and investment firms were cramming her inbox, asking for ways to diversify both their own companies and their investment portfolios. Pretty much every VC firm that had ever rejected a Kapor pitch contacted Ulili, along with others she'd never heard of. Many of the emails started with an apology.

"I'm sorry, I know you sent us some potential companies before" or "Sorry, you know our firm wasn't ready to invest before but now we are hoping to look at the awesome talent you've been trying to send us."

Many told her they were committed to doing things differently: "We realize we are a monochromatic team, and we want to change that."

Ulili wanted to leverage new, potential partners, but like us, she was wary of wasting time on so-called initiatives with no real commitment.

Kapor Center's Summer Associates program, the one she started, the one that Brian participated in, was receiving eight hundred applications a year for their five to seven slots. She hated turning away talented people, and she understood the lack of diversity in their field stems from a lack of opportunity to get trained. She asked the investment firms that approached her if they would form partnerships with Kapor Capital's Summer Associates program. This led to many, many more Associates. She was filling up the pipeline.

Ulili and Brian have continued to use their platforms, as some of the most successful and longest-tenured Black VCs in the country, to be activists as well as investors.

Ulili joined a call to action with Black Tech for Black Lives.

"We as Black people in tech have a unique position and opportunity to respond to violence against Black people's bodies. While we're proximate to the pain, we largely avoid its most brutal physical outcomes. But we, too, feel the blows," said the group. "We carry the scars on our psyches and hearts as our voices go largely unheard in the workplace and beyond."

When critiques poured in over then presidential candidate Joe Biden's choice of a Black, female vice presidential partner, Ulili was among the first Black women leaders to sign a powerful opinion piece.

"We are servant leaders—motivated by a desire to uplift and advance our communities and nation," said the letter. "And we will not tolerate racist or sexist tropes consistently utilized in an effort to undermine our power."

We are in awe of the power and grace Ulili and Brian carry. They know exactly what they're doing as venture investors: turning capitalism on its head.

10

LESSONS LEARNED

In 1970, economist Milton Friedman published his notoriously big idea that a company must be beholden solely to shareholders, "to use its resources and engage in activities designed to increase its profits." Fifty years later, Nobel Prize–winning economists were lining up to tell the world how very wrong this was.

The late General Electric CEO Jack Welch's practice of boosting earnings with mass layoffs—a novel idea that became the cruel norm—now puts him "on the Mount Rushmore of men who screwed up this country," wrote David Gelles in his 2022 book, *The Man Who Broke Capitalism*.

Focusing only on profits and shareholder returns works well for the few; the rich do get richer. But everyone else—the workers, customers, and community members—is left behind, something Aclima CEO Davida Herzl had seen firsthand growing up before deciding she had to do something about pollution. Greed-driven capitalism has been a major contributor to every equity gap in the U.S. today—in education, housing, labor, criminal justice—not to mention climate change, community safety, and generational wealth.

In 2019, nearly two hundred CEOs of America's largest companies at the Business Roundtable recognized that they had been practicing a destructive doctrine. Together they declared an end to shareholder capitalism and committed to a new idea, stakeholder capitalism. They pivoted their missions to benefit everyone impacted by their business—customers, employees, suppliers, communities, and shareholders.

In the passing years, Business Roundtable CEOs, whose companies have some 20 million employees and $9 trillion in annual revenues, have begun to shift.

"Stakeholder capitalism is not about politics. It is not a social or ideological agenda. It is not 'woke.' *It is capitalism*, driven by mutually beneficial relationships between you and the employees, customers, suppliers, and communities your company relies on to *prosper*," wrote BlackRock CEO Larry Fink in a letter to CEOs in 2022. Reducing a company's carbon footprint, for instance, ensures long-term viability, something investors and executives should care about, he wrote.

Critics immediately said BlackRock should stop investing in fossil fuel producers.

"Businesses can't do this alone," Fink wrote, "and they cannot be the climate police."

He encouraged investors to use environmental, social, and governance (ESG) ratings—which measure a range of societal impact issues for corporations—as a decision-making factor. ESGs, as well as B Corp certifications, are supposed to designate that a business is meeting high standards of transparency and social good. But we've said for a long time that you can get to be a B Corp by having enough recycling baskets. These ratings can be gamed, and by 2022 there are tobacco producers, mining firms, and companies with over-the-top executive compensation that pass ESG ratings. We are in dire need of a rigorous definition of "good business" and that's just one of many reasons why we've been very specific and measurable about how we define gap-closing.

We appreciate the intent from a powerful business leader whose firm manages $10 trillion, but we are also aware it's actions that count, not just words, and we're still watching the BlackRocks of the world, waiting for significant action. There have been countless pledges signed by broad swaths of corporations or by specific industries with specific initiatives—anyone remember the 2017 "Decency Pledge" in the wake of a VC being called out for sexual harassment of half a dozen women? It was initiated by Reid Hoffman, founder of LinkedIn and a partner at a prominent VC firm, Greylock. Such seemingly well-intentioned efforts never seem to be accompanied by powerful accountability mechanisms.

Even as corporate America is promising changes, we're increasingly frustrated that the venture capital industry has been a marginal voice in that conversation. Most VCs worship in the church of greed, first and foremost (although they would phrase it as financial returns). For decades, they, along with other institutional investors, have asserted that social impact of any kind must be thought of as concessionary in that it necessarily leads to an unacceptable sacrifice of financial returns. We and others have demonstrated that this assertion is false, by investing soundly in companies like the ones we've described in this book, and hundreds of others led by incredible visionaries—all of which are healthy, growing enterprises devoted to social change, training underrepresented communities for good jobs in tech, eliminating crushing debt that limits opportunities, and addressing climate change.

It's going to come down to a new generation of VCs, entrepreneurs, and business leaders to make the changes necessary to eliminate bias in tech, and build in equity from the first conception of a potential new company. This means business schools will need to revamp their curricula, from courses on basics like marketing and finance to the growing body of classes on entrepreneurship and venture capital. Day one needs to be about impact. Before they start launching businesses of their own, graduating MBAs need to have a deep-set understanding that every company has an impact: negative, neutral, mixed, or positive. They need to think about who benefits from a business and who might be hurt, which gaps are widened or closed in corporate and entrepreneurial endeavors. There are some hopeful signs of change, and we've noticed a more holistic view of business impact on politics, economics, and the climate. More businesspeople are considering, as our founders do, that systemic racial injustices have led to disproportionate environmental burdens for communities of color.

There's an important role for employees and consumers, too, in influencing the success of companies. If more employees voted with their feet, companies would have to modify their practices and their cultures. Similarly, consumers can vote with their pocketbooks by not supporting companies that may produce cool products but do so by polluting communities or creating toxic work environments.

It's also time for massive endowments, especially those at foundations and universities controlling trillions of dollars, to invest in companies, either directly or through venture capital funds, in a way that is consistent with their own social and educational mission statements—in the case of universities to prepare global leaders to solve social, cultural, economic, and environmental issues. Yet annual surveys of more than one thousand U.S. college and university endowment officers show that most of their investment strategies ignore impact. Similarly, investors for major foundations with massive portfolios have no interaction with the program officers who are making charitable grants to mission-driven organizations. A foundation could be committed to eradicating poverty by giving grants representing 5 percent of their assets, while 95 percent of their funds are invested in gap-widening businesses that exacerbate income and wealth inequality.

When scrutinized for these shortcomings, venture capitalists often resort to blaming their limited partners (LPs), asserting that the LPs only care about financial returns. In turn, the chief investment officers who oversee university and foundation endowments and who supply the venture capital firms with their capital sometimes say they would like to invest in firms like Kapor Capital so their investments can make an impact, but they can't. Instead, they claim that the institutions they work for—pensions, foundations, university endowments, trusts, insurance companies, and more—demand that they only work with big-name VC firms. This elaborate web of false assumptions, outdated excuses, finger-pointing, and blame-shifting makes progress all the more daunting—but not impossible.

We encourage our peers in venture capital to join the movement and address concerns raised about shareholder capitalism. Entrepreneurs and investors need to clean their own houses, commit to diversifying their own teams and their own portfolios, and establish criteria to evaluate companies that promote equity versus those that contribute to inequality. Set diversity and impact goals and exceed them. We call on our peers to have an impact. Inaction is an active choice. We need to hold each other accountable.

What if each one of us who writes a check to our alma mater demanded that our donation be invested in funds that only invest in companies consistent with the college or university's mission? What if public sector employees were represented on the investment committees of the multibillion-dollar pension funds that control whether they will have a comfortable retirement or not? Perhaps they should demand that fund managers and their underlying portfolio companies reflect the diversity of the employees whose hard-earned wages are being invested?

We believe in the missions of the founders we invest in and see their companies in stark contrast to the conventional capitalism that drives inequality in our country. We've learned a great deal from our founders and our partners; we've had some painful lessons, but we're also able to cheer some great successes. We've proven our path can be successful in building equity; now it's time for people managing hundreds of billions of venture capital dollars to join us. We can be the change.

INVESTING FOR IMPACT

The year was 2013, and President Barack Obama's Affordable Care Act was *finally* rolling out. At least it was supposed to be. But Healthcare.gov, the customer-facing side of Obamacare, was crashing. On launch day, just six people managed to enroll in health insurance as tens of thousands tried to log in. Over the next few weeks, tens of millions of Americans tried to use the site, only to receive frustrating error messages. Healthcare.gov itself was hacked. Fake copycats appeared. Costs soared from a $100 million website to upwards of $1 billion as layers of contractors raced to fix it.

"I promise you," said Obama. "Nobody's been more frustrated. I wanted to go in and fix it myself, but I don't write code."

In San Francisco, three tech entrepreneurs—George Kalogeropoulos, Ning Liang, and Michael Wasser—did write code, and they were among the frustrated Americans trying to log in. What a mess, they later told us. They couldn't figure out what was available, or how much it would cost, and that was when the website didn't simply lock them out. "I think we can do better," said George. The stakeholders went to work.

Three days later—after lots of caffeine and a few hundred dollars—they launched HealthSherpa, to help low- to middle-income Americans, seniors, and large swaths of Black, Latinx, and Indigenous communities find a new health plan.

The site debuted amid a moment of great national outrage over the disastrous rollout of Healthcare.gov. *The Daily Show* host Jon Stewart kicked off an interview with Secretary of Health and Human Services Kathleen Sebelius with a challenge: "I'm going to try and download every movie ever made, and you're going to try to sign up for Obamacare, and we'll see which happens first." She resigned a few months later over the failure of the website. There would be congressional hearings and federal investigations of fraud and waste.

We understood firsthand that the situation was much more nuanced. Todd Park, founder of Athenahealth, was the chief technology officer of the United States at the time, reporting to President Obama. He was called in and spent countless round-the-clock shifts in his office rebuilding the site. Todd hosted the first-ever White House Tech Inclusion Summit in 2013, in partnership with one of our nonprofits. After leaving public service, Todd cofounded another health care company, DevotedHealth, which focuses entirely on helping people get the best Medicare coverage possible; Kapor Capital is an investor.

But back in 2013, uninsured and underinsured Americans were very frustrated and Todd and his team couldn't fix things overnight.

HealthSherpa wasn't exactly the same as Healthcare.gov, but it did offer a new approach to helping people find health insurance that would be covered under the new law. In just a week, the cofounders gave numerous newspaper, television, and radio interviews; they were featured on all the large networks and twice in the *New York Times*. Conservative on-air personalities loved the story, and George, Ning, and Michael were happy to appear on a half dozen different Fox News shows. This not only drew interest from investors, but it also generated 1.5 million visitors in its first month. HealthSherpa would become one of our earliest and most successful impact investments, and over the course of almost a decade we've learned a lot of lessons and identified best practices through our work with them. But we've also noticed the emergence of some troubling patterns—even a company that is measurably helping people overcome life-and-death struggles may not be creating a culture in-house that is consistent with their goals.

We've talked about our failures, and hopefully shined the light on successes. In this chapter we're sharing the best practices we've learned, through recurring patterns, on our own investing journey. Some learnings came from HealthSherpa; others are ideas we've developed over the years. We now insist that founders address challenges they personally empathize with. Companies need to hire teams that reflect their potential customers or users, and the bottom line needs to be social impact, in addition to dollars, or they often end up missing out on both. There are some alternative strategies we encourage investors to consider, including getting creative about how money is spent, how people are compensated, and how promotions and pivots are decided. Some of the solutions to fight inequity in the workplace are now tech startups themselves, and these can add a layer of fairness into how a company runs. At the end of the day, it's important for individuals to grow and lead, but also to step aside and make room for the next generation.

AN EMPATHIC BUSINESS MODEL

The brilliant thing about HealthSherpa was that people could find a health insurance plan quickly, using only their phone, with a clear understanding of what they were going to have to pay. Great technology, built from an empathetic understanding of those who are being served—the stakeholders—is an unbeatable combination. George had grown up in Greece, where citizens benefit from universal health care. When his family came to the U.S. for a year, they couldn't afford health insurance and had to figure out how to sign up for Medicaid. They qualified, but in the passing years George realized just how complicated, unintuitive, and broken the health care system was.

Every tech startup wants to find a problem and create a solution. HealthSherpa was different. They measured impact not in dollars but in how many people they were serving, uninsured people who were so marginalized they couldn't even access a government program aimed at helping them.

None of the HealthSherpa founders were especially politically active, and they knew the Affordable Care Act, signed by President Obama in 2010, had plenty of critics.

"Whenever somebody asks us politically charged questions, our reaction is, well, we wouldn't know the first thing about any of the policy involved," George told a business journal. "That's not our role in this. It's to make an easier-to-use website. It's not to take a side."

George, Ning, and Michael hadn't thought about how to make money. They just saw a problem they could quickly solve for a group of people who were struggling to use the new government program.

During our conversations, HealthSherpa's cofounders would weigh different ways to monetize their product. Initially, they didn't know anything about health insurance. The first thing they did was take all the traffic from their site and direct it to insurance agents who would pay them for these leads. They had pictures, phone numbers, and contacts established for the licensed insurance agents who, once a user had selected the right plan through their site, would help a user purchase it. But they found it was very difficult to audit the performance and behaviors of the insurance brokers. For example, customers would call the insurance broker with a plan in mind and the insurance broker would then try to switch them to a non-Obamacare plan in order to get a higher commission, or to avoid filling out a long application on Healthcare.gov. They decided to become licensed as an insurance agency themselves. They had to learn the ins and outs of health insurance all from scratch and become licensed in all fifty states. This brought unexpected benefits. Now they could understand what people got hung up on when they were spending time on the phone talking to customers. No amount of spending, training, or networking can replicate all of those insights they got. This is what we mean by empathetic tech—it applies not only to the people who are served, but also to the people providing that service.

They also had to do some creative things like get a custom insurance policy from Lloyd's of London (the same place where Rolling Stones guitarist Keith Richards insured his fingers), because no traditional insurance company would insure a brand-new, national insurance agency whose founders had zero insurance experience. Because they had become so high profile, they were able to establish contracts with the top one hundred major insurance companies. When people enrolled in a plan, the insurance companies paid them a commission. By the end of their first real year's open enrollment, they had finally gotten all the logistics in place and signed up just under 1,000 families, at about $300 to $400 per family in actual revenue.

When we talk about proof of concept, they were there. Now it was time to scale this business.

Their next step was to begin licensing the technology to insurance agencies, benefits consultants, and insurance companies who also wanted to sign up customers directly, and that drove a lot of growth.

In their second year, enrollment grew 100x, to over 100,000. And in less than a decade, HealthSherpa had signed up more than 9 million people in Affordable Care Act coverage; by 2022, the company born out of frustration was enrolling about one out of three Americans who signed up for health insurance. It was the first company to partner with the Centers for Medicare & Medicaid Services and the Department of Health and Human Services to offer these services.

Their average consumer's household income is around $21,000 per year and once they use the system, they typically only pay about $30 to $40 a month on average out of pocket. About a third of their consumers pay zero dollars out of pocket for health insurance that typically costs $600 to $800 a month. For many of their users, this is the first time that they have health insurance. That's what we call impact.

We see no shortage of social problems waiting for smart solutions. What's more, there's government money, state and federal, that's already been allocated, sometimes poorly spent and sometimes never spent, to create tech solutions that make it easier for citizens to access government services, from job training to food programs such as SNAP and WIC, and medical support. The lessons from Health-Sherpa are to find a real problem impacting millions of people's daily lives that needs a solution; use empathy to come up with a good solution; and design a business model that aligns with the mission. The overarching lesson? Impact creates more impact.

In 2022, a team of Boston University and Drexel University researchers published a study that found that Medicaid expansion under the Affordable Care Act dramatically reduced arrests. The largest decrease came with arrests for drug possession and selling, which dropped 25 percent to 41 percent in the three years following expanded access to health insurance. The explanation: the Affordable Care Act mandated coverage of mental health and substance abuse services as an essential health benefit, and so people who might have ended up in handcuffs were able to get help. Impact creates more impact.

REFLECT THE COMMUNITY YOU SERVE

When Cat Perez arrived at HealthSherpa in 2015 as chief of product, she recognized a shortcoming. As a queer woman of color, she saw a company that was expanding rapidly without enough focus on

223

workplace culture. Because HealthSherpa had launched like a flash and then expanded exponentially month after month, the hiring managers rushed to recruit engineers without much thought about diversity. They were hiring with a whole bunch of wrong assumptions that we've seen over and over again: they were looking for pedigree credentials and only people with explicit computer science training. Many recruits had taken their job just for a paycheck; they didn't consider themselves stakeholders—they were "just" programmers. Cat understood the business model—after all, she had won a $1 million hackathon prize for developing HealthCareLove, a site similar to HealthSherpa. She and George had opted to join forces rather than compete, and she shared the vision of equity and access. Unfortunately, she was realizing that teams of people working at Health-Sherpa weren't necessarily mission-driven; they were there for the job, and saw tech through a narrow lens. She asked us for advice.

Cat asked Freada to talk to their HealthSherpa teams about diversity, and of course we were happy to help.

However, as we feared, many of HealthSherpa's engineers and salespeople pushed back: they said they didn't want to lower the bar by hiring women and people of color.

"I'm color-blind," someone said. "I'm gender-blind," said another.

Someone asked if hiring for diversity was even legal.

The HealthSherpa teams also pointed to the women among them, mostly white or Asian. There's no gender disparity here, they said. Freada explained that an intersectional lens is critical, and that diversifying would mean most women would be women of color.

We suggested some strategies that other major companies, including Intel and Pinterest, have used to boost hiring of people of color: employee referral programs, hiring bonuses, setting inclusion goals, adding diversity goals as criteria for advancement. Freada asked them how they found potential candidates and emphasized that if they're networking with people they went to school with, that gives some people an unfair advantage that has nothing to do with qualifications or an ability to do a job. Cat came back to us, really upset, and said our lesson had not been well received. Staff were offended or dismissive.

"Well," said Freada, "maybe you don't want those people working for you."

At the time, Cat was a bit stunned. But this was a business issue, we explained. For decades, we've told hundreds of founders that their teams must resemble and reflect the community they are working for, in order to design and create solutions appropriate to that community. If they have biases and attitudes that contradict their own company's users, customers, or clients, then they are undercutting the mission and should find another job. This is not a random social and racial justice belief. And this is not asking if a team agrees on putting a Black Lives Matter poster in the window. This is asking if a company has done a decent job communicating the mission when screening employees, not just reviewing whether they have the right number of years of engineering or sales experience. Do they understand the mission? Are they aligned, and can they internalize it and act on it?

HealthSherpa's success depends on making sure everyone working there understands who the uninsured users are, how they think, and what their daily lives are like. That's what Ning was thinking back in 2013, when he tried to use Healthcare.gov. He just wanted to type in his zip code and see what was available. And so that's what they built.

Cat leaned on us heavily early on to make sure they were establishing a culture and a value system that would scale with their company as they grew. Nearly a decade in, she told us it worked—they've been able to attract talented coworkers who would have gone elsewhere if it weren't for their team composed almost entirely of women and people of color.

Their colleagues understand what it's like to live without even knowing what preventative care is available, and to avoid seeing doctors because they cannot afford it. The thought process, as one team member explained, is that with health insurance, their clients can live to see grandchildren graduate from college. Yes, they're creating technology to help fill out a form, but they understand this means so much more: they're literally improving lives.

Fortunately, as the years have passed, we have to explain this concept less frequently to the founders we've invested in. But we are not naïve. These myths and biases persist and their consequences show up in unexpected ways, which means that none of us are really, ever, off the hook when it comes to the work of closing the equity gap.

WHAT'S WRONG WITH GREED-FIRST INVESTING?

As we've noted, in today's VC ecosystem, founders ceaselessly get the message that they should be raising as much money as possible at the highest possible valuation. This means setting extremely challenging goals for revenues and growth. Every year, and every quarter in that year, must be larger than the last. Revenue growth can easily be expected to increase 200 percent in just one year. If, for any reason, those expectations are not met, there is a domino effect of adverse consequences. Founders try too many things at the same time. Talented team members leave. Investors push the company to rebrand and relaunch with a poorly focused business model.

Massive revenue and growth goals don't take into account shifts in market sentiment or the overall economy. Many of our founders who had the luxury of choosing their investors, with multiple term sheets, went with the highest valuation and the largest check, often against our advice. Some even told us they wished they could take an investment from a VC firm with the best people to help with their business, but since that firm didn't offer the highest valuation they turned them down. Just as we talk about redefining the measurements of success to include both social impact *and* financial gains, we encourage founders to include values *and* valuation when evaluating investors.

For the greed-first VC, the purpose of pushing companies in this direction is to increase the chances of a single company being the kind of enormous success that will reap enough revenues to cover their investments in all of the companies in a portfolio, and then some. That's known as "returning the fund." We explain it like this: A $50 million fund makes 10 investments of $5 million each. One of those companies multiplies in value by 10, and is now valued at $50 million. The VC firm has made back all of its investment capital. Any other money made after that is gravy. What other VCs don't tell entrepreneurs is that this approach increases the odds for others in the portfolio to fail. The greed-first investor only cares about grand slam home runs; he doesn't care about a base hit, let alone a strikeout followed by a pivot. We explain to our founders that this so-called power law of VC, when one company in a fund can return the whole fund and therefore all other investments can go out of business, is cruel and not something we're interested in at all.

Here's an all-too-common scenario: A company has taken the term sheet with the highest valuation, hired a lot of people, and spent a lot of money on sales and marketing, chasing and failing to achieve extreme targets for customers and revenue. Now it's running out of money, so additional financing is needed, possibly on an emergency basis to meet payroll. But the company is in a weak bargaining position. Existing investors are looking at what's known as a "down round," meaning the valuation of the company now is less than the previous round. Investors hate this because it decreases the value, on paper, of their holdings, which they have to report to the limited partners who wrote them checks. This can be the beginning of the end.

The company has to lay people off and cut back spending. Company morale goes in the tank. Talented staff leave. The CEO may be removed by the board as not being the right leader. It doesn't matter what the underlying causes are or if they were beyond the founder's control, whether it's an economic recession or pandemic lockdown. We've learned through experience that today's high flyers may have an awful letdown.

This is even more concerning with impact investing. Investors have an incentive to protect their investment, we understand that, but with companies that aspire to create great social change as well as economic value, particularly those focusing on vulnerable populations, the primary responsibility must be to the stakeholders who are at risk. We've told the leaders at HealthSherpa that the only valuation that really counts is the one at the time of the exit. Everything else is like the score in the middle of the ball game. It's a kind of vanity metric.

GET CREATIVE WITH COMPENSATION

Every time George, Ning, and Cat talk about raising money, we talk about equity.

In some cases we've seen, founders who grew up without means, in underrepresented communities, ask for a salary and equity that is way out of line with the market norms for the stage, size, and revenue of the business.

"I could be making three times this if I didn't leave my other job," founders will often tell us. They point out they are highly educated, and that they're centuries behind in building generational wealth.

The trouble with this is that the funds left over in the company's bank account after taking that 3x salary aren't enough to recruit and pay a team to make the progress needed to reach the next milestone.

It's going to create tension and hostility with the team, the board, and early investors. But that doesn't mean "no" is the answer. It means it's time to get creative.

We start with a conversation, especially with Black founders, about the legitimacy of their demand for equity, historically and currently. But at the same time, we stress that to burden this particular startup, at this time, with the entirety of trying to fix systemic racism is not the right solution. We talk about how we must accept and recognize that there's unfairness that can't always be immediately mitigated, but can be over time.

At the same time, we loathe the dysfunctional dynamic in today's VC ecosystem that expects founders in the pre-seed and seed stages to work for next to nothing, and the assumption that they can raise initial funding from friends and family. This fails to recognize that this approach only works for young, single people who come from privilege. It disfavors families with children, those with large student debts, and individuals who are supporting family members, as is frequently the case with Black and Latinx founders.

There's even a popular term traditional VCs use to describe this mentality: "ramen profitable," which means if everybody lives together, shares an apartment, and only eats ramen, then the startup can be profitable. But that's just not a way for grown-ups to live, especially if they have families.

We often see investors offer a founder a sort of sliding option. Either take little to no salary in exchange for a larger share of the company, or maximize their compensation in exchange for their equity. People from low-income backgrounds are always going to choose the higher paycheck. They need the money and they need it now, which means in a decade, when the company they've worked so hard for is successful, they will have lost out on the generational wealth building because they were covering their parents' rent or hiring a lawyer for siblings caught up in the criminal justice system. These biases in the existing VC model are inherently discriminatory toward people from low-income backgrounds, which in the U.S. means disproportionately people of color.

It's time for new solutions. We encourage investors and board members in startups, especially with founders from underrepresented communities, to get really creative when it comes to founder compensation. Here are a few examples:

HELP PAY OFF STUDENT DEBT.

More than 45 million Americans owe $1.7 trillion in student loan debt. Two-thirds of those debtors are women. Black borrowers owe more and are three times as likely to default. We can't make up for generational wealth in the compensation of a seed-stage company, but we can pay off student loans, which is a great investment in a founder. In recent years, more companies have been adding student loan repayment as part of their benefits packages, and during a tight labor market this perk can draw talent. Chegg, an educational tech company, sold stocks that had been set aside for executive compensation to increase student loan repayments for all of their employees, from entry-level team members to vice presidents. We offer all employees at Kapor Capital, Kapor Center, and SMASH a benefit that helps them pay off student debt.

PROVIDE A MORTGAGE SUBSIDY.

The racial gap in the homeownership rate between Black and white families is growing; more than 68 percent of white families own their home, but fewer than 38 percent of Black families do, according to

Urban Institute research. That gap is even worse in the Bay Area, where housing prices are among the highest in the country. Providing a founder with a mortgage gets them into that market, building equity in their own home and offering the security of homeownership during one of the most unstable times of their career.

PROVIDE CHILD CARE AND ELDER CARE FUNDS.

After housing, child care is often the largest single monthly expense for families. Children's Council San Francisco estimates that parents spend between $20,000 and $30,000 a year for their children to be cared for between birth and age five. In-home care or assisted living for an elderly parent or disabled family member can be twice that. Our founders tell us they choose large paychecks over a significant stake in their companies because they're supporting extended family members or hiring people to care for their own kids. Subsidizing care can diversify a workplace and attract talent. It reduces parents' stress and anxiety and helps them focus on the work they're passionate about. We've heard these subsidies questioned: What about people who don't have kids, how is that fair? The answer is that *fairness is not about treating people the same. Fairness is getting to a level playing field*, a place where everybody can focus on their career or training. Think about it: If somebody is in a wheelchair and needs to be transported in a special van, does that seem unfair?

LET THEM OFF THE ELEVATOR BEFORE THEY REACH THE TOP FLOOR.

Founders whose companies are successful and growing after a few years inevitably come to us with the same dilemma. A schism has developed between the team who has been at the company from the start and recent hires brought in to manage the roaring growth.

They want to alert us to their problem but doubt we can help. The good news, we tell them, is that there are solutions. We've seen this issue arise consistently in our startups, and we learned about it first-hand decades ago with our own early stumbles. When Lotus grew rapidly and newcomers from larger, more bureaucratic companies were brought in to help us into a new phase, the same tensions arose.

Here's what happens: Some employees are really incredible in the early days of a startup. They're big contributors and help a company get off the ground very, very rapidly. But the people who get a startup from zero to $1 million in sales aren't the same people who get that company from $50 million to $500 million; that's typically a different skill set and often a different personality type. During the later phase, a company is dealing with different standards for bigger contracts, a different set of people are making decisions, and, let's face it, more money is at stake. Unfortunately, it's very common for later hires to come on board at what was once a scrappy little startup and treat the early staff, and their ways of doing business, with condescension. They can be patronizing or aloof, leaving their colleagues feeling defensive and hurt. It must be said that these situations are excruciating. But they may be practically inevitable in high-growth startups and there are some tools we've developed. We call this strategy: *Let them off the elevator before they reach the top floor.*

First, we advise founders to accept that this problem is more than likely to occur. The sooner they embrace the idea that they're going to go through something uncomfortable, the sooner they can get through it.

Second, find a way for the early staffers to step away with dignity. Think of moving them elsewhere in the organization, or offer them retirement. But here's the critical piece: honor them for their contributions. Make a very public and loud gesture of appreciation and gratitude for what they did to launch this startup. At the same time, let the new hires know, very clearly, that they wouldn't have their job, doing six- and seven-figure deals, if the early team hadn't scrambled, hustled, and used every creative tactic when there was no money in the bank.

As for new hires who treat others with disrespect, that's when we tell our founders they need to show leadership. If an individual cannot abide by company values of treating people respectfully, first give them feedback. Perhaps it's not intentional, so help them understand how they are coming across to others. We always tell founders that the impact of their behavior—and the behavior of everyone else in the company—is what matters. Quite often, very well-meaning people engage in ways that are hurtful, and perhaps even biased or harassing. If they cannot change, ultimately they need to be sanctioned because they're not building an inclusive culture.

That is, in the end, our goal, to have corporate America forging workplace cultures that prioritize diversity, inclusion, and a true sense of belonging.

NEVER TOLERATE INJUSTICE.

When Mitch was a partner at a large Silicon Valley VC firm, Freada launched a project to survey and study close to thirty of their portfolio companies about their quality of work life, following the employees and companies over five years. At the time, the firm would spend hundreds of thousands of dollars on glitzy events, bringing in Hollywood stars to entertain the partners and portfolio CEOs. In advance of a Pebble Beach retreat, the firm's leaders—familiar with the work Freada was doing to help their entrepreneurs—asked her to find a high-powered keynote speaker on workplace culture. Freada invited a leading investment banker, Robin Chemers Neustein, who started at Goldman Sachs in the 1980s after cold-calling financial firms. In just eight years she was a general partner, and then a senior director; she was chief of staff to several eras of heads of the firm. Robin oversaw Freada's consulting and training work at the firm for a decade.

Without irony, one senior partner told Freada, "If she fucks up it's your fault." It was a little bit joking, a little bit threatening, just a reflexive demonstration of power from a wealthy VC.

Neustein came armed with an incredible video of Goldman Sachs's coheads, financial world veteran Stephen Friedman and former Treasury secretary Robert Rubin, talking about the important connections between business success and culture in the workplace. Robin's presentation was off the charts, and the takeaway was that paying attention to company culture matters because it impacts revenues. The partners thanked Freada and said Robin's keynote raised their awareness.

Later, Freada was presenting the survey results from portfolio companies to the firm's partners. Her presentation included data on employee perceptions and experiences of their managers, of company culture, job satisfaction, and a host of other issues at the companies in their portfolio.

"Raise your hand," said Freada, "if you're on a board of a company being sued for race or sex discrimination." Everyone raised their hands.

"Raise your hand," she said again, "if you've brought concerns about this to a partner meeting." No one moved.

There was a sense of fatalism and resignation that race and gender workplace conflicts are just the cost of doing business, and there's nothing to be done about it. Why would anyone, especially shareholders, just accept that there will be problems in any company, rather than use the tools available to solve them?

It's foundational for all of Kapor Capital's portfolio companies to have a working understanding that there are things that can and should be done to foster organizational health. We talk with Health-Sherpa's leaders about this regularly. We anticipate there will be problems, and we work with our entrepreneurs to solve conflicts, hopefully before they turn into lawsuits. Litigation is expensive and a distraction, but more importantly, dealing with issues of diversity and inclusion is baked into the Founders' Commitment we require for every investment.

USE TECHNOLOGY TO MITIGATE BIAS.

In the 1980s, investors dubbed a sector of tech startups that offered financial services "FinTech." In the passing years, there's been Med-Tech (medicine), EdTech (education), GovTech (government), and many others.

Meanwhile, in the 2000s at Google, the Human Resources Department reinvented itself as People Operations, a term that caught on, first in tech and then more broadly. The idea was to focus support on employees—key stakeholders in a company—rather than focusing on complying with labor laws. In Google's first case example, People Operations wanted to convince women who left on maternity leave to return to the office.

Why didn't VCs have a people ops tech sector, wondered Freada? We talked about the possibility of tech startups that could build in some of the hard work Freada and her colleagues had been doing for decades, using technology to mitigate bias throughout the workplace, from recruiting, interviewing, and hiring to setting salaries and promotions, conducting performance reviews, and establishing career paths. It was also clear that harassment and unfair treatment was a problem across all industries. Founders, CEOs, and human resources departments were looking for solutions, and we saw a huge opportunity for founders who were passionate about solving the problem.

To get things rolling, in 2015 we hosted our first annual "People Operations Tech," aka POT, a pitch competition for tech startups offering human resources services, especially ones that could mitigate bias. CNN called it "the sexy new startup sector that's disrupting HR."

People ops tech startups from around the country brought their innovative ideas to eliminate workplace bias, discrimination, and harassment. The competitions continued, and we've seen the sector blossom. There are job-matching apps, tax withholding programs for independent contractors, and recruiting tools that use mini-mentoring sessions to validate nontraditional tech talent. Many of the people ops tech companies we've seen seek to eliminate bias in various forms of talent screening, but there are many other missions; one works to wipe away criminal records, while another supports parental leave transitions.

OMBUDS: SPOTTING TROUBLE, SERVING UP SOLUTIONS

While Mitch launched and funded one startup after another, there was one particular service Freada had been thinking about for decades: ombuds. We think every company should have an ombuds, an independent, confidential resource where employees can raise concerns about the workplace. They offer two, separate services to companies. First, they provide a safe, informal, nonbinding channel for staff to seek help. Workers may find themselves subject to bullying, harassment, or abuse of power, sometimes for years. Some don't speak up because they are afraid they will lose opportunities if they complain. Others fear that they will be considered to have poor judgment, unable to handle their own problems. Often the supervisor or manager they're supposed to report concerns to is the perpetrator of the conflict or unacceptable behavior. HR or people operations departments are paid by the company and are therefore not neutrals. Ombuds can offer an employee an empathetic ear. They'll listen and take issues seriously, protecting staff from retaliation. Ombuds provide an impartial analysis, suggest options, and give referrals to resources.

In addition to employee support, an ombuds can spot the first hints of trouble at a company and get them solved before they escalate into lawsuits, bad publicity, or mass departures. If a particular supervisor is making sexist comments, for example, an ombuds can flag the issue to a CEO. If a group dynamic is leaving a few people sidelined, again the ombuds can help bring teams together. Fundamentally, they improve a workplace culture, because they provide early-warning signals when there's still time to resolve issues. In addition, they take the risk out of raising concerns by relying on aggregate data.

Freada's training as a researcher and decades of customized surveys for organizations from tech startups to the United Nations, Wall Street firms, and international law firms had made it clear to her that the only way employees would speak up was if they had some control over what happened to their complaints and the opportunity to pursue a proportional response. Sometimes that meant merely conveying that certain comments in all-hands meetings were inappropriate without launching a damaging, career-limiting formal investigation. The other key hesitations that can keep employees from coming forward are fear of retaliation and fear of not being believed. Ombuds services offer ways to address all of these concerns. The aggregate data is of great use to the C-suite and board of companies who genuinely care about culture and inclusive workplaces.

An ombuds should be an essential resource in any workplace, but they're still not ubiquitous because, as of yet, it hasn't made sense for smaller firms and startups, with tiny teams and stretched budgets, to bring one on board full-time. And in larger firms, it can be hard for an in-house ombuds to be trusted by everyone as a neutral party. There are also some tricky legal waters to navigate, but many larger corporations have done so successfully for decades.

In 2017, Freada and Lisa Gelobter were seated at the same table at a dinner hosted by Todd Park, the former CTO in the Obama administration. Lisa is a technologist with an extensive track record in disruption and transformation of large-scale legacy systems and in creating groundbreaking and culture-shifting solutions.

"Have you ever heard of this thing called an ombuds?" asked Freada.

Lisa, a Black computer scientist who worked in Obama's administration as the chief digital service officer for the Department of Education, had previously worked on several pioneering Internet technologies that had reached billions of users, from Shockwave and Hulu to BET Networks.

"A what?" asked Lisa.

In the mid-1990s, Freada had envisioned a third-party ombuds service and had even reserved a toll-free number, OMB-UDDY. "Ombuddy" was to be a sort of on-demand service with a trained ombuds at the other end of the phone. Freada wanted the core idea updated to be tech enabled.

Lisa dove into the concept. The approach she ultimately developed was to take the foundational principles of ombuds and democratize access to it, amplify the proven techniques to reach a much broader audience, and make it approachable, relatable, and usable for workers in any size company, work setting, industry, or geography. She and her cofounder, Heidi Williams, conducted extensive ombuds training and research, conducted hundreds of interviews with employees and company management, tested user experiences, went through iterative product development, and soon tEQuitable was born: a third-party, tech-enabled ombuds platform to help make workplaces more safe, equitable, and inclusive.

Born to immigrant parents who both surmounted long odds, Lisa says her Jewish father "was a feminist before the word existed." He was Shirley Chisholm's campaign manager in 1972 when she ran for the Democratic presidential nomination as both the first woman and first Black candidate. Notably, it took Lisa twenty-four years to get her computer science degree from Brown University, not because she couldn't handle the classes, but because it was simply unaffordable. By the time she graduated, she was already working at high levels in tech and was deeply experienced.

Despite her professional success, like many Black women Lisa was repeatedly mistaken for an administrative assistant; other colleagues assumed (wrongly) that she would have trouble understanding technical concepts. And like all too many people in the workplace, she had faced sexual harassment. She fundamentally understood why an ombuds could make a difference.

After beta testing and thoughtful due diligence, tEQuitable launched in short order; Freada was an active adviser. Here was a company that allowed employees to privately bring issues forward, acquire new skills, and get guidance on how to address difficult situations at work.

It turns out that most of the bias and harassment issues that come up in the workplace are not new. They repeat themselves, and there are solutions. A white colleague mixes up the names of their Asian colleagues. A male colleague talks over the women. A coworker's cultural communication style is mistaken for rudeness. And on and on.

If a tEQuitable user is feeling uncomfortable in the workplace, they can open up the app and get a script to address the issue directly with their boss, coworker, or even human resources staff. The intent is to foster a culture of healthy and open communication and give the worker some agency, as so often they feel like the control is taken out of their hands. For example, if they type in any of their frustrations, they can find action modules that resonate with their experience and give them tools to address microaggressions. One of the key insights tEQuitable heard from employees was "How do I know it's not just me? Am I being too sensitive?" So Lisa and her team created a library of stories, where people could see themselves reflected without having to take aggressive action. Every story includes four components: What happened to me, how did it make me feel, what did I do about it, and what were the outcomes? These solution pages resonate with workers and help them build a plan and feel more confident in their next steps. Different individuals have different learning styles, and at any point they can also schedule a one-on-one session with a coach. Ultimately, the goal is to empower employees to address issues directly or make change.

"I wish I had this last week when this thing happened to me," a user told Lisa.

Heads of human resources were also enthusiastic, because tEQuitable provided them with data and insights they'd never had access to before, like identifying systemic trends. A finance team might be having bullying issues. A marketing team might face an unfair distribution of work. Lisa told an interviewer that she loves the idea of inventing something new to solve a problem "that has plagued workplaces since the beginning."

For someone who is directly affected by interpersonal conflict or as an ally, advocate, bystander, or manager, "tEQuitable is helping to create a company culture where if you see something, say something, *do* something," says Lisa, who would have appreciated it if more people had stood up for her as well over the years.

In the wake of the #MeToo movement, Freada introduced Lisa to Anita Hill, professor of social policy, law, and women's, gender, and sexuality studies at Brandeis University. Thirty years earlier, Hill had testified in groundbreaking hearings that then Supreme Court nominee Clarence Thomas had sexually harassed her. Hill was chairing the Hollywood Commission, cofounded by Freada, to take collective steps toward tackling the culture of abuse and power disparity in the entertainment industry. Lisa brought her experience and expertise to the organization, helping identify steps that could be taken to eliminate Hollywood's toxic workplace culture.

Lisa, like any Black woman in technology, unfortunately knows firsthand about discrimination, bias, and harassment in the workplace. Her empathy for people who, like herself, are confronted with uncomfortable situations at work is at the core of her mission, and the reason tEQuitable is so effective. The driving mission of the company is manifested in its name—they are using technology to make workplaces more equitable.

CLOSING THE JOB INTERVIEW GAP

Other people ops tech solutions have been taking bias out of resume screening and job interviews. Technical interviews are a whole new level of discomfort than the typical suit-and-tie conversations where managers ask prospects: "What are your biggest weaknesses?" For jobs in tech, candidates might start with those simple questions, but they will soon be challenged to step up to a whiteboard and demonstrate coding skills or open up a computer file and debug the errors.

The tech interview was a huge barrier in 2022 for a middle-aged

Silicon Valley man who spent twenty years working as a janitor at night before learning to write code. He was, by hobby, a nerd, passionate about computers and technology. In 2012, when Harvard University and MIT began offering free, online computer science courses—the same exact classes their students were taking, just one week later and online—he signed up. Over the next six years he took every free or low-cost online course he could manage, and by 2022 he was trying to get an interview at Google. He had the skills, the certificates, and the experience, but he was scared to death of the interview.

That's where Aline Lerner and her people ops tech company interviewing.io stepped in. Aline was an MIT-trained engineer who was tasked with hiring people early in her tech career. She worked as an in-house recruiter, and then created her own technical recruiting firm. After three years of hiring computer engineers, it hit her: these technical interviews are not creating a hiring meritocracy.

"Most hiring managers pay lip service to how they're looking for strong computer science fundamentals, passion, and great projects over pedigree, but in practice, the system breaks down," she wrote. Unless you know someone in the company, the odds of you even getting an interview are very slim, she learned.

She began studying tech-hiring research and conducting studies on her own. She found a system where great engineers who don't "fit the mold," as she put it, don't even get a chance to talk to a tech recruiter, let alone have an interview.

She launched her own company to solve this problem and close the equity gap in tech hiring. At interviewing.io, candidates could book technical mock interviews with engineers from top companies. The sessions are virtual, anonymous, and live, with a senior engineer who gives feedback and mentoring at the end. There are specific Google and Facebook coaches, who design customized lesson plans for the role a candidate is applying to. They'll have between three and ten sessions. Before the pandemic, Aline worked with tech recruiters, offering ready-to-go candidates for tens of thousands of dollars each. When the pandemic hit, companies stopped hiring and Aline pivoted. Interviewing.io's next iteration was aimed at job candidates, and her timing was perfect. As businesses reopened, candidates who did well in the practice sessions could unlock interviewing.io's job board and book interviews at Amazon, Dropbox, and many other companies scrambling to hire talented computer engineers. The mock interviews started at $150, but candidates could defer payment until they got a job.

"Resumes are dumb," Aline likes to say. "Meritocracy is possible."

In 2022, the Silicon Valley janitor logged in to interviewing.io and began his training for Google's technical interview. A few weeks later he wrote to Aline. He was starting a job as a Google engineer the next day.

"I was a janitor who was just writing code on the side," he wrote. "I really needed help with the interviewing practice."

He said her company changed his life, which is exactly what we had intended.

CHAMPION A GREATER, MORE EQUAL, AND MORE JUST NEXT GENERATION

When Ulili launched our Summer Associates program in 2011, we became one of the first venture capital firms to offer what were essentially paid internships for students interested in becoming entrepreneurs and/or venture capitalists.

In the passing years, applications poured in, and it crushed us to have to turn away hundreds of promising students. By 2022, we were ready to expand. We retained a handful of the Associates to work with us at Kapor Capital, and we also partnered with other impact investment VC firms to take on other Associates, while we provided professional development for the incoming class.

And so it was we found ourselves on another summer week, this time on the West Coast, facing seventeen potential VCs. It was a group so diverse—more women than men, members of the LGBTQ community, Black, Latinx—that if they all went into investing, as a cohort they could single-handedly shift the demographics of investing by a few percentage points.

They reminded us of younger versions of successful CEOs and founders we know—people like Jake and Irma, Davida, Phaedra, Ruben, and Cat, founders we had gathered with on the other side of the country, on another summer day.

Ask us anything, we told the new Associates. And they didn't hold back.

What do we look for in founders?

"Values driven to the core," said Mitch.

Why choose founders from underrepresented communities?

Entrepreneurs tend to scratch their own itch, we said, solving problems they've overcome. We invest in people of color, from low-income communities, because they're inclined to offer solutions to the world's greatest unsolved challenges, based on their own lived experience.

They asked us about term sheets, a concept some had just learned earlier that day. We told them about a founder who was offered a huge investment in exchange for a large share of their equity.

"Don't do it, this is a trap," Mitch remembered advising this founder, who agreed. A year later the investor came back to the founder with more money and better terms. It was a risk that paid off.

One of the younger, new Associates asked us, simply, how do we make our investment decisions? She would be learning that summer, about due diligence and checklists, playbooks and unit economics.

"You're going to get to see how the sausage is made from inside the sausage factory, and there's no substitute for that if you're thinking of getting into VC," we told them. But that was only a starting point.

"If you're just going through those checklists you are missing the big picture, and you're going to miss the company that ninety-nine percent of the people on this planet need," said Mitch.

"As you do your analysis, never forget where you came from," said Freada. "Hold true to your values."

Finally, we told them, "You are the change in the whole venture capital ecosystem."

It was a lot of responsibility, we said, but also an incredible opportunity. Quietly, first one Associate, and then all of them, began to nod their heads in agreement. We stepped back and watched them get to work.

ACKNOWLEDGMENTS

Closing the Equity Gap was both a labor of love and a passing of the torch. We did not do this alone.

We want to thank:

The entrepreneurs in the book who graciously allowed us to share their stories and who inspire us daily with their passion to close gaps of access, opportunity, and outcomes for their communities.

All of the founders in the Kapor Capital portfolio and their teams whose vision and hard work continue to amaze us.

The IDEAL scholars at UC Berkeley—including the three who work closely with us in our organizations and one who contributed to the book.

The SMASH scholars—their curiosity and enthusiasm despite daunting obstacles, resets the biases that so many in tech and VC have and gives us hope for the future of STEM.

Our partners at Kapor Capital, Brian Dixon and Ulili Onovak-puri, and Allison Scott, CEO of the Kapor Center, who are leading our organizations into the next generation of innovation, bringing their own brilliance, compassion, and dedication to creating a world we all know is possible.

ACKNOWLEDGMENTS

Kapor Capital Summer Associates over the decade plus and Kapor Fellows who represent the next generation.

The behind-the-scenes team at KEI that supports us and without whom none of this would be possible. Many, many people help us juggle daily work life, organize our events, and care for and feed our guests.

Special thanks to Greg Humpa, who has been our air traffic controller for a quarter century, juggling more people, meetings, events, and requests than we can possibly count.

Our extended family of many generations, faiths, races, and cultures with whom we share Thanksgiving and Passover.

Our co-investors and fund managers who dared to break the mold with their investment criteria.

Michele Norris-Johnson, a force of nature in her own right, whose Race Card Project is unearthing new insights into the myriad ways we each experience our identities and opens the possibilities for us to build empathy. She introduced us to Gail Ross, who has been a guiding light through this book-writing journey, offering encouragement, enthusiasm, and much-needed feedback along the way.

Martha Mendoza, our collaborator and expert interviewer, who managed to pry fascinating tales, previously unknown to us, from those we've worked with for many years.

Hollis Heimbouch, for believing we had something important to say, and helping us define it and frame it along the way.

The team at Ross Yoon for their perseverance in helping us shape a proposal.

Barbara Henricks and Nina Nocciolino for their expert guidance in getting the word out.

Generation Investment Management for their pioneering work on sustainable capitalism, which opened a door for us to rethink investing.

President Obama and Valerie Jarrett for their timely visit in 2021, sending the entrepreneurs with whom they met over the moon and catapulting forward with their businesses.

And to Ollie, our rescue doodle, who told us daily when to get up from our computers and go for a walk. Woof.

HOW WE INVEST

The conventional wisdom about investing is based on a large number of flawed assumptions that don't hold true. There are so many talented entrepreneurs who come from unconventional—by mainstream standards—backgrounds. They have the fire to create businesses that simultaneously become highly successful financially and help fix some of the deepest social inequities today. When we started out in 2011, we had a thesis about why it was possible and how to do it. Now we have lots of evidence, both in terms of financial returns and the social impacts.

In *The Equity Gap*, we've shared our proof of concept, told the stories of several entrepreneurs, explained their distance traveled, and recognized their social impact. We don't think capitalism is necessarily a dead end. There's just a different way to practice it. There are different ways to think about how we should be allocating capital. There are different metrics for success in business. It can't just be about the money.

We've developed a detailed methodology about who the kind of founders we invest in are, how they run their companies, and what kind of commitments they have around diversity. It's a very different approach than the usual checklists and playbooks. At Kapor Capital, diversity isn't a numbers game or a PR ploy, it's a fundamental approach to building an effective organization whose composition reflects the people that it's serving.

AN OPEN AND FAIR PROCESS

As the very first step at Kapor Capital, every pitch comes through our website, a burden to our junior investment team members who have to sort through thousands a year, but truly leveling the playing field. Many investors only take pitches from people they've already met, which excludes anyone outside their network. To our knowledge, we were the first to end the requirement of a "warm intro" and to call it out as inherently biased. Just like unpaid internships and many other practices that have been in place and unexamined, we always ask who has access and who is excluded. Our approach invites any and all who believe that their startup meets our investment criteria, published on our website, to submit their pitches, and even more than that it helps ensure a fair process because every inbound submission, regardless of who it comes from, goes through the same process. Fair process, in turn, leads to better decision-making. Just as with hiring, where there is a growing body of research about the importance of "structured interviews" as reducing bias, a standardized process that everyone can access removes some of the subjectivity.

BE DELIBERATE ABOUT YOUR SECTORS

All VCs sort potential investments by the type of business category, sectors like cloud, enterprise, telecommunications, quantum computing, or cryptocurrency. Our list is very different: education, finance, health, sustainability, people operations, justice. To be clear, merely being in a sector doesn't make a company gap-closing. A $300-per-hour online tutoring business is an EdTech company, but it's gap-widening.

HOW WE CONSIDER GEOGRAPHY

There was a time when venture capital firms told companies they would have to relocate to the Bay Area if they invested. And we used to say that it's critical for the tech engineering team to be on-site, interacting with each other and the rest of a company. We learned a lot of new things about geography during COVID lockdowns, including the fact that geography matters a lot less than it used to. Many companies are entirely or substantially virtual, with nominal headquarters, and they are no longer having people come into an office every day.

We do still have some firm principles on geography. We invest in U.S.-based companies, although as they grow, many have become global. We believe the location of a company needs to focus on who the company serves, and that their office location needs to enable their business. If they are building tech ecosystems in underestimated cities, they should be in an underestimated city. We also talk to our founders about the risks of outsourcing their technical teams outside of the U.S. We believe this only works if the founders themselves are technical and have connections with the country they are outsourcing to. For example, if a founder's parents are Pakistani immigrants, she'll have a deeper understanding of the culture, how to navigate the time zones, how to travel back and forth, and some business connections.

YOUNG COMPANIES

We choose pre-seed and seed-stage investing so we can engage with our founders as they establish foundational social impact and diversity plans, and set the culture of their companies. Because we've been so focused at this stage of investment, we have seen what works and what doesn't as we advise on strategy, problem-solving, growing the business, and fundraising. These early rounds of capital are generally used to help advance the startup to a stage where it will either prove or disprove value and customer demand for the product or service. As you have seen, pivots are expected. At the point we invest, companies almost always have a working version of the product or service and a small number of active users. However, we evaluate on a case-by-case basis and cannot provide specific target numbers. If the product has not been built or deployed, it is very likely too early for us to invest.

FIVE BIG QUESTIONS

1. IS THE BUSINESS GAP-CLOSING?

Key to our core values is our definition of success, which involves closing gaps of access, opportunity, or outcome for low-income communities and/or communities of color. We are particularly interested in those that address gaps of disproportionate relevance to Black and Latinx communities. When pitches come in, we are evaluating their potential to produce large-scale social impact. This is the way that most differentiates us from Silicon Valley VCs, because the centrality in our discussions is about gap-closing.

We ask our founders, who is going to be better off if this works? And we consider, how scalable is the impact? The potential social impact needs to be large enough to justify the amount of money they're going to raise. A lot of VCs say they're making impact investments, but here are two red flags:

- A company that donates one item to a charity in exchange for every item purchased does not meet our standards; it's too easy, if the company is tanking, to save their bottom line by eliminating the donations. In this instance, impact is an add-on, not baked into the core of the business.

- A company that aims to serve everyone, but on a sliding scale, making money only from wealthy people, is a huge risk because they can shift their mission if they're not profitable enough. As with Buy One, Give One Away, a sliding scale can always be adjusted to eliminate the most needy.

2. WHAT'S THE STATE OF THE BUSINESS MODEL?

Many investment firms rely on a set of formal assessment criteria combining numeric scores across multiple dimensions into a single "investability" score, but if the investors are being honest they will tell you there's always something subjective about the process. We believe there's never going to be an algorithm (no, not even one based on the latest techniques in artificial intelligence) that can identify whether a particular business model is going to work. Among other things, with scanty or no operating history at all, there's a lack of quantitative data on which to base the algorithm. Assigning a number or score to subjective criteria doesn't magically transform them into something objective. They're still scores based on subjective assessments and conventional wisdom.

Our investment team is well grounded in the basics of business and business models. We look at the size of the potential market. We look at the maturity of the market. Is it a well-established one in which there are entrenched competitors? If so, what is the 10x disruptive factor this startup is going to bring? Or is it a nascent market in which no one has yet established a strong, recurring, growing revenue stream? If so, what is the evidence the market is ready and what is this team bringing in its technology and its customer relationships to be the first or among the very first? Due to our reliance on lived experience, our founders are often identifying new products, services, and markets.

If they do succeed at first, how can they protect and extend their advantage against the certainty of follow-on competition? The list goes on.

The business model is inevitably going to change, so while we want to see something that makes sense at the outset, we know how important it is to place a bet on a founding team that has capability, the smarts, passion, and the resilience to invent and reinvent the model as they go.

3. IS THERE TOO MUCH COMPETITIVE OVERLAP WITH ANOTHER COMPANY WE HAVE INVESTED IN?

We don't want to have two companies in the portfolio who are directly competitive. It's not fair to them, and it's self-opposing to our own interests to do so to the extent helping Company A hurts Company B, in which we have an interest, and vice versa. Where we are different than other investors is that we give a lot of weight (yet not a veto) to whether a CEO we're already working with regards the direct competitiveness of a company we are considering. It's the opposite of the kind of lip service we often hear from investors on the topic of not investing in competing companies.

What complicates matters is knowing that business models evolve and change, sometimes dramatically. Frequently, two companies in the same sector that have each pursued separate destinies find themselves in direct competition. This movement is often accelerated by a collective learning process in which the entire industry figures out the optimal business models. Or it comes from two companies starting on parallel paths but as they succeed and grow, they expand into each other's products, services, and markets. If this does happen, we take care to have a different partner be the lead investor for the competitors, and to avoid transferring proprietary information between them.

4. ARE THE FOUNDERS UP TO THE CHALLENGE?

One measure of a founder's commitment and passion is whether they are solving a challenge they had to face. It's fundamental to our investing that a founder has to have lived experience of the gap they're trying to close, because that's going to help them identify rapidly scalable, market-based solutions that others have overlooked. It's also going to build empathy and lead to a nuanced understanding of the customer.

We meet with the team and consider their background and skill sets. Although we don't require a technical founder, it's often critical to their success. We look at what the team has accomplished and what they may have learned from failures. Investing in entrepreneurs from marginalized communities allows for new ideas, markets, and revenue streams, bringing a competitive advantage to tech.

5. IS THIS COMPANY COMMITTED TO DIVERSITY AND INCLUSION?

We only want to invest in companies that are truly going to reflect the people they serve, at every level. Before we invest, we require our entrepreneurs to sign on to our Founders' Commitment. This means they are going to set diversity and inclusion goals and be held accountable to them. We can support them in figuring out how to set those goals, but we don't prescribe them; the goals need to fit their business, and we ask for quarterly updates on how they are meeting them.

Our founders commit to investing in mitigating bias in their companies—from recruiting to compensation—using people ops technology, training programs, and other resources. They're going to organize opportunities for their employees to volunteer with underrepresented communities, especially those that reflect their customer base. And they are going to participate in workshops that we host at Kapor Capital, sessions that support them in meeting this commitment.

G.I.V.E.: THE FOUR PILLARS OF THE FOUNDERS' COMMITMENT

1. **GOALS**: *Establish diversity and inclusion goals that are appropriate for your company's funding stage, employee size, customer base, and core business. Include progress on diversity and inclusion in quarterly investor updates.*

2. **INVEST**: *Invest in people ops technology (POT), training programs, and/ or resources that assist with mitigating bias in the employment life cycle (e.g., sourcing, hiring, promotion).*

3. **VOLUNTEER**: *Organize volunteer opportunities for your employees to engage with underrepresented communities, especially those that reflect the company's customer base.*

4. **EDUCATE**: *Participate in diversity and inclusion sessions to learn what works and what doesn't. These sessions will be hosted by Kapor Capital and will be made available for virtual participation as needed.*

In addition to sessions focused on living up to the Founders' Commitment, we do many other sessions as needed due to events in the ecosystem or the country. After George Floyd's murder, for example, we held a series of sessions on Stepping Up and Speaking Out as a CEO. Addressing a real concern of our founders, we were asked to prepare a version for their employees, as they didn't all feel as comfortable talking about racial equity issues as we do. We did so right away.

OUR MESSAGE TO INVESTORS: THIS IS ENTIRELY POSSIBLE

Next time you're taking a pitch from someone who doesn't seem to fit the startup mold, and who is focusing on a segment you never thought of, instead of grilling them on jargon, ask yourself, is this the next Irma and Jake, Phaedra, Donnel, Davida, or Ruben?

Fight the good fight and get into good trouble until we achieve a more equitable future. Through our investments, we can dismantle systemic barriers in technology, in entrepreneurship, and in the world at large.

ABOUT THE AUTHORS

MITCH KAPOR
@MKAPOR

MITCH KAPOR is a pioneer of the personal computing industry and an entrepreneur, investor, and advocate for social change. As a founding partner at Kapor Capital, Mitch, along with his partner and wife, Freada Kapor Klein, invests in tech startups that close gaps of access, opportunity, and outcome for low-income communities and communities of color, and in founders committed to building diverse workforces and inclusive cultures.

In 1982, Mitch founded Lotus Development Corporation and designed the Lotus 1–2–3 spreadsheet, the "killer application" that made the personal computer ubiquitous in the business world. He cofounded the Electronic Frontier Foundation in 1990 and is the founding chair of the Mozilla Foundation, creator of the Firefox web browser.

Mitch is the cochair of the nonprofit Kapor Center in Oakland, California, and also serves on the board of SMASH, the Summer Mathematics and Science Honors Academy, a three-year, STEM-intensive residential college prep program that empowers students to deepen their talents and pursue STEM careers.

He would like to be known for his saying "Genius is evenly distributed by zip code, but opportunity is not," and for his efforts to close that gap.

FREADA KAPOR KLEIN, PHD
@THEREALFREADA

FREADA KAPOR KLEIN is an entrepreneur, activist, and pioneer in the field of organizational culture and diversity.

As a founding partner at Kapor Capital, Freada invests in seed-stage tech startups that create a positive social impact by closing gaps of access, opportunity, and outcome for low-income communities and communities of color.

She is the founder of SMASH, now in its twentieth year, which provides rigorous STEM education and access to social capital for low-income high school students of color on ten university campuses across the country.

Freada's initial job in tech was as the first head of employee relations, organizational development, and management training at Lotus Development Corporation. Her job description was to make Lotus, then the world's largest independent software company, "the most progressive employer in the U.S."

In 1976, she cofounded the Alliance Against Sexual Coercion, the first organization in the U.S. to address sexual harassment. She holds a PhD in social policy and research from the Heller School for Social Policy and Management at Brandeis University, and has conducted numerous large-survey projects on perceptions and experiences of bias, harassment, and disrespectful treatment in workplaces.

Freada is a member of the Obama Foundation Tech Policy Council, the U.C. Berkeley Chancellor's Board of Visitors, and the council that formed the Hollywood Commission chaired by Anita Hill. She serves on the advisory boards of Twilio.org, Generation Investment Management, and Trident Capital. She is a board observer of Aclima. Freada is also the author of *Giving Notice*, which details the human and financial cost of hidden bias in the workplace.